THE BOOK OF NOBLE PURPOSE

Foreword

This foreword is a collection of testimonials from a variety of different business sources. The sources concerned are all people who I regard as inspiring and in their own way each has been touched and moved to passionate action by a noble purpose.

'All the same, it's strange that at the beginning of the 21st century, questions were asked about the rationale and the purpose of companies, the famous "why?". Every company has a mission, and the stakeholders of this mission are apparent: its human capital (its employees), its clients, its shareholders, and its partners (suppliers, environment ...). Shareholder value is an absolute aberration, which we now pay for with inequality, social and environmental discomfort, and distrust towards the company. An enterprise in the 21st century will be either moral, or it will not be at all. That is why I salute Olivier Onghena, who has taken on the subject to remind us all of this fundamental truth, which we have always applied to Châteauform, namely that happy associates make happy customers, who, at their turn, make the shareholders happy. In that order. A noble purpose is a purpose that satisfies everyone involved, and it will be nothing if not fair.'

Daniel Abittan

Co-founder & President, Châteauform

Founder, Acuitis

'I first met Olivier in Mount Abu in Autumn 2015. I was touched by his genuine desire to serve humanity and bring the concept of noble purpose into the work he is doing. It is excellent that a book has been written about this. As we develop mastery over our thoughts and feelings, our innate nobility emerges in our thinking and behaviour. Spirituality is the awareness that allows all this to happen and brings a life of deep happiness.'

Dadi Janki

Spiritual Head, Brahma Kumaris World Spiritual University

'While philanthropy should by definition be driven by a noble purpose, the reality is that motives are often not so transparent, and much of it is still driven by other interests including ego, reputation and power. In this book, Olivier gets at the heart of why purpose matters in all aspects of life.'

Silvia Bastante de Unverhau

Global Philanthropy Expert

'Olivier Onghena has written a must-read primer for anyone on the quest for meaning and purpose in business and in life... Read this book – and learn from one of the best.'

Tomas Björkman

Founder, Ekskäret Foundation

Author, 'The Market Myth' & 'The Nordic Secret'

Full member, Club of Rome

'Olivier's book offers an interesting perspective on the importance of Purpose. For a business leader, it all starts with the why: a clear definition of the noble purpose of the company, which is its meaningful contribution to the people and the world. It generates more engagement from the employees and helps attract and retain talent. It also leads to a stronger bond with customers, as they become contributors to the noble purpose.'

Francis Blake

Chairman, Derbigum

'Our society is constantly changing. Climate, inequality, polarisation. A multitude of challenges in a complex and ever-evolving world. At the same time, we develop technological innovations that we can perfectly apply to achieve a better world. So why don't we do so on a large scale? More than ever, we need a connecting story, a noble purpose. From a personal, authentic viewpoint, this book will inspire as many people as it possible can.'

Piet Colruyt

Impact investor & Founder, Impact Capital

'There are special moments in our lives when we decide on an essential bifurcation without suffering the effort we've put in or the risks we've taken. Because this decision is part of a mindful personal path, and it is the natural consequence of the mainspring we chose in the deepest depths of our being. That is why Olivier's teachings are essential.'

Jacques Crahay

CEO, Cosucra

President, Walloon Union of Enterprises

'I am convinced that the notion of purpose will become the central concept of the future.'

Herman Daems

Chairman, BNP Paribas Fortis

Chairman, KULeuven

'Having meaning and purpose in your personal life and at work transcends age and culture; it engages the brain, feeds the soul and lifts the human spirit. At the Adecco Group, what we do goes far beyond just the financial. We exist to help people around the world be inspired, motivated and prepared to embrace the future of work. In short, we are intrinsically driven to make the future work for everyone. I am heartened to see the topic of noble purpose coming alive through this book, reinforcing how we should all strive to make a lasting and positive difference to the world around us.'

Alain Dehaze

CEO, the Adecco Group

'For many years, I've known Olivier Onghena as a passionate man with a mission. I very much appreciate the consistent way in which he calls upon and inspires those responsible in various segments of our society to find their purpose. *The Book of Noble Purpose* will certainly prove to be an important contribution. For this reason, I would like to share my motivation why I do what I do. I remain socially active because I want to contribute to a society where everyone receives equal opportunities to grow, as described in the Universal Declaration of Human Rights. When I commit to various projects, my starting point is human dignity and knowledge, freedom and responsibility, involvement and tolerance, and the right to live a meaningful life.'

Luc De Bruyckere

Founder, TAJO

'For a strong brand like La Monnaie in Brussels, the noble purpose has become a more reliable compass than any mission statement can formulate. The ephemeral character of any stage performance and its non-quantifiable added value are perfectly reflected in the 'why' of our organisation: to elevate consciousness about ourselves and society through the profound experience of opera. A noble purpose, therefore, enthuses all stakeholders to participate in our project. Thanks to Olivier's inspiring book, I hope that many more leaders of all kinds of organisations will get inspired to give noble purpose the centre stage it deserves.'

Peter de Caluwe

General Director, De Munt-La Monnaie

'Companies with a purpose attract better people and retain their people better. As a result, they outperform their competitors that operate without a purpose. Based upon his own personal and unique experiences, Olivier Onghena takes us through the why, the what and the how to find that purpose for your company, and for yourself, and shows you that, once you found that purpose, you just create a better and more balanced life for yourself and those around you.'

Patrick De Maeseneire

Chairman, Barry-Callebaut

CEO, Jacobs Holding

'In my role as CEO of Ageas, I have been frequently triggered to reflect fundamentally about the concept of purpose, the mission of our company. In the early days after the collapse of the Fortis Group, it was about survival. After some years we could start thinking more positively about the future, the real purpose of our business. The conclusion was that we were not just there for our shareholders, our customers and our employees. As an insurance group, we have a fundamental role in society by providing people with security in case of adverse events and by investing in responsible initiatives. Our current strategic plan reconfirmed and even strengthened this stakeholder model with an explicit reference to the society in which we act. I'm convinced that the DNA of Ageas and all its employees is driven by a noble purpose to create societal value in combination with economic value. Thinking about purpose and the reason to exist is a must for every actor in society, both in private and professional life. Let this book be a motivation to take some distance from the daily rat race and be an inspiration to reflect on the purpose of our being and of the organisations we are involved in.'

Bart De Smet

CEO, Ageas

Incoming chairman, Federation of Enterprises in Belgium

'In business, it is as it is with humans: our visions, our goals and our actions can be guided by the awareness of a purpose in life. This sense is all the nobler as it is in relation to and in service of others. Businesses, too, live only to serve – except when they only seek vanity. It's the others who give us our reason for existence and the energy to continue on our path. This path can be sustainable and for the benefit of all, if we respect equality and, now more than ever, our planet. Thank you, Olivier, for making me proceed on this path of consciousness.'

Philippe Dorge

Deputy Director-General, La Poste Group

'It's odd… Nobody wakes up in the morning thinking 'let's destroy the climate or get some toddlers in Asia to work'. Yet this is exactly what is going on each and every day. In our addiction to short-term profit, we all resemble a junkie destroying his own vitality for a profit high. We are ready to integrate a few fundamental values in our market system. People? Planet? Ubuntu? Karma? Let's start with a new profit definition that includes costs of people and planet. Read this book! Let's dream, dance and deliver: share ideas and dreams, dance coalitions of the willing, deliver a systems change!'

Volkert Engelsman

CEO, Eosta

CEO, Nature & More

'I am very grateful to Olivier for enkindling the nobility in people with this book. When we are born, we often do not know what we are meant to be doing on this earth. You will be presented with plenty of choices later. The extent to which you make these choices is subject to on your upbringing and education. Whether or not you persist depends on your willingness to do so through your intellect, personality, genes and willpower. Achieving your goals requires inner processes involving multiple motivations, which often clash because of the many circumstances that you have to overcome. But never forget your pride, which will hopefully always lead you to noble goals.'

Axel Enthoven

Designer

'The purpose of life is to be happy. The moment to be happy is now. The place to be happy is here'. That's what Gérard Blitz, founder of Club Med, said. Seventy years ago, Club Med set out on a quest for happiness in harmony with nature. This quest was limitless, centred around values that are still as valid now as they were then, in a world marked by the folly of men and nature: freedom, kindness, accountability, a pioneering and multicultural spirit. It is a tremendous mission that, together with the women and men of this company, we strive to carry on, all over the world, by reinventing ourselves constantly, with respect for the environment and our hosts. And that gives so much meaning to our actions. The testimonies gathered in Olivier Onghena's book remind us just how much the existence of a noble purpose incorporates a fundamental level of engagement from the women and men in the company. This is not the least of its merits.'

Henri Giscard d'Estaing

Chief Executive Officer, Club Med

'My leadership team and I had the pleasure of working with Olivier throughout 2019 and witness the impact of having a noble purpose on the whole company. As a biopharmaceutical company focused on developing new medicines for patients with severe diseases, formalising our noble purpose ("transform the patients' world by helping them realise their hopes and dreams for a healthy Life) was extremely valuable to the whole organisation. From workers in the factory, researchers in the labs, commercial people in front of our customers, we are all aligned around our noble purpose, which fills us with pride, energy and a sense of duty and urgency. I am convinced that this book will further broaden and deepen society at large of the importance of leading a purposeful life.'

Peter Guenter

CEO, Almirall

'Is "noble purpose" the next buzzword? Is it a temporary fashion? Will Wall Street, the next career move, fear for risk, or year-end bonus erase one's "noble" ambition? I really hope not, because I remain convinced that over time, the most, if not the only successful ventures are the ones where you want to reach a purpose that supersedes everything. This is why Brussels Airlines' vision was "to bring people together" instead of just "transporting people from A to B". This little sentence changed everything when we had to decide against many "wise advisors" and faced a lot of adversity to become the only non-African airline connecting the three countries hit by the Ebola crisis in West Africa to the rest of the world in 2015. Happily, we have people like Olivier Onghena, who remind us why we are there and what a venture stands for!'

Bernard Gustin

Chairman, Elia Group (and former CEO of Brussels Airlines)

'Within both the academic and the medical world, a noble purpose may appear an obvious driver of ambition as academic teachings, scientific research and medical acts all aim at serving mankind. Reality, however, is different, as research is not always driven by noble purpose and medical acts might have other incentives besides helping those in need. Following his personal journey in the search for a purposeful life, Olivier Onghena-'t Hooft introduces us to the world of noble purpose, which could be a source of inspiration for those academic researchers and health care providers aiming for a more purposeful professional activity, including focus on disease prevention, higher patient satisfaction and health-economic savings for society.'

Prof Dr Peter Hellings

Professor, Universities of Leuven, Ghent & Amsterdam,

Founder & President, EUFOREA

'I have been working with Olivier for many years, and he supported me in different organisations to establish a noble purpose. Be
different, do good and be successful! The roots might already be
existing in the company, but you need to discover and develop
them in group work, and Olivier is an incredible adviser and
profound teacher. I was very surprised by the organisational motivation, increased energy and astonishing business success that
followed. A prerequisite is a sincere approach linked to credible
values. Then the noble purpose will connect welfare, happiness
and success. This book is a real must-read (and do) for any leader
and entrepreneur.'

Stefan Hoetzl

CEO, TEKA Group

Group Executive Committee member, Heritage B

'Being ready to make a difference is what gets me up in the morning, improving the world step by step. Setting a noble purpose and
facilitating teams to make a difference aligned to that purpose is
what all leaders should do. And there are enough noble purposes to
pursue: addressing climate change, reducing inequalities, making
society disease free…'

Bruno Holthof

CEO, Oxford University Hospitals

'Being inspired by a vision larger than one's own little person is often difficult to maintain over time. This vision, however, is like a tree that grows slowly but surely: if you want to share it with others, the impact will be strongest after a certain amount of time. By persevering in its philosophy and sharing its vision, the tree will develop, and its fruits will begin to feed the next generations. Thank you, Olivier, for being an inspiration to people who tend to think they are alone in this fight. Thanks to you, your actions, your charisma and your kindness, you drive us to become better people.'

Yassine Lahlou

Managing Director, Byland

Citizen of the world

'If we are lucky, there comes a time when we stop striving for a certain image of what our life should be like and start to listen instead to the life that wants to be lived through us. What a blessing when purpose comes knocking and we can heed the call.'

Frederic Laloux

Author, Reinventing Organizations

'Aren't we always better when we are driven by a true meaning behind what we do? Driven by ambition, energy and focus that are all the stronger because they go beyond our own destiny and are part of a collective human adventure? This is the strength of the noble purpose: it enables us to make free choices because they are illuminated by the light of purpose. This purpose is the quest of the new generations our companies desperately need if they want to face the future. Congratulations to Olivier for this much-needed inspiration!'

Denis Machuel

CEO, Sodexo

'My commitment is rooted in the core of my inner life, and it is sustained by serving an ideal that is greater than me. This movement encourages me to grow and picks me up by giving me progressively to its two poles.'

Vincent Monziols

Vice President, Saint-Gobain

'The world is in a clear transformation from linear to exponential. The availability of key technologies, capital and resources are enabling entrepreneurs (and corporates who dare) to cross the linear line from deception to disruption in a breadth and width of historically unknown size and speed. Leadership has to become aspirational, causing significant transformation based on the 'why?' behind the work being done, something that unites and inspires aligned action of free people for a shared purpose.'

Karsten Ottenberg

Former CEO, BSH Home Appliances Group

Purpose-driven Leader and driver of transformations

'Identifying a noble purpose at enterprise level helps to strengthen employees' motivation by achieving inner alignment between their values, beliefs and behaviours, which leads to sustainable performance. That's what we pursue at PSA on a daily basis, by developing sustainable and affordable mobility for all. Olivier's book is very inspiring and a great support for entrepreneurs and business leaders who want to embark on such a noble purpose journey.'

Maxime Picat

Member of the Managing Board, Groupe PSA

'Next to a high degree of curiosity, a noble purpose is probably the essential driver for scientists to do the exceptional things that many of them do. The complexity and regular setbacks that come with research are strenuous. I have been privileged to help discover the Ebola virus, lead efforts to contain the first-ever recorded Ebola epidemic, become a pioneering researcher into HIV/AIDS, and try to inspire many governments and leaders to think long-term when it comes to global health. All this has often been nourished by a desire to serve a greater good and be of service to humanity. As Olivier puts it very rightly in his exciting and multi-facetted book, having a noble purpose is what makes all the difference. This is a very inspiring and courageous venture that Olivier undertook!'

Dr Peter Baron Piot

Director, London School of Hygiene and Tropical Medicine

Former Executive Director, UNAIDS

'Today's society craves leaders with a long-term vision. Where are we heading, why, and for whose benefit? Organisations often need a sustainable goal that reaches beyond short-term thinking and purely results-oriented performances. Non-quantitative focal points, such as respect and involvement, also play an increasingly important role for the environment, employees and 'customers'. This requires a servant and vulnerable leadership. Personally, thanks to the meetings with Olivier Onghena, I gained more insight into this matter. I am curious about his book that will undoubtedly inspire us towards a more value-driven, meaningful leadership.'

Jan Raes

Managing Director, Royal Concertgebouw Orchestra

'One might say that I found my purpose in life as I grew up listening to my father's stories of fleeing the Nazis. They made me very aware of the evil that governments can do if left unchecked. Yet even the worst governments try to hide their crimes. That reality has driven me to scrutinise and publicise their atrocities as the best way to avert them. That scrutiny is also the best way to ensure that government officials serve the public rather than the power and wealth of themselves and their cronies.'

Kenneth Roth

Executive Director, Human Rights Watch

'Business gives us an ideal vehicle to express our innate human need to care, to express ourselves through a purpose that transcends narrow self-interest. Indeed, businesses with a noble purpose are instruments of healing: they alleviate suffering, elevate joy and promote healthy growth in all the lives they touch.'

Professor Raj Sisodia

Co-founder, Conscious Capitalism Inc.

Co-author, 'The Healing Organization', Author, 'Firms of Endearment'

'Finding your noble purpose deeply relates to that question you always ask yourself, "what is the meaning of life?". If we believe in something more profound, that propels us and makes us excel in finding solutions for this world's most complex problems, we believe in purpose, and therefore we need to find it and dedicate our lives to it. I would like to thank Olivier to dedicate his life to noble purpose and to have written a very complete and inspiring book about it.'

Sebastien Saverys

Founder & Co-CEO, Durabilis

'This book is the powerful spiritual awakening we need to enlighten the world. You plunge us into the depths of our infinite nobility that is the source of all our abilities, the most supreme being our inexhaustible love. This book teaches us that it is possible to free ourselves from the obstructions that limit us because they are only illusions. It is highly appreciated!'

Marianne Sébastien

International Prize for Human Rights

Founder, Voix Libres

'In a creative and irresistible way, Olivier Onghena's book advocates a meaningful mission ("noble purpose") in one's private life, in business and in politics. After having been elected Best Employer ten times, I realise all too well that Torfs' mission ("putting employees and customers firmly in their shoes") is the basis for both happy employees and sustainable and innovative entrepreneurship.'

Wouter Torfs

CEO, Schoenen Torfs

'I fondly remember that – when I became responsible for ORMIT Group and you were responsible for ORMIT Belgium – we spoke to our management team about what kind of leadership we wanted to augment in our trainees. Soon, we were perfectly aligned: good earnings were not a goal in themselves, but rather the result of working towards enthusiasm, ensuring that people would lead with their heads and their hearts and that they would find meaning in their work. We wanted to set a good example with ORMIT. Practise what we preach! It's great to see that you have pursued this topic so energetically and that you have given it so much value. I know it comes from your heart and it is wonderful to see that you yourself have found so much meaning in this theme! First class!'

Hetty van Ee

CEO, ORMIT Group

'Entrepreneurship is an attitude or a way of life offering someone a unique opportunity to create, build and improve for the betterment of oneself, one's community and global society. It gives a higher purpose and long-term value to what we are meant to realise in life. This is what *The Book of Noble Purpose* clearly stands for and, rightly so, invites business owners and entrepreneurs to pursue.'

Guido Vanherpe

CEO & co-owner, La Lorraine Bakery Group

'"Culture eats strategy for breakfast" is attributed to management guru Peter Drucker, and while it's probably apocryphal, it does make sense. Driven by personal and professional experiences, Olivier Onghena credibly elaborates the Druckerian metaphor into the image that the higher goal creates a corporate cultural appetite.'

Frank Van Massenhove

Author & columnist

Former President, Belgian Federal Social Security

'In their lives, people have to choose what purpose they want to give to it. In fact, there is only one option, namely that you choose for the other, for their happiness and development, so that they, in turn, will one day make the same choice. Only then will we get a more harmonious and, simply put, a better world. That choice is not apparent. It is preceded by a fight between Me and You. Obviously we must also receive respect and love ourselves. Obviously we should also assert ourselves, and there is vanity in each of us. The only thing that is not allowed is that this pursuit of recognition comes at the expense of another. That is the bottom line. Positively, a meaningful life is about what we can do for the other, for our fellow human beings. In politics, this translates into championing the public interest; every other interest is subordinate. What binds leaders is something that transcends them and their countries. This translates into concrete compromises and a long search involving trial and error. But if there is a common belief and determination that we can overcome those problems.'

Herman Van Rompuy

President Emeritus, European Council

Minister of State

President, the European Policy Centre

'On the one hand, my noble purpose is to take care of human beings, the Earth and the common good, and on the other it's the creation of fairly shared abundance. I am convinced that a noble purpose must be engrained in every leader of every organisation. And I am delighted that Olivier has decided to inspire the world by writing a book devoted to this exciting, vital subject.'

Marc Vossen,

CEO, NRJ Group Belgium

'Growth is a 20th century concept that is linear in nature and invariably based on a win/lose foundation. Success in the 21st century is to "thrive". A business that aspires to thrive is a business that leaves a better planet and community as a result of its activities, and in the process earns the reputation and the right to grow economically. *The Book of Noble Purpose* is a great inspiration for the courageous leaders – business, academic, political, civic society – that are passionate about this urgent need for transformation and inspired by an inner force to see it through.'

Guy Wollaert

Founder, Idea-Value-Impact

Former senior vice president & Chief Technical & Innovation Officer,

The Coca Cola Enterprises

1

My passion to inspire

'Great knowledge is not the same as wisdom.'
(Schopenhauer)

Why have I written this book?

To inspire people with the power, impact and beauty of purpose. To prompt them to reflect on their own Life and how they can get the most out of that Life by giving it purpose.

To encourage the leaders of companies to think about what they and their organisations stand for. And how they can stimulate the people in those organisations to commit themselves fully and give the best of themselves with a powerful feeling of engagement and flow. By motivating them to build organisations where purpose is the leitmotif, a leitmotif that can influence society in a positive and sustainable manner.

To inspire political leaders to act from a real spirit of engagement with the following generations and not simply from a desire to be re-elected. By opening their eyes to the need to build cities, regions, communities and societies with a purposeful future, where participation, collectivism, equivalence, welfare and prosperity are combined.

I have experienced for myself, in my personal, relational, social and business Life, the remarkable role that a noble purpose can play and the huge impact it has had. Since I have been encouraging the people in my immediate environment to live and work with a noble purpose and have developed a socially relevant activity around that theme through GINPI (the Global Inspiration and

Noble Purpose Institute), I can see every day in concrete terms what such a purpose can do with and for people, organisations and systems. I have also seen how people in society are clamouring with an ever-louder voice for greater purpose and how the economy is shifting towards a mechanism that is oriented on sustainability, added value, a more aware form of capitalism and responsible stakeholders. These observations and convictions are what I wish to share with you transparently in this book.

My purpose is to initiate in people – people of all kinds, without distinctions based on social class, family background, ethnic origin, cultural, religious or philosophical conviction, or a person's role and place in society – a process of reflection, in the hope that this will allow them to look in a different way at Life and at the giving and taking of work. It is not my intention to try and convince people of a particular theory or point of view. All I expect is that people will engage in healthy conversations and develop clear and well-grounded positions.

In this way, I hope to energise as many people as I possibly can to ask themselves the following questions, not only for themselves, but also for the systems in which they work, or in which they give leadership or of which they are owners: 'Why do I do what I do? Why do we do what we do?'

I have written this book for everyone who is interested in living a purposeful Life.

For people who are concerned to make a positive and sustainable impact. In fact, for everyone who is interested in Life, since Life without purpose is not really living. In other words, for every Human being who wants to escape from 'the mediocrity of Life' and wishes to find great(er) satisfaction and 'flow' in a new kind of Life, by looking in a totally different way at what you do and why. For everyone who wishes to make a purposeful contribution based on what he does and how he does it.

For every leader who wants to have an impact on society through the realisation of the noble purpose of the organisation, company or authority for which he is responsible or to which he makes a contribution.

For every entrepreneur-owner who wishes to follow a new path with his company, a path that focuses on something more than short-term profit but is based instead on a strategy and a new organisational culture created around a noble purpose.

For every leader of people and teams, who wants to inspire his people to give the best of themselves and inspire his teams to achieve outstanding levels of performance.

For everyone who has understood that entrepreneurship and leadership in pursuit of a noble purpose offers limitless possibilities but does not yet know how to release and harness those possibilities within his own organisation or team.

For every entrepreneur and leader who still wishes to be convinced about the way in which a noble purpose for his company or organisation will contribute towards the creation of (substantially more) human happiness, a better society and greater economic relevance, with all the direct and indirect positive effects this will cause.

This book is about the importance of giving purpose to our existence as human beings, to the organisations in which we work or give leadership, and to the society in which we live.

The starting point for my book is the philosophy and the purpose to which I have devoted my Life in recent years. In other words, the things I stand for as a human being, as a person: inspiring as many of the world's high impact leaders as possible to focus on the creation of joy, harmony and beauty for the benefit of the future evolution and prosperity of humankind, society and the world.

Chapter 2 is about my own transformation to a conscious and happy Life of purpose. I will tell you how, like a bolt from the blue, in 1994 I was unexpectedly involved in a brutal kidnapping, an event that led me to ask what is probably the most crucial of all Life's questions: why am I alive? And in my case, following that drama: why am I still alive?

That kidnapping was the moment that changed everything, a tipping point. It set me on a path that forced me to leave my own comfort zone, so that I could realise my true purpose. Ever since that moment, I have been searching for inspiration, for Life-changing lessons and for Life-changing teachers who could help me to find the focus and the power that would lead me to discover the true essence of myself. As a result, I now see Life through rose-tinted spectacles. My glass is always half full, never half empty. This magical transformation has made it possible for me to reconnect with my deepest inner being, so that I can live a purposeful Life, based on concrete values and principles.

Chapter 3 is about the beauty and power of noble purpose. What is it? What is it not? How does it work? How important is transformation in the development of a lasting noble purpose? Using a highly spiritual approach, based on the theory of the four bodies, I will explain why having a noble purpose actually forms the very core of human beings, organisations and society.

In *Chapter 4*, I will go deeper into the essence of our lives: why do we live and how do we achieve self-realisation? We do not have different Lives, but there are different facets in our Life. Ideally, we need to keep those different facets in balance. If that balance is lost, it is important to know how it can be restored by making the right choices. Making choices, paying a price, restoring balance: these can all be achieved with relative ease, providing we are in contact with our noble purpose. I will also explain why the vast majority of people do not have this contact and, as a result, have become disconnected from their true selves, so that they no longer have any real commitment to what they do. In these circumstances, people search for comfort instead of purpose; the easy option instead of self-disciplined persistence; material success instead of spiritual balance. By doing instead of being and by failing to ask the right questions, they allow themselves to become the victims of a new form of post-industrial slavery. In my opinion, the only way they can free themselves from this servitude is by evolving from a position where they are negatively weighed down by the burden of their work to a situation where they can positively embrace their work with zeal. This involves making clear choices about the best way to achieve purposeful self-realisation.

In *Chapter 5,* I will discuss just how vital the concept of noble purpose will be for the future of organisations in a VUCA world in transformation. Organisations must evolve into ecosystems, in which people can obtain genuine self-fulfilment in a sustainable manner by serving the unique noble purpose for which the organisation stands and which the organisation actively promotes.

I will argue for the transformation of organisations from soulless machines focused on production and short-term results to empathic ecosystems with an organisational culture based on purpose and 'LovInShip'. I will re-interpret the traditional 'assets' and 'liabilities' of the balance sheet and put forward the concept of 'IT-WE-I'. I will explain the true nature of organisational culture and how organisational energy can be released, as well as highlighting the important values and principles this involves.

The penultimate chapter is about the new kind of society that is gradually developing, in which the old ways have had their day and are being replaced by new government authorities and public bodies that will give meaning and purpose to humankind and society. I will discuss the huge societal changes that are heading our way in the coming decades and also highlight people's new expectations within that changed society. How will a new class of enterprising political leaders, blessed with a long-term vision, deal with these changes and give them shape?

Finally, I will draw a number of conclusions that summarise the ideas and concepts contained in this book and will hopefully prompt you to self-reflection and action.

The book will also offer a wide range of examples from my own Life, career and entrepreneurship. My aim is to share these experiences in a way that makes as clear and as concrete as possible the various insights that I have been able to draw from my personal, social and business contexts.

Why is this so important? Because ultimately it is my hope and my intention that *The Book of Noble Purpose* will make a contribution to the general progress and welfare of humankind, society and the world, based on an authentic, transparent, self-experienced and well-developed approach!

2

A present from Life for Life

'Write the bad things that are done to you in sand
but write the good things that happen to you
on a piece of marble.'
(Kahlil Gibran)

11 January 1994

Since I was a teenager, I have kept a diary. Sometimes my entries were frequent and intense. Sometimes I would write nothing for weeks on end. It all depended on how I felt, how much time I had and how much I needed to get something off my chest by writing it down. Over the years, it has now become my habit to write down whatever inspires me and whatever I find remarkable about a particular day or experience. I have discovered that this has a marvellously therapeutic effect and offers deep insights into who I am and the things that are important to me.

At special moments, I like to look back through my old diaries and leaf through their pages. It always amazes me how my words can take me back through time to the moment they were written, so that I can relive what I thought and felt, almost as if it were yesterday. The power of the human memory is unbelievable. And the insights that this allows you to acquire are truly remarkable.

That is precisely what happened to me when I recently read through my diary from January 1994, while staying at Terkameren Abbey, an inspiring and restful haven of calm not far from our Brussels residence. More specifically, the eleventh day of that month and year is one that I will never forget. What a Life experience that turned out to be...

I would like to share it with you.

Suddenly, I saw the light. The light was all around me, but I didn't know where I was. Slowly, I regained consciousness, but I was still drowsy from the pungent smell, the nature and origin of which I could not immediately place. My mind was in a state of total confusion. Everything seemed to be moving in slow motion, not least my own thoughts and sense of awareness. Where was I? What had happened? How long had I been lying here? I was sprawled uncomfortably half on and half off the back seat of a car. I could smell its expensive leather, mingled with the sharper undertones of spilt petrol and burnt flesh. Around me, I could feel what seemed to be a sticky mess. I could now also feel the pain coursing through my body, without being able to say precisely where it was situated or what had caused it. There was a haze in front of my eyes and a ringing sound in my ears. I felt afraid and had no idea what was going on. But there was one thing that I did know; something was very badly wrong.

My confusion was complete. But somehow my survival instinct took over. 'Get out of the car,' I thought to myself. 'If you stay here, you are going to die.' I tried to pull myself up but was immediately overcome by dizziness. Losing my balance, I fell back onto the seat. But I knew instantly I had to make a second attempt. Gripped by panic and suddenly all too clearly aware of how much danger I was in, I heaved myself into a sitting position, so that I could roll out of the open door. I crashed to the ground with a bump, still not realising that it was Oscar's BMW that I had just fallen from. I opened my eyes, but was instantly blinded by the glaring headlights of a second car – a car that I now know to have been driven by our kidnappers.

From then on, things moved fast. I began with all my might – you have no idea just how much strength you have until your Life is in danger – to drag myself away from the car with my arms and elbows. Without knowing or caring where I was going, I crawled through a patch of mud and damp leaves until I tumbled into a kind of roadside ditch. Then the lights went out again.

How could things ever have come so far?

To understand this, it is necessary to go back to Christmas 1993, just a few weeks before the 'incident'. I was 27 years old, leading a happy Life, and had just started a new relationship with a Belgian-Columbian man. After my studies at the Free University of Brussels and various internships abroad, I has also recently embarked on the first steps of what I was sure would be a fascinating and fruitful professional career. For a time, I had worked as a young political attaché for the EU delegation to the United Nations in New York, but now I was back in Brussels.

This would be the first Christmas that I did not celebrate with my parents and family. Instead, I would be spending a few weeks in Bogota with my Columbian partner and his family.

During the 1990s, Colombia was a country where the drug cartels were engaged in a merciless Life-and-death struggle with each other over market supremacy. This was the period of Pablo Escobar and countless other heartless thugs, for whom a few hundred lives more or less didn't make the slightest difference, as long as the drugs millions continued to fall in their greedy and bloody hands. Escobar has since been murdered himself, but at one time his fortune was estimated at a staggering 25 billion US dollars! In other words, the 'economic interests' were huge. If this meant that a few hundred innocent (and sometimes not so innocent) bystanders had to die, so be it. At the same time, the Columbian government was engaged in an equally bitter struggle with the FARC (*Fuerzas Armadas Revolucionarias de Colombia*), a group of left-wing revolutionaries who demanded independence for vast areas of agricultural land in the Columbian interior. The FARC wanted to give back power to the small farmers, whose land – or rather their control over it and the income they derived from it – were all too often expropriated by the large landowners and a corrupt political elite.

The combination of drugs wars, revolutionary unrest and crushing poverty on the one hand, contrasted with a breathtaking land-scape, delicious food and warm, friendly people on the other hand, meant that in those years Columbia was an exciting, adventurous and vibrant place to be. It was a destination for hundreds of thousands of tourists, who seldom saw or realised that just miles away from their tourist hotspots, hundreds and thousands of Columbians were being massacred in bomb attacks, gun fights and assassinations organised by the drugs traffickers, the *guerrilleros* and the army in a ferocious 'eye for an eye' struggle. Even so, there was little reason for the tourists to be worried. Unless they foolishly wanted to visit the rebel-held area, or took other unnecessary risks, or just happened to be in the wrong place at the wrong time, there was very little risk of anything happening to them...

This, too, was very much my expectation when I arrived in Columbia that Christmas. I wasn't looking for or expecting trou-ble. Thanks to my partner and his family, I had the privilege of staying in one of the best and safest districts in Bogota, in a chic residential building guarded by both the army and private security firms. The parents of my friend were very generous people, who were well respected by the local community and displayed a high degree of social commitment. The likeable pater familias, Oscar, was a highly esteemed, self-made businessman, who through his own intelligence and hard work, allied to the right contacts, had built up a stable business empire, with commercial and financial interests in various sectors, none of which – in case some of the more suspicious among you were thinking it – had anything to do with drugs, weapons and terrorism. Even in a country like

Columbia some people work hard, honestly and lawfully to try and move the country in the right direction, seeking to create a fairer society (social discrepancies were – and still are – huge) based on fair and sustainable economic principles.

My friend and his family lived in a beautiful penthouse in the most fashionable part of town: in the same apartment block lived the Columbian prime minster and his family. The building, set in a small park of its own, was guarded 24 hours a day. You couldn't leave or enter without passing a private security patrol or checkpoint. These heavily armed guards not only watched our every move, but also monitored the moves of everyone who came near. The main entrance, which was about 30 metres from the road, was protected by a screen of bulletproof glass, metres high and metres wide, so that cars could pull up and their passengers could get out without the risk of being shot. The windows of all the apartments were also made of the same glass and there were security cameras everywhere. Once you were inside, however, you were completely shut off from the potential danger of the city and felt totally safe. Even so, the curious atmosphere beyond our heavily guarded perimeter still made me slightly uneasy, coming as I did from a country where such security measures were not necessary and the risks of falling victim to attacks and random murder were (then, at least) almost non-existent.

I soon discovered Bogota in all it many facets. I was taken to the Museo del Oro (with its unbelievable golden treasures). I was invited to the residences of various friends of the family, including other leading businessmen, politicians and media figures. We explored the leafy suburbs around Bogota and even went as far as Los Llanos, the beautiful hills just outside the city, with its excellent restaurants and breathtaking panoramas. In short, it was the most marvellous time and as a world traveller I still have the most wonderful memories of those carefree days. My visit was a succession of one amazing discovery after another, and I quickly became charmed by the country, the people and the culture.

During my stay, another close friend of the family arrived in Columbia. This was the esquire Bryan Montgomery. He made a three-day stop-over in Bogota, to give him a breather after a tiring business trip that had taken him from London to Japan, Indonesia, Bahrain and Australia, before moving on to spend a week at his holiday home on Key West in Florida. Bryan, who sadly died a couple of years ago, was a much respected British businessman, philanthropist, politician and humanist. Amongst his many other functions, he was the third generation owner-chairman of the second largest company in the world specialised in the organisation of international trade fairs. During that visit, I got to know Bryan, who I had never met before and who was thirty years older than myself, as someone with a huge amount of resilience and a liberal dose of British phlegm and humour. He shared my passion for contemporary art, the collection of which he saw not only as a way to broaden his own mind and thinking, but also as a way to support promising young artists, while making sound investments for the future in a manner that diversified his already impressive portfolio. As for me, I was just learning to explore the fascinating mystery and diversity of modern art, which would later become my greatest passion. In other words, we had something very much in common, something that would unconditionally bind us for the rest of our lives.

It was this shared passion for art that prompted Bryan to invite me that fateful morning of 11 January 1994 to accompany him on a visit to the studio of Dolores Nunez – an artist of Spanish origin living in Columbia. To me, it seemed like an opportunity that was too good to miss: the chance to get to know an up-and-coming artist in the company of a fine art-lover and collector from who I could also learn much. I agreed without hesitation.

The Nunez studio was on the other side of Bogota, so Oscar, our host, agreed to lend Bryan and myself his car for the day, together with his driver, Enrique. The car in question was a heavy and partially armoured BMW, which had previously served Oscar as his official vehicle during his time as Columbia's ambassador in Mexico. It was the only transport option we had: Bryan was a true bon-vivant, who wasn't too worried about watching his weight. It would have been a hard job to squeeze his 165-kilo bulk into the two-seater sports car of Katja, Oscar's wife! It was late afternoon by the time we finally set off. The drive to the studio was an interesting one, taking us through some of Bogota's most elegant and attractive neighbourhoods, although we passed others that were clearly much less appealing…

Once we had arrived at Dolores' place, we had a marvellous time. I was charmed by the powerful expressiveness of her work and how she managed to inject the energy of her Spanish temperament into her pieces. She took the time to explain to us how she first gathered her ideas, before translating them into sketches that she later used to make her finished works, which she then displayed in exhibitions and galleries in her own unique way.

I tried to translate for Bryan, who was not a Spanish speaker, the nuances of what she was saying. At the end of our visit, she gifted us a number of reproductions of her own work and the work of her partner at the time, Alberto Pancorbo. She carefully rolled up the reproductions and put them into a cardboard tube, and my delight was complete when she unexpectedly added an original study piece of one of her paintings. The rest of the day just couldn't get any better – or so I thought.

After we left Dolores's studio, Bryan suggested that we should not dine with our hosts that evening, but should go to a well-known Italian restaurant, where he had eaten so well during a previous visit. So that we could get to know each other better and talk about art, he said. For the second time that day, I didn't need to think twice. It was Christmas time, my partner was held up at his office that night by an unexpected new deadline and I also wanted to learn more about this fascinating Englishman and his passion for painting and sculpture. We asked Enrique to drive us to the Italian, which was located in the centre of one of the better commercial districts in Bogota. So off we went.

On the way in the car, Bryan and I had an intense discussion about Nunez's art and her expressive power. I also wanted to hear from Bryan how he had started his collection and how he selected the pieces he decided to buy. It was only years later, after I had visited him a few times at his country house in Amersham (near London) and at his villa in Crete, that I became aware of just how large and impressive that collection really was. He later donated part of the collection, now known as the Bryan Montgomery Collection, to the Budapest Museum of Modern Art, which houses it in a special wing named in his honour. He also created a sculpture park in the grounds of the house at Amersham and all his company premises throughout the world were graced with magnificent pieces from his collection. He really was a true art-lover.

The drive to the restaurant was a long one, made even longer by the chaos of the traffic and the appalling state of the Bogota roads. By now, it was evening and already starting to get dark. Not that we were worried. Far from it: the atmosphere inside the car was good and Enrique had put on some jazzy music. It was one of those special moments when you feel connected with a deep source of happiness and experience an intense sensation of inner harmony. At last, we were getting closer to the city centre and were just 15 minutes from our destination. I can remember that we passed the headquarters of the *guardia civil*. It was about half past nine. Quite late, but not too late to dine at that exquisite

Italian restaurant. Little did we know that we were destined to never arrive...

And then it began. All of a sudden, we were overtaken by a white car. Two men were hanging out of the windows, shouting aggressively at Enrique that he had to pull over, while keeping us covered the whole time with heavy automatic weapons. Because our driver knew instantly that this was a matter of Life and death, he ignored their warnings and put his foot down hard on the accelerator. The powerful BMW engine roared and our car shot forward. Enrique realised that our only chance was to try and outrun the terrorists' car, which was now hot on our tail. He had been trained to deal with situations of this kind and screamed at us to lie down. The terrorist driver tried several times, unsuccessfully, to force our car off the road. Eventually, however, he managed to pull alongside the BMW, allowing one of the other thugs to fire at our tyres and pour bullets into the bodywork.

After that, everything happened quickly. It seemed as though we had stumbled into the middle of a bad gangster movie. We were now the ones who were in the wrong place at the wrong time... The screeching of the tyres, the roar of the engines and the rat-a-tat-tat of the machine guns made a discordant and very frightening cacophony of sounds.

I am only able to tell you what followed because Bryan later told me everything that happened. For me, the events of those next few minutes have been totally erased from my memory. Gone. Vanished.

When the terrorists finally forced the BMW to a halt, they pulled Enrique out of the driver's seat and demanded at gunpoint that he should tell them who was in the back. He said that Bryan and I were friends of his boss. 'So where is the boss himself?'

they screamed. 'He's at home,' replied Enrique, as calmly as he could, but as frightened as hell. 'These are just foreign tourists. Innocent people. They are only visiting.' One of the armed men then looked inside the back of the car to see if Enrique was telling the truth. They were hoping to find Oscar. What they found was... us!

In their frustration and rage, they beat Enrique to a pulp and threw his bleeding body over me on the back seat of the car. Two terrorists then climbed into the front, one to drive and one to keep us covered with his machine gun from the passenger's seat. Or rather, to keep Bryan covered. Enrique was still unconscious from his beating and I had also been dazed when we had been rammed off the road and I was shot. The BMW sped through the city, followed by the terrorists' own vehicle: tyres screeching, the alarm on our car wailing, lights flashing. I can remember fragments of the noise. But what I can remember most of all – because the door was not tightly shut – was the nauseating smell, a combination of blood, leather and exhaust fumes.

At some point I must have come round again. I could hear the man on the passenger's seat shouting aggressively at Bryan, who couldn't understand a word of Spanish. The terrorist was saying that if the 'fucking bastard of a rich tourist' didn't stop staring at him, he would kill him there and then. We had been forbidden to talk, so I looked intensely at Bryan with my eyes, trying to get the message across as best I could. But there was no reaction. According to Bryan, I then grabbed the terrorist by the neck with all my strength and pulled him back against the headrest of the front seat, in a frenzied attempt to strangle him. He was surprised, but not surprised enough to drop his gun, the butt of which he brought down on my head with a sickening thud. This explains why I was later treated in hospital for a deep and bloody gash in my forehead, although I didn't realise it at the time.

Bryan always said that my action was heroic and had saved his Life. Because he couldn't understand what the man with the gun was saying and because in his shocked condition he couldn't stop staring straight into the terrorist's eyes, he was certain that without my intervention he would have been shot and killed. Was he right? I have no idea! I can't remember anything at all about it!

The only thing I can recall before I fainted again is that I said: 'Oh my god, Bryan!' And then the lights went out. And this time they went out properly. It was quite some time before I regained consciousness and became aware of what was happening.

I don't know how long it took me to crawl from the car, from which I had now managed to extricate myself, to what I thought was a 'safe place'. But at a certain moment, I realised – totally unexpectedly and wholly unplanned! – that I was next to Bryan and Enrique, who were alive but lying motionless on the ground under the muzzles of the terrorists' machine guns. I saw that Bryan's large, round face and neck were bloody and swollen. I can remember thinking that his head looked like the head of the crucified Christ, with red blood from his forehead dripping down across his pallid features.

The first question I asked was: 'Bryan, what happened?' 'We got kidnapped!' he replied. 'Now shut up, because they threatened to shoot us if we speak,' he added in a frightened whisper.

'Kidnapped!?' I thought. 'What the fuck!'

Suddenly, I heard a voice from the kidnappers' car shout. '*Liquidales! Y vamonos!*' – 'Let's just finish them off and get out of here!' This was one of the moments when understanding Spanish was not an advantage. It was all too clear – to me, at least – what fate now awaited us.

This sudden and brutal realisation paralysed me with fear. I could feel my heart racing and my throat constricting. I just managed to call out in panic: 'They are going to kill us! My god, Bryan! They are going to kill us!' His eyes looked directly into mine. All I could see was dazed incomprehension. Our time had come. We were going to die. I was still only in my twenties and I was about to be slaughtered like a pig in a cold and wet forest somewhere outside Bogota. Like in all the books and movies, I saw my Life flash before my eyes in an instant. Had it all been for nothing? I could even imagine the newspaper headlines back home: 'Olivier Onghena-'t Hooft dies in a hail of bullets in Columbia.'

Following his leader's instructions, one of the five terrorists moved towards us, to finish us off. He was only about 20 metres away. I could see his silhouette, but not his face, because it was too dark. A thousand and one thoughts raced through my mind. My heart continued to pound, like it was trying to break out of my chest. Such was my fear that I could scarcely breathe. My eyes searched for contact with something real, something that would take me out of this nightmare. But there was nothing. This was reality… All notion of time had long since disappeared and the pain I had previously felt had vanished as well. I could hear the footsteps of our executioner getting closer and closer. It seemed to take forever, but it can only have been a few seconds. The end was now very near and I awaited the explosion of bullets that would tear into our three helpless bodies. By now, 'Number 5' (as I came to regard him) was just a few steps away. He stopped to load and cock his weapon – that terrifying 'click-clack' sound will stay with me as long as I live! – and lowered the barrel to point it in our direction. There was to be no mercy, no last-minute reprieve: his leader had told him to kill us and that is what he would do.

What happened next changed my Life forever and gave it a new and lasting sense of purpose. The events in question can only have lasted for a few a seconds but they are engraved with crystal-like clarity in my memory, so that I can still recall them, right down to the finest detail.

As our murderer stood over us – I never saw his face, but Bryan swore that he recognised him years later in a *Guardian* article about terrorists killed by the Columbian army – I was more frightened about the pain I thought the bullets would cause than about the prospect of my imminent death. Perhaps he wouldn't kill us immediately. Perhaps he would only wound us fatally, so that our torn bodies would slowly bleed to death in great agony. What the hell did I know? How are you supposed to think at a moment like that? It is so far removed from anything you have ever experienced that all you can do is fall back on your essential self and your natural instinct for survival.

In an attempt to try and limit the impact of the bullets, I made myself as small as possible by rolling into a foetal position and putting my arms over my head. Was this to be my last independent action? A desire to avoid the mutilating effects of a machine gun at close range? The only thing I can remember consciously thinking is: 'Just do it, man! Let's get it over with!' But at the same time I also had an awareness of something else: 'Shit, this is going to hurt. Where will the first bullets hit. How long will it last? Will we die instantly?'

Remember, we are only talking about fractions of seconds here! And, strangely enough, immediately after these thoughts had flashed through my brain, I became completely calm. An intense feeling of peace and tranquillity swept over me. It was as if I had entered the twilight zone between Life and death. In fact, that is precisely what happened, although I didn't realise it until later.

I experienced the kind of restfulness you experience during a dreamy day in the countryside, surrounded and enchanted by the wonders of nature...

The external world seemed to slow down. The chaos around me ceased. The noises inside my head became more distant. My consciousness moved into another dimension. I suddenly found myself in a different reality. A wonderful new reality. A reality I had never known or encountered before. Amazingly beautiful and harmonious. A huge field full of flowers stretched out before me, acre after acre of unspoilt natural magnificence. The combination and intensity of the colours was dazzling. And the variety of the flowers was equally spellbinding. This was a field like no other. Endless. Enchanting. Exhilarating. In the distance I could see a kindly sun. I was no longer aware of fear, pain or anything else connected with ordinary reality. Suddenly, I saw my mother, who is still alive, walking, almost nymph-like, across the field, her arms stretched out towards me, speaking words of comfort and encouragement as she came. The contrast with what was happening in the real world around me could not have been greater and I could feel myself retreating deeper and deeper into my inner self. At that moment, I had no idea whether I was already dead or still alive. I didn't even have the conscious awareness to think about it in any meaningful way. All I had was a vague sense of being in some kind of intermediary state between Life and death, making a journey towards a pleasingly bucolic world that seemed to be beckoning me. Was this death? Or was it heaven? Surely it couldn't be hell!? Had I reached my final destination? Wherever it was, it was peaceful, serene and unbelievably beautiful.

But sadly – or perhaps not? – it didn't last. After an indefinable period of time, this sweet bucolic world of flowers, nature, maternal love, peace, sunshine and great calm gradually faded away, to be replaced by confusion, astonishment, pain, anger and darkness.

In the meantime, Bryan and Enrique had already returned to the reality of this world. They had heard a woman shouting: '*Viene la policia, viene la policia!*' A woman in the middle of the night in a forest in the middle of nowhere, miles outside of Bogota, suddenly shouting: 'The police are coming'? It seemed like a miracle (even though I don't believe in them). How was it possible? And who on earth was she? We never saw the woman and she never made herself known to us. But at that moment she saved our lives.

In a matter of seconds, with engines revving and tyres screeching, our five would-be assassins had roared away, taking both vehicles – theirs and ours – with them. Bryan, Enrique and myself were now abandoned in a desolate spot, miles away from anywhere, with no transport, no means of communication and little prospect of immediate help. No-one knew we were here and there was no-one around to whom we could turn. But at least we were still alive. How I would have loved to have met that woman, to have put my arms around her neck and thanked her from the bottom of my heart...

After the first waves of confusion and relief had passed, we slowly returned to a state that can best be described as a kind of unconscious awareness. We began to realise that the terrorists had gone and we started talking to each other. I said to Bryan: 'Bryan, I think I am paralysed.' To which he replied: 'Are you sure? You managed to get here, didn't you?' Apparently, he had not seen how I had needed to use my arms and elbows to crawl away from the BMW. 'Can you move your feet?' he asked. 'Yes, I can!' I said. Notwithstanding the searing pain, which felt as though someone had poured acid into my veins, so that every movement brought with it a burning sensation that ran from my groin to my abdomen, I kept on wiggling my feet, for fear that I would lose the use of them if I ever stopped. What I didn't realise at the time was that by continually moving my feet in this way, I was slowly draining my body of blood. The doctors told me afterwards that, in effect, I was slowly bleeding myself to death, because my 'foot wiggling' kept on pumping blood out through the various bullet wounds in my body.

Bryan held my hand and I held his. His head was swollen and covered in blood. I asked him how he was and he replied with typical British phlegm: 'I'll be alright'. I could see that Enrique was clearly in shock. He kept running around like a headless chicken, moving constantly back and forth over the boggy piece of ground that had nearly become our place of execution. But at least he could still walk, which increased our chances of getting out of here alive. I shouted to him several times, but nothing seemed to register. He just kept on running around in circles. Once, when he passed close enough to me, I grabbed hold of his trouser leg. I screamed at him that he needed to pull himself together and check whether he was wounded or not. I then added, with as much urgency as I could muster: 'Enrique, go and get help. Find out where we are and see if you can get find anyone to help us. If you can, call Oscar. He will know what to do. Now go!' He ran off into the forest, but I wasn't certain whether he had understood or whether my shouting had just panicked him.

I am a firm believer that in this kind of crisis situation, where death is never far away, people's true nature and real strengths automatically come to the surface. The fact that I was able to take control and try to find a solution to our predicament, even though I was in shock and suffering great pain from my wounds, speaks volumes about the human spirit – and was an important lesson for me in later Life. How else can you explain that someone whose legs were riddled with bullets, had a flesh wound in his back and was slowly bleeding to death could summon up the will to live and the necessary Life Force that helped to ensure we survived this terrible ordeal?

Because survive we did, all three of us, each in his different way.

Enrique had indeed gone for help. He found his way to a residential building at the edge of the forest and was able to speak to the caretaker via the intercom. He asked him to telephone Oscar, and the caretaker agreed. Shortly after midnight, Oscar and Katja were awoken by a stranger who informed them that there had been an attack, that their car had been stolen and that its three occupants had been badly wounded. Not surprisingly, all hell broke loose!

In the meantime, while Enrique was away, Bryan and I saw two motorbikes approach the fringes of the clearing where we lay. In Columbia, you are never certain whether the people you meet these kinds of circumstances are 'good guys' or 'bad guys'. In the hope that they were the former, I waved my arms and screamed out in Spanish that we needed help. We were lucky – or so we thought. They were two local policemen on patrol. Imagine our surprise and dismay when they briefly conferred, turned their bikes around and drove off! When I later told my story to agents of Columbia's state security service, they said that this was the usual reaction of the police and emergency services in such situations: the drugs barons and the FARC terrorists made it a habit of murdering anyone who offered help to their victims. This was their way of creating the terror and chaos that allowed them to keep their grip over the authorities and the local population.

Time dragged on but eventually we saw another vehicle approaching. This time it was a police van and this time they did stop and come to our aid. But it was very painful aid. I had only been able to explain in pretty vague terms my wounds and what I thought had happened to me, and clearly they hadn't understood properly. They just grabbed hold of my arms and legs, pulled me across the ground and bundled me onto the back seat of the van.

Because the van was small, my legs were still hanging outside. As a result, that they pushed them roughly into a folding position, so that they could close the door. I screamed with pain and kept on screaming, until they realised that this wasn't going to work. They opened the door again and pulled me back out onto the ground. They said that they would need to call for assistance. By this time, the pain was excruciating and I thought that every moment might be my last.

A short time later (although for us it felt like hours), two ambulances arrived. At first glance, they seemed more like the security vans used for transporting money. Once again, I was seized by fear: were they 'goodies' or 'baddies'? But once again, our luck held. The ambulance crew explained that they were paramilitary medics, who were specially trained to give first aid in terrorist incidents. Their ambulances were indeed armour-plated and they all carried weapons! Not for the first time that night, I wondered just what kind of madness we had unwittingly stumbled into…

The ambulance men wanted to evacuate me in one ambulance and Bryan and Enrique (who by now had returned) in the other. Because Bryan couldn't speak a word of Spanish, I was reluctant to be parted in this way and held on tightly to his hand. Even though I was on the verge of going into shock, I insisted that we stay together and wouldn't accept their argument that Bryan's weight made this difficult. The harder they argued, the harder I argued back, until eventually they agreed. Bryan and I set off for the hospital in the back of the same ambulance, still hand in bloody hand.

Yet even then, the excitement was not at an end. As we were ready to drive away, two large SUVs pulled into the clearing under police escort. Uncertain what was happening, the ambulance crews drew their guns and prepared to defend themselves. There was a good deal of shouting back and forth, before it became clear that the SUVs (also armour-plated) were there to help. In fact, they actually belonged to Oscar and Katja's near neighbour, the prime minister of Columbia. As soon as they had received the call from the caretaker Enrique had asked for help, our hosts immediately contacted their influential neighbour to seek his advice. He agreed to transport them to the scene of the crime in his own personal vehicles, since this was the only way to get cross Bogota quickly and safely.

I can remember clearly that I gave my wallet to Katja, who was standing by the open ambulance door and looking as pale as death. I also asked her to look after my other things and to make sure that we were now taken to the best hospital in town. As an afterthought, I added that I didn't want to receive a blood transfusion from people I did not know. During the journey, the ambulance people tried to convince us to go to the nearest hospital, since they said that every minute could make a difference to my chances of survive. Once again, I stuck to my guns: even though the best hospital was much further away, I insisted that this was where I wanted to be taken, as I already knew of its outstanding reputation. There, and nowhere else! The driver shrugged his shoulders and set off on the long journey across the city.

It seemed to take an age before we got there but we finally arrived at the best private hospital in Bogota, where the best professional medics in the country, who had all been trained abroad, were waiting to treat me and Bryan. But not Enrique. He had been taken by the other ambulance to a different hospital in a state of complete shock and it was several days before we saw him again.

From the ambulance, I was transferred to a trolley and wheeled into the accident and emergency unit. By now, I was drifting in and out of consciousness. Like in the movies, I can remember looking up at the ceiling and seeing a succession of brightly coloured tubes and cables pass before my eyes. Once I was in the operating theatre, the surgical team wanted to get started immediately. I could see the anaesthetist moving towards me and I will never forget my reaction. Turning my head to look directly at the head of the team, I said: 'My name is Olivier Onghena. I am 27 years old and come from Belgium. I am a guest of the Perez family, my blood group is A positive and I only want to receive blood from my host family. I also expect you to consult with me in advance about everything you intend to do to me. Now is that clear?' The team leader, who had trained as an A&E specialist surgeon in America and later turned out to be a charming man, could hardly conceal a smile. He replied that everything was crystal clear and that what I asked would not be a problem. I could rest assured that they would do everything possible to 'save' me! He explained that they would first give me a sedative, before removing my clothes and cleaning my wounds. Afterwards, they would send me down to the radiology department, where they could see what kind of internal damage I had suffered. Only then would I be brought back for surgery.

This seemed to me like a fair deal, so I nodded my agreement! It was at that point that my body finally gave out. Without warning, I went into a shock so severe that I was soon bouncing up and down on the operating table in a fit of uncontrollable spasms. My muscles and limbs would no longer do what I wanted. I had lost all mastery over my bodily functions. It was an unnerving experience – but by no means my last one.

Once they had stabilised me, they removed my clothes and cleaned my wounds, as they had explained. But transferring me back to a trolley to be taken down to X-ray, being turned over and prodded by a team of six nurses, to see where I had sustained broken bones or other injuries, having the bullet wounds in my legs and back probed, however gently: these were painful experiences that I hope I never have to repeat.

Even so, in the final analysis the results turned out to be not too bad, and could certainly have been a lot worse: one bullet through the left leg, with no bone damage but serious muscle and some nerve damage, entering the left side and exiting the right; one bullet in the right leg, entering in the left side and pressing against the skin on the right side, without exiting; a bullet wound in the lower back, at the fifth and sixth lumbar vertebrae; a wound on my forehead (from the machine gun butt); scratches and glass wounds on the throat and neck; a serious loss of blood. At this stage, it was not clear whether there would be any permanent damage.

The results of my blood and oxygen tests were also in and it appeared that I had lost so much blood that immediate surgery was out of the question without a prior period of rest and recuperation. As a result, I was taken off to a private room in the intensive care department to 'sleep'.

That night was the most terrible and most frightening of my Life! Sleeping was impossible and I became confused and disoriented by all the strange noises and images that kept flashing through my brain. My thoughts were in total chaos and my emotions ranged from panic to despair and back again. Would I survive? If so, in what condition? What would I tell my parents? And might my attackers not return to try and finish me off? Even with an armed guard to watch over me, it was still nearly morning before I finally drifted off into an exhausted sleep in fits and starts. I was alarmed and distressed at the total lack of control I seemed to have over my own thought processes. It was like being in a mental strait-jacket.

Fortunately, I received the very best care and soon began to recover at a rapid rate. The physical and emotional support I was given could not have been better. According to the specialists who treated me, I would be able to walk, run and even play sports 'more or less normally' after just a few weeks or months, provided I did the necessary exercises and had the iron discipline this effort required.

After a few days in hospital, I was allowed to go 'home' to Oscar and Katja's, where I again received the best treatment money could buy. But now came the difficult task of telling my parents that I would be returning to Belgium a few weeks earlier than planned. I can still remember almost word for word the telephone conversation I had with my father: 'Hey dad. Everything okay? Here? I'm afraid I've had a little accident. Nothing too serious, but I need to rest up for a few weeks before I can come home. What happened exactly? Er, well…' I gave him a very quick summary, playing down the seriousness of the incident. I could have saved my breath. One of my then sisters-in-law later told me that after our conversation, my father immediately went upstairs to the library where she, my brother and my mother were already sitting. He tried to speak, but the words just wouldn't come out of his mouth. They all thought he had had some kind of seizure, until he finally blurted out: 'Olivier was kidnapped, seriously injured and is paralysed. It will be a few weeks before he can come home…' Okay, that is not exactly how I explained it to him, but at least everyone on the home front now knew. It took all my powers of persuasion to prevent my brothers (with the very best of intentions) from jumping on the next plane to Bogota. They wanted to help, and that was very kind of them – but there was nothing they could have done.

The revalidation period was at times exhausting. I needed to find some mental peace of mind, while at the same time building up my bodily strength – a combination that wasn't always easy. I also had to make myself available to the Columbian state security service, the federal police, various other government departments and the Belgian embassy (who performed their duties perfectly, both in operational and human terms). In addition, numerous well-meaning friends of the Perez family also came to see me, offering their support and expressing outrage that such a thing should happen to a guest in Columbia (before going on to detail their own experiences with murders, kidnappings, etc.). At one point, it all became too much for me and I asked for access to be restricted to just my host family and a few close friends. I needed time to myself, so that I could order my thoughts. But I also needed space to deal with my physical pain (the wounds in my legs had torn open on more than one occasion when I was just out walking with crutches, as my doctor had instructed). Above all, I wanted to focus on what would happen after Bogota and what I would do when I returned to Belgium.

It was that intense period of revalidation, when I was still physically limited by my injuries but was mentally very sharp and focused, that I began in some mysterious way or other to think about my Life. I wanted to go in search of the deeper meaning of Life, although I really had no idea what that might mean. I had become intrigued by the functioning of the brain and the link between fear and behaviour. I found that I wanted to know more about the importance of emotions, not only in crisis situations, but also in general.

In fact, what I initially wanted was to find out why Bryan, Enrique and myself had each responded very differently to the same facts in the same context. Both during the kidnapping and for a time afterwards, Bryan was totally apathetic, 'spaced out', staring into nothingness. Enrique had reacted very strangely, both immediately after the terrorists fled and when we were taken back to Bogota. He just ran out of the hospital without saying a word to anyone, only to reappear at his employer's several days later. He didn't want to speak about what had happened and for a few years, he never did. Of the three of us, I had been the most badly injured, but I was also the one who remained most calm, following my remarkable near-death experience. How could we all behave so differently? But this was not the only question that occupied my thoughts. At the same time, I wanted to know why so many terrible things happened in the world and, more specifically, in a country like Columbia, where the people were generally friendly and the culture was fantastic. Linked to this, I also wanted to know if there was a reason why things like this happened to some people and not others. Could I answer these questions? If I could, could I also draw any lessons from those answers? And if so, what lessons?

The events of my Life have prompted me on more than one occasion to ask that most fundamental of questions: what is the meaning or the purpose of the things that happen? Not just during my recovery from the kidnapping, but also later on.

Why, for example, did my grandfather die so unexpectedly in January 1984? Following an intestinal perforation as a result of undetected stomach cancer, 'Parrain' (as I called him) left us much too quickly and much too soon. I can remember it as though it were yesterday. We were sitting at home in the front room – my grandmother, my parents and my brothers – asking our existential question about why God let such a good person die, while he let the most terrible criminals and paedophiles live.

Why was my close friend, Caroline F, a unique woman in every respect, slowly eaten away from the inside by another aggressive form of cancer? We discussed the point – the purpose – of her disease several times before she died. What message could she find behind her terrible suffering? Was there any message? In the end, she gave up the search for meaning in her condition. One of my last memories of her is of her lying, exhausted and zombie-like, on her death-bed, staring up at me and my Life partner Luciano, and whispering: 'But it's just not possible! It's just not possible.' We had to strain to hear her words and the next day she fell silent forever, at the age of just forty-one.

Why was a leader like Gandhi murdered? Why are so many African leaders corrupt, enjoying lives of unimaginable luxury, while their people live in poverty and misery? Why do IS terrorists carry out such terrible attacks and throw homosexuals from the roofs of tall buildings? Why is there so much domestic violence in supposedly 'developed' countries? Why are so many children abused and mistreated by men and women who have sworn to protect them and set them a good moral example? Why does one half of the world have an abundance of almost everything, while the other half has a lack of almost everything? Why do we continue to consume, consume, consume, behaving as though there is nothing wrong with the environment? Why do people meekly accept their position as slaves to the economic system? Why does a man like Trump become president of the richest and most powerful country in the world and think it is a good thing to destroy the social achievements of his predecessor, Barack Obama? Why are so many multinationals only concerned with their own interests and those of their shareholders? So many questions about the purpose of Life!

The big billion-dollar question that I asked myself after the kidnapping in 1994 was this: why am I still alive? I wanted to discover more about my deeper inner motivations. What made me want to live? What was it that gave my Life meaning and purpose? Why did I want to get up each morning with so much enthusiasm? What did I want to make of my Life, enriched as it now was not only by my experiences in Columbia, but also by all my other previous experiences and by all the experiences that were no doubt still to come? After all, that is what Life is: living in the here and now but founded on the wisdom of lessons from the past and our hopes for the future.

In addition to all these questions, there was something else that continued to puzzle me: why had I never asked these crucial questions before? Were there moments in the past when I had consciously thought about the meaning and purpose of my Life? If I was honest with myself: very few, if any. This was something I understood quickly: we humans, the most evolved species on earth, always wait until something terrible happens in our Life before we ask the questions that really matter. Curious, don't you think? Why do we first have to experience some drama or tragedy before we can be persuaded to think about the truly important things? Do we first need to see our Life in a different perspective before these things acquire their importance? Why is it only when some disaster has struck that we finally turn to the more spiritual side of Life? And why do we only search for comfort and hope in some higher power (god, the universe, music, prayer, reflection, silence, memories…) when we are travelling through the vale of tears? When will we learn to trust in ourselves?

These are the questions that I will try to answer in the following chapters. Inevitably, these answers will be strongly coloured by my own experience and my own outlook on the world, by my own spiritual development and my own philosophy of Life. I do not pretend that I have all the answers and it is not my intention to try and 'convert' you to my point of view. I simply want to share with you the things that are important, even crucial, in the hope that this will encourage you to reflect more deeply and to look at your Life in a different way.

The basis of everything is the journey and the search that we make together as people, as human beings. And as far as this journey is concerned, the old adage holds true: to travel hopefully is better than to arrive. Our perceived destination only sets a general direction for our travels; how we actually get there says immeasurably more about who we are and what we want. It is this search, in my case inspired by the events of the kidnapping, that forms the subject of the following chapter.

The quest for meaning in Life

'Two men look out through the same bars. One sees the mud, and one the stars.' (Frederick Langbridge)

As a result of the kidnapping, my views on just about everything – Life, human beings, our potential, our resources – changed dramatically.

This chapter is about my journey towards meaning and how I would give my Life a new purpose. After Bogota, it was no longer a matter of simply wanting to live or to be like everyone else. I wanted my Life to be special. Destiny, in the shape of my experiences at the hands of my kidnappers, had marked me in such ways (both positive and negative) that I had no choice but to live my Life differently, more intensely and more uniquely. If you have been kidnapped and shot, there are essentially three things you can do. You can act as though nothing has happened and try to put the events out of your mind as best you can. Or you can surrender to your trauma, embracing it in an unhealthy manner that will ultimately lead to your psychological extinction and your transformation from a human being into an amorphous nothingness. Or you can choose to live the Life you so nearly lost to the full and turn it into something remarkable. With this final option, it is as though you use 'the experience' as a foundation for building up a new and more conscious vision for the future.

As you have probably guessed, I chose the third option. My psyche had not been irreparably damaged, so that I still had the possibility to exercise my free will and to stand in Life more fully and with greater awareness than ever before. I began to try and find a meaning and a purpose for everything. I took every opportunity to ask myself questions about the 'why' of things and the finite nature of moments and relationships. I wanted to understand how people can help each other and how they can be there for each other, rather than against each other. I went in search of the potential in myself and those around me, because I had begun to sense that human potential is a powerful source of strength and progress. It struck me that it was much more worthwhile and much more personally enriching to spend my time on useful and purposeful things than to lead a Life governed by the uninspiring meaninglessness of gossip, indifference and negativity. I wanted to find out how I could achieve the most output with the least input, in all fields of endeavour. What did I need to do, so that I could get the most out of Life? Because I now realised that Life – my Life – could end from one moment to the next. In my case, that end had been very close and terribly real.

Makrigialos

This book is about my trajectory, my journey, my search for my noble purpose.

After my initial deep reflections about the meaning of Life during my rehabilitation in Bogota, I was finally able to give concrete shape and form to my *noble purpose* in the summer of 1997.

After the kidnapping, Bryan Montgomery, my companion in misfortune, invited me to visit him, so that we could get to know each other better. I stayed a number of times at his estate in Amersham Common, just outside London, and also at his holiday home in the Cretan village of Makrigialos. He had bought and converted a number of old fisherman's cottages where he spent the summer months, although he later moved to a villa that he had built further inland. The village was on the coast in the southern part of the island, far from the capital city of Heraklion and, fortunately, far enough from the awful tourist trap at Agios Nikolaos. Bryan's domain had something theatrical, almost cinematographic about it, standing as it did high on a hill surrounded by an olive grove. The design of the villa itself was a stylish cross between Beverly Hills brashness and Scandinavian refinement, all bathed in the relaxing Greek atmosphere that has so much in common with the Italian concept of *dolce far niente* that I love so much. The villa had wide terraces on each side, with a magnificent garden and a huge patio that led to an equally huge swimming pool, which was lined by a colonnade and looked out over a deep valley with a fine view of the distant sea. The weather was always perfect and the wonderful fragrances of the Cretan countryside are still embedded in my memory. It was, above all, the early mornings, with their unimaginable serenity and beauty that I remember most of all. The natural charm and intensity of the surroundings impressed me deeply.

During that unforgettable summer of 1997, I drew up the plan for what I then referred to as my 'Life's mission'. I had chosen different books from which I could seek inspiration and had brought with me a blank notebook to add my own thoughts and conclusions. My intention was to write down everything I learnt about myself and what I wanted to do. I read a number of works by Sanaya Roman, who had received many of his own spiritual lessons from the medium Orin. I also read *The Alchemist* by Paulo Cuelho, about the search for Life and the Soul of the Universe, as well as *The Celestine Prophecy* by James Redfield, *Emotional Intelligence* by Daniel Goleman and *The Seven Spiritual Laws* by Deepak Chopra, the last of which I still regard in many ways as my own personal 'bible'. As if this was not enough, I also devoured *Le Sens du Bonheur* by Krishnamurti and various pieces by the Dalai Lama. I sought inspiration in spiritual texts and old writings, often while listening to classical music, traditional Greek songs or opera (yes, there was lots of opera). In between, I made long walks in the often rugged Cretan landscape, where I could gather and order my thoughts.

But if it was a time of great intellectual stimulation, it was also a time of wonderful culinary delight. At the local markets, Bryan and I chose the ingredients for light lunches and sumptuous dinners. I made them both with the same great enthusiasm and served them in beautiful old terracotta dishes and richly decorated bowls. We had candle-lit dinners in the dining room, around the pool and even at different places on the grass. Each moment was a moment of beauty, a moment of sheer pleasure in the enjoyment of what is. No effort was made to make things more complex than they needed to be. Instead, our search was a search for purity.

It all made me feel very calm and happy. Sometimes, I stayed up all night, just lying in a hammock and looking at the stars. Sometimes, I got up before dawn, to watch the sunrise over the sea, to feel how the world was slowly awakening and how the sense of energy increased as the sun climbed higher and higher.

In my diary, I wrote down all the thoughts that came to me as I was reading, walking or being otherwise creative. I made a note of everything that stimulated me mentally, emotionally and spiritually, the things that took my thoughts and feelings to a higher level. I selected particular sentences and words that appealed to me or prompted me to deeper reflection. I spent days (and sometimes even nights) just reading, forming my ideas, or philosophising with Bryan and his other guests (Bryan's house, like God's, had many mansions and they were frequently occupied). Bryan, who was remarkably learned in his own right, acted as a sounding board for my ideas. He seemed to enjoy challenging me with his understated British humour and his attempts to catch me out in ways that would allow me to learn from my mistakes. This was his way of checking how deeply I was taken with an idea and then helping me to develop new ideas of my own from it. In short, Bryan was a kind of mentor for me. He called himself: 'The non-official godfather whom Olivier helped to survive'.

The love for books and other writings that I acquired during that summer has never left me. From that moment on, I continued to read as much as I could, thousands of pages at a time. Gradually, I began to see a pattern in what I was doing. Often, the core of what I was extracting from my reading could be traced back to a special and often exalted view of Life, the world and humankind that I was gradually developing. In fact, my views on Life and people had evolved out of all recognition since the kidnapping. What's more, these feeling of enlightenment, positivism and of somehow being different appealed to me enormously. Having the courage to say things that went against the norm and elaborating new ideas and philosophies that stimulate reflection and bring us closer together through our shared emotions and our common humanity: these were all things that exhilarated me more than I could ever have imagined. As Bryan would have said: I had found my 'cup of tea'. I began to develop a clear sense that the link between spirituality and pragmatism, between the exalted and the earthly, between the extraordinary and the everyday, between what is and what can be, that these contrasting yet complementary elements would form the basis for my 'Life's mission'.

Of course, I also understood that my journey was not yet over. On the contrary, I still had a long way to go before I could give that mission concrete shape and form. Above all, I needed to go deeper into what I thought and felt. But how? I have never taken drugs and hardly ever touch alcohol (and still don't), so how could I find a way to truly connect with my deeper inner self? A sustainable way that could have a major impact on the physical, mental and spiritual aspects of my Life? I discovered the answer in mediation, yoga and self-development. These three techniques are all connected with each other and all strengthen each other. In fact, I would even go so far as to say that all three are indispensible for each other if you wish to undergo a transformation that will be both complete and lasting. I will return to this process of transformation in the chapter 'Joy through noble purpose'. But first I would like to say something about the power of that deepening and connecting.

Inspiration

Inspiration has always been essential for me. Even when I was a small boy, I can remember looking out the window of our beautiful house in the countryside and being rapt in awe at all the wonderful things I saw outside, especially the beauties of nature and animals. However, it took my post-kidnapping Makrigialos journey to make me more fully aware of the role that inspiration had played and would continue to play in my Life. All those amazing moments and insights which inspired me during that summer of 1997 helped to make me who I am today. By acquiring deeper understanding and greater connectedness through inspiration, it is possible for a human being to achieve great things. And if you can link that inspiration to what I call 'noble purpose', you can increase your power and your ability immeasurably, so that there are almost no limits to what you can do.

In my opinion, inspiration is essential for everyone, and certainly for leaders. How we inspire ourselves – or, sadly, fail to inspire ourselves – says much about who we are, how we approach Life, and how we view the world. Inspiration gives us hope and allows us to dream. It leads to new ideas and new insights. Inspiration converted into action is a source of creativity and a generator of previously unseen ideas. Inspiration can lead to transformation, radical renewal and great progress. Inspiration is what motivates us to leave our comfort zone and explore new and unknown territories. It is the essence of all things, the foundation of our Life, the energy and power of our aura, and the radiance of our personality. Inspiration shapes our thoughts and guides our deeds. It allows us to shine and to create impact. And by allowing ourselves to be deeply inspired, we become a source of inspiration for others.

In other words, inspiration has huge intrinsic power. Deep inspiration brings us into contact with our 'divine' or pure self. It is the indicator of our 'heartbeat of Life'. The more we are connected to our true inner self, the more we are open to being inspired in the most diverse ways. Or to put it in slightly different terms: it is only then that you can really understand what inspiration does with you. You might feel joyful. Or amazed. Or impressed. Or you might just stand there, open mouthed, to look, listen or feel. Or any of a hundred and one other reactions. In fact, it is probably fair to say that if you analyse someone's sources of inspiration, you will be able to form a pretty good opinion about that person's personality. 'Show me your inspiration, and I will tell you who you are!' For this reason, my definition of inspiration, without wishing to be in any way limitative, is the following: the recognition of those things, moments, situations, places, persons and conversations – and all the possible associations between them – that can lead to astonishment and can prompt us to do unique and amazing things.

Through my intense process of reflection about my Life, it became increasingly clear to me that harmony, beauty and joy would play an essential role in that Life. At the same time, I also became increasingly amazed at the way in which those three things could induce in me a certain form of sublimation, even spiritual ecstasy. I searched for ways to make this remarkable trinity more concrete by mapping out my sources of inspiration more accurately, a method that I now regularly employ in our advisory work we do with GINPI. In my case, this involved going in search of all the sources of inspiration that would allow me to connect with and live by what harmony, beauty and joy meant for me.

Sources of inspiration are specific to each of us. Some sources are permanent; some are temporary and will be replaced. They evolve in keeping with our self-development as a person. There is an art to allowing yourself to be inspired by sources that let you look at Life in a more satisfying and more holistic way, that encourage you to dream, that help you to escape from the grind of daily routine and prompt you to take inspired action. Being inspired is a conscious deed. For me, there is nothing finer than to be constantly amazed by different sources of inspiration and to look at Life through a multiplicity of different perspectives. Or to summarise: it is crucial for each of us as a person to know what inspires us and then to keep those things close to our heart.

On my website, you can find as an example – or perhaps I should say as an inspiration – the different kinds of things that inspire me. They include: Andrew Lloyd Webber, Angkor Wat, antiques, artists, Aston Martin, Baroque music, Beethoven's 9th Symphony, Béjart, beauty, Biodanza, Brancusi, Buddhism, Cirque du Soleil, Club Med, conscious capitalism, contemporary art, Copenhagen, creation, Danish design furniture, Deepak Chopra's Seven Spiritual Laws of Success, Earl Grey tea, controlled eccentricity, aesthetics, exclusivity, Firmdale Hotels, French Polynesia, fresh flowers in an

Ettore Sottsass vase, Galapagos, Gandhi, Georg Jenssen, Ghent, Giacometti, Händel, Havana, humanism, Intelligence, James Bond, James Ivory, John Goossens, Le Pendule de Foucault, la pochette Hermès, inspired leadership, liberalism, long-term, luxury, Luxor by boat, LVMH, Marrakech, Martha Graham('s Dance Company), Maurice (the movie), meditation, modern art, MOMA, Mozart's Requiem, nature, Nelson Mandela, New York, originality, passion, Peggy Guggenheim, piano, Pierre Alechinsky, quality of Life, Rangali Island, Richard Branson, Rocco Forte ('s hotels), Samosir Island, Sex and the City (the soap and the films), summer nights, Sydney, symbolism, simplicity, The Godfather (movies), Tintin, Tom Ford, Ubud, values, Verdi's Requiem, VUB, yoga and Zen.

I knew ever since Bogota that I wanted to live an exceptional or extraordinary Life. But I didn't know at that stage what this Life would look like and what it would involve in concrete terms. In Makrigialos I began, for the first time, to give that wish a more definite shape and form. And I did it by making a list – I must confess to having a weakness for making lists! – of my sources of inspiration. My growing awareness of these sources and of the strength they gave me made it possible for me to start thinking practically about what I wanted to do with my future. What would be my Life's mission and how would I fulfil it? How would I make it extraordinary? Gradually, I began to develop a framework that had to be inspirational, authentic and appropriate for me, but would also be able to serve my outside world, the world of others. I wanted to do things based on my inspired conviction that were right. Things that would make me unique and would allow me to make an exceptional contribution to the Life I was going to lead. After a time, this process would help me to ultimately define my 'noble purpose'. Within this ultimate vision, which I still use as my compass today, the words 'harmony', 'beauty' and 'joy' remained central. But as a 'mission', it was too embryonic;

the concrete side of things was still missing. Making it concrete would obviously need to be connected with actions. But what actions? What could I and must I do to live a Life that, for me, would be extraordinary? What behaviour should I adopt? What challenges should I seek?

These are not easy questions to answer, but what can help you – what can finally allow you to make your 'noble mission' concrete – is a set of values. It is these values that guide your behaviour. If you need to decide something, if you want to act, if you have to solve something stressful or if you need to resolve a conflict, your values will help you to do it in a manner that is worthy and matches who you are as a person. In other words, it is not about what you do, but how you do it. They way you do things determines to a large extent the way you will be viewed by the outside world. You are recognised and valued by how you deal with others, how you take your decisions, and how you stand up for the things that are important to you.

So, as the next step in my journey, I went in search of the values that were closest to my heart, knowing that at the moment when my noble purpose became final, these values would help me to fulfil that purpose by guiding my actions in the right direction.

Success beyond success

If I ask people during my workshops or conferences to think about why they have great admiration for a particular person, then almost without exception I hear a summary of various positive attributes. Sometimes a number of competencies – such as strategic insight or the ability to focus – might become confused with attributes and also get thrown into the description, but that is not a problem. Most people, however, often with a degree of emotion and humility, confine themselves to an explanation of how they recognise and appreciate certain important values in the person they admire so much; values such as courage, respect, humbleness, accessibility, openness, clarity, simplicity, love, generosity, lightness or transparency. Nobody ever mentions power, dominance, manipulation, arrogance, cold-heartedness, egoism, competence, avarice, wealth, self-interest or greedy ambition. The key characteristic of values is that they are positive. This is a dimension that warms our hearts, that encourages our respect, that makes us like people, or makes us want to work for such value-driven paragons.

In other words, values are a kind of behavioural compass. It is thanks to our possession of values that we are able – usually unconsciously – to direct our actions and behaviour. Values make us do things in a manner that is specific to us, which allows us to distinguish ourselves from others. I behave in this way, driven by my values, and you behave in that way, driven by your values. These different modes of behaviour can often vary considerably. But there is nothing wrong with having different types of behaviour, coming from having different sets of values. 'Different' does not mean 'bad'. By behaving in a consistent and value-driven manner, we create clarity for our environment and those around us. If I behave authentically, with all people in all circumstances, then my environment will see and recognise that authentic behaviour, my authentic communication and my authentic reactions. This recognition will in turn have an impact on that environment and how it reacts to me.

By living in accordance with your values, you create for yourself a moral compass which, as it were, becomes your behavioural trademark: he or she does things that way, and no differently. Your environment will know that there is no point in trying to persuade you to do things against your values. Because they know that you will refuse. Nobody has exactly the same values, or the same hierarchy of values, or the same experience of values. It is our values, together with our noble purpose, that makes us unique.

Even so, I come across a surprising number of people – very often in a professional context – who have never questioned themselves about their own fundamental values and how those values relate to the values of the organisation they work for, as they understand them. They know 'more or less' what is important to them, but they find it hard to describe these things clearly. Fundamental values are the values that you will never betray and will always respect. They are our essence, and they are with us at all times and in all places. Even if we are not always aware of them. Alongside these fundamental values, we also have a broad set of additional values, which supplement the fundamental ones to create our complete value shield. This combination and this shield will be visible to everyone through our behaviour.

Values are there to be displayed. It is in this way that we make who we are (more) visible. And by being more visible for each other, it becomes easier and more pleasant to deal with each other. There are no longer any surprises in other people's behaviour. Viewed from the perspective of an organisation – as we shall see in the chapter on 'The House of Noble Purpose' – it is essential that people who work together learn to know each other on the basis of their respective values, since this will lead to the most agreeable and also the most fruitful form of collaboration. Many problems in collaborative ventures and interactions arise simply because we do not know, cannot see or are not able to detect what the other person really stands for.

Do you actually know what your fundamental values are? Which values will you never compromise, not even when you are put under pressure? It is only by thinking how you will react under pressure that you can gain insight into which values are important to you and which ones are not. If you refuse to budge when it comes to a particular value, even if you have to pay a price for your determination, then it is probably fair to say that this value is fundamental for you. If, however, you decide to give way – in other words, if you fail to respect the value and throw it overboard at the first sign of trouble or adversity – then that value will probably not be a fundamental one. Although in some cases it might still be, if you have not yet developed sufficient self-respect and/or self-confidence to stand up for your fundamental values.

An excellent way to discover your values is to think about how you would like to be remembered at your funeral by four specific people: your best friend, your Life partner (if you have one; if you don't, chose another very close person to you), one of your children (if you have any; if you don't, imagine what could be said by your imaginative child) and the best colleague you ever had. Will what those people say about you(r values) be consistent? Will they all say the same thing? Or will some say one thing and others say something else? For example, it might be that your colleague valued your accessibility, whereas your child valued your unconditional love. Check the extent to which the values mentioned by one person are also evident in the other three contexts. You will find that some values are indeed context-related. Some will weigh more heavily in your professional Life; others in your private Life. Some values will be omni-present, irrespective of the context.

What values will they ascribe to you? More to the point, what values would you like them to ascribe? This represents the difference between your existing values and your aspirational values. Existing values are the values that you already hold. They guide your present actions and make you who you are today. Aspirational values are the values you hope to acquire in the future, for which you are prepared to make changes in your behaviour to make this possible.

Action: map out your values

Now that you know the difference between existing and aspirational values, you should be able to easily select between five and seven of them. Visualise them – without words – on a large sheet of paper as a value shield, something along the lines of a coat of arms that noble families often have. By giving shape and form to your values in a creative way, you can develop an excellent compass that will help you to apply your values consciously, day after day, both in good times and bad. During sessions with management teams and family councils, this exercise can help to improve inter-connectedness, often creating new insights and giving deeper meaning to the group.

Naturally, I did this same reflective exercise for myself and came to the conclusion that my values are deeply representative of the things for which I stand in my Life. My values are my unconscious guide. Thanks to my values, I continue to come increasingly closer to myself, and, in that sense, also more easily recognisable to others. My values, which are displayed openly and transparently on my website, so all those with whom I interact know who I am, are authenticity, autonomy, excellence, integrity, joie de vivre, serenity and sustainability.

Last but not least on this subject, let us be clear on one crucial point: we each have only one single value set. We cannot switch our values, depending on whether we are at work, at home, with friends, on holiday, etc. We are integral beings and we have just one set of values, which, ideally, we should apply in the same way in every interaction and in every context. If we were to assume that we could have a number of different value sets, this would result in us having a number of different personalities, turning us into schizophrenics who, in the end, would no longer know which values to use with which personality. The power and beauty of having just a single value shield is that it is recognisable for everybody (including yourself), so that we are able to live our Life in a coherent manner.

Living in accordance with your values demands courage and focus, especially when we come into contact with new people. In situations of that kind, there is often greater pressure to conform to the prevailing culture or tendencies. The extent to which we are prepared to make our own values subordinate to those of our friends, acquaintances and professional contacts will depend on how well we know our values, how important they are to us and how much we consciously try to live by them. Or not. Particularly within organisations, there can be serious expectations of new-comers to conform to the existing values. It is therefore important for everyone involved in business relationships – recruitment interviews, customer-supplier interactions, performance reviews, etc. – to give sufficient attention to the values that are at play on both sides, to see whether it is possible for each individual to reconcile himself or herself to those values. Or not.

What I call 'success beyond success' therefore consists of living your Life in accordance with your values and doing things in a way that allows you to be true to yourself, so that you remain in contact with the things that are important to you and do not deviate from the principles for which you stand. When you are interacting with others, this can often require a serious effort. Sometimes people will try to change how you are guided by your values. Sometimes you might want to change their relation to theirs. But you cannot change other people's values directly, particularly if they do not want to change. You can, though, certainly exercise a degree of influence on others, by showing clearly what you stand for and how you lead your Life. But it remains a delicate balancing act. If, for example, you are hurt by something that someone says, it is better to explain to that person what effect his/her words have had on you, rather than attempting to convince them to stop saying such hurtful things, although that might be our natural reaction or tendency. It demands mental strength and awareness, especially when dealing with people who are close to you, or who have influence over you, to say and to show what you stand for, and to do this in a constructive and non-aggressive manner. But if you remain true to yourself, you will always remain true to Life. And that, in symbolic terms, is also what I mean by 'success beyond success'.

Life principles and convictions

If you listen to your inspiration, you will also become aware of your Life principles and convictions. Life principles are the moral, ethical and practical foundations on which we base our Life. Examples might include: respect for nature, a willingness to forgive, a lack of willingness to accept any form of discrimination, racism or social exclusion, attaching importance to the self-reliance of the individual, opposing alcohol and drug use, etc. Our Life principles are our most essential principles, those of the highest order. They colour our way of looking at the world. Or to put it in slightly different terms: they help to define our world view. If, for example, a person is against discrimination, he/she will accept that everyone should be given the same opportunities and that social determinism should not be allowed to play a role. Similarly, people who think that individuals should be self-reliant will value a political system that encourages individual initiative and citizenship.

Convictions are articles of belief in your own ability and the ability of others. In other words, convictions do not relate to the things or people *in which* you believe – for example, a particular god or a particular trainer for the national football team – but to *what* you believe. What you believe will strongly influence your behaviour. If, for example, you believe that you are capable of pushing yourself beyond your existing limits, you will search for ways to move beyond those limits. If you believe that you are not good enough to seize a particular opportunity, there is a good chance that you will do things that cause you to doubt or show uncertainty, so that the opportunity will indeed be given to someone else. In short: 'You become what you believe'. This is a slogan I have used daily right from the very start of my reflective process and it has since become one of my most typical character traits.

Alongside our values, our Life principles and convictions are the essential parameters of who we are. By reflecting on and becoming aware of these values, Life principles and convictions, we can get a very good picture of who we really are.

Connecting with my bliss

Thanks to my many years of deep and intense reflection, I have a deep and strong connection with myself and with Life. I have learned to go in search of answers to my questions within myself, and not in others outside myself. It is in our own self that our wisdom, strength and potential reside. If we want to know if we are really living the Life we want to lead, we need to stand in front of our own mirror, not someone else's. Only then can we see who we really are. And then we must decide whether we are satisfied with what we see... or not.

It was only when I felt that I had discovered the connection with my 'right' noble purpose that I was able to find the words to give depth to the things for which I stand. It was only then that I stopped doubting and found the strength to proclaim my noble purpose to the world. This gave me more and more energy. And the more energy I got, the more ready I felt to pursue my noble purpose to a successful conclusion in practice. As Steve Jobs put it in his graduation speech[1] about the importance of purpose: 'As with all the matters of the heart, you'll feel it when it is right.' For me, my noble purpose did indeed now feel 'right', as though it was the thing that I had been put on this earth to do: namely, to inspire leaders with impact worldwide to create harmony, beauty and joy, for the benefit of the welfare and progress of humankind, society and the world.

In the beginning, I read my noble purpose every morning during my meditation. After a while, I read it once a week. Now I talk about it when I speak at conferences, or advice leaders in their search for their own purpose, or lead organisational transformations. My noble purpose has gradually evolved to become a part of myself. But it wasn't always that way. Even though I found my noble purpose in the 1990s, back then I never talked about it much. For many years, I simply did what I felt I had to do, in keeping with that purpose.

For me, the big turning point was a keynote speech I gave at the architecturally impressive headquarters of ING in Amsterdam in 2012. The then ING vice-president for Talent & Development was Ricardo Sookdeo, who I had gotten to know through a common friend. My kidnapping story and my subsequent search for transformation made such a deep impression on him that he asked me to re-tell it during a keynote to 150 high-potential ING leaders. I hesitated, because until then I had never made use of my personal experiences in Columbia (and afterwards) as part of my public presentations. If I referred to them at all, it was only obliquely. Finally, I decided to accept Ricardo's request and agreed to talk about what had happened in Bogota in my speech. During the introduction, about who I was, what I do, etc., I did a short power meditation to ensure that I would remain as authentic and as focused as possible. When it was my turn to speak, I mounted the stage with composure, confidence and full concentration. I looked around the room, said nothing for the first few moments, and then launched into my story about what had happened to me and how I dealt with it. My tone was restrained but with the necessary degree of strength and emotion to make my words convincing, as I explained what GINPI is and why we do what we do. The auditorium, which was packed to the limit, was soon hanging on my every word. And then something strange happened. As I was talking, I had the feeling that the energy of everyone in the entire room, including the people in the technical cabin and those high up in the balcony at the back, was moving towards me, right up to and into my heart, so that I was able to conduct an intimate and respectful discourse with each and every one of them, while they sat on a kind of lotus flower in front of me. The sense of unity within that auditorium was unbelievable, truly amazing. The focus was total, so total that you could have heard a pin drop. Afterwards, during the break, dozens of people came up to me to say how deeply my story had touched them and had inspired them to think differently about the purpose and meaning that they, as young and promising business leaders, should give to their Life. I regarded this as a fine gift and I am still grateful to Ricardo for the opportunity he gave me.

That Amsterdam feeling is a feeling I have had thousands of times since I began to fully live and experience my noble purpose. By living more consistently and more consciously in connection with that purpose, I have acquired a remarkable energy in my Life, a previously unknown strength, an indescribable clarity and an ease of decision-making that allows me to choose between what is appropriate and necessary, and what is not. This makes it possible for me to carry on doing what I do as though it were no effort; to enjoy the excitement and the satisfaction that comes from successfully completed projects and investments; and to meet the right people and somehow always get offered the right propositions. This even goes so far (and I hope this does not sound pretentious) that for my consulting firm I never foresee any budget for marketing and sales, because I know that people will always find their way to our door anyway. When I launched GINPI in 2010, I made it an unwritten rule for myself and for my future partners and colleagues, whoever and wherever they might be, never to ask or prospect for a mission, a deal or an opportunity. I wanted – and still want – that leaders who think and feel that we can mean something for them should come to us of their own free will and make that feeling explicitly known because they feel and understand that we are the right partner for them.

Living in accordance with your noble purpose has much in common with what the Indian Hindu philosopher Swami Bodhananda called 'living your bliss'. That bliss, that connected-ness with my inner core, allows me to live a Life that is remarkably rich and varied. It allows me to meet wonderful people all around the world. It allows me the opportunity to do things that have a rather important impact on the economy, politics and society. For me, every day is a new adventure in exploring how I can use my noble purpose to contribute to something exceptional. Just as importantly: for me, every day is a new and conscious reminder of the beauty of Life. Even on days when the sun is not always shining.

Loving Life

'You are as young as your confidence and as old as your fear;
you are as young as your hope and as old as your despair.'

(Albert Schweitzer)

In the following pages, I will be delighted to share with you the love I feel for Life and how I live that Life. It is, I freely admit, a very personal view of Life, of my Life. Even so, I believe that it also contains something of the universal, because what I feel and think is also recognisable in many other men and women who likewise lead authentic Lives and have inspired (and still inspire) me greatly.

Ode to Life and respect for every day

The fact that I almost miraculously survived a brutal kidnapping without a psychological trauma is perhaps the biggest gift that Life has given me. So how could I not be grateful every single day for having received something so wonderful? How could I fail to value it and make use of it? For this reason, I regard each new day as a symbolic celebration of Life. For me, it is a celebration to be able to get up out of bed each morning; to give deeper meaning to each new moment, no matter how ordinary or extraordinary, to be able to do unique things; to meet fantastic people and bring them into connectedness with each other and with themselves, to build up something special with my partner, Luciano; to have marvellous conversations with my parents, my brothers, my cousins, my nephews and nieces, my many friends and clients worldwide, to encourage them all to live more than ordinary Lives and do extraordinary things.

For me, Life is something unbelievably unique and fantastic. Life is not something you should waste with negative thoughts or a lack of awareness to see its beauty. Life calls us to search for its deeper meaning. And you don't have to be kidnapped to know that! Although perhaps in many cases you do need to be kidnapped or experience something similar before you do it! That is a real shame, and such a wasted opportunity. I live every day to the full and want to inspire everyone else to do the same. This is an appeal to live Life at two hundred miles an hour and experience it for a full two hundred percent, or even more! Try to discover how meaningful your Life is and what, from this moment onwards, you can do with that Life that is unique and special to you.

The downside of this philosophy is that I have a certain aversion for people who cannot see Life for what it is and who fail to celebrate it. There is no place in my environment for people who live Life negatively because they lack the courage and the will to transform themselves. I do not like complainers or people who try to play the victim, constantly moaning about their bad luck and envying the good luck and happiness of others. I do not believe in luck and happiness as abstract concepts that are either randomly given to or withheld from us. Instead, I believe that we can attract and generate our own luck and happiness. People who have luck and happiness for the taking, but fail to realise it, are Life's fools. People who search for and cherish Life's luck and happiness are Life's winners.

Life is not some kind of transactional process with which you play roulette. Life is the greatest gift that we human beings are given. My focus is to make the best possible use of that gift in the time that is available to me. Two hundred miles an hour and for two hundred percent. Every day, for as long as I live.

Gratitude

And for that, I am enormously grateful. I am grateful for my Life. And for everything that Life allows me to do or not to do. I am grateful for the nature that surrounds me and gives me wise insights. I give thanks for the first rays of dawn and the first birds that come to sit on the tree near my meditation room after the winter. I give thanks for the sun, the moon and even the rain. I give thanks for Anna, our cleaning lady, who comes each week to make our wonderful Brussels house so beautiful. I give thanks for all the people I meet and who give me the opportunity to share theories and re-examine accepted positions. I give thanks for the sisters who run a bio-shop around the corner and sell such fantastic walnut bread. I am unbelievably grateful for the music of Bach, Verdi, Madonna, Sia and Barbara Streisand. I am grateful for the amazing places to which my work takes me. I am grateful that I can share and learn so much from my dear colleague-partners in our CoBrAS partnership. I am grateful for the delicious jam my father makes each new season, and for the love with which my mother writes greetings cards. I am grateful for Luciano's tolerance and understanding when I have to go on one business trip after another. And for his sublime smile. In short, I am grateful for a thousand and one things in Life. And I share that gratitude. In fact, my Life is a Life of gratitude. Even in difficult moments or when things are not going well.

Every morning, when I get out of bed, l welcome the new day. I welcome Life. During each of my meditations I thank Life and what I call the 'universe'. Before I go to sleep at night, I thank the day for everything it has brought. Yes, even for the things that were difficult or bad. I see this as a way to be ready to start the next day with renewed enthusiasm.

By living in this grateful manner, every moment, every meeting and every occasion becomes an opportunity. The inspiration I mentioned earlier is everywhere, at all times and in all places. I view the world through my lens of harmony, beauty and joy, and, as a result, I see things that others do not see. And it is in this that I find new opportunities. New opportunities to contribute as much as I can to the harmony, beauty and joy of the world, all around me and everywhere I go. Around me by encouraging those nearest and dearest to me to do the same. Everywhere I go by inspiring impactful leaders to do the same in their organisations, interest groups and spheres of influence.

Rooted in my philosophy of Life and my deep connectedness with my own inspiration, I have developed the capacity to identify subtle correlations and can immediately sense the deeper origins of things. I put this wisdom at the service of my noble purpose.

Because I look at the world so differently, I also see the things that are not fully harmonic, beautiful and joyful. Or things that are going wrong. I use my noble purpose to try and put these things right. It is not always possible, but nevertheless that is and remains my approach to the world, my philosophy of Life. And it is an approach I use towards everything.

I seize every opportunity to give advice, whether it is asked for or not. If I arrive in a hotel (something that happens almost every week) and if I see potential that is not being exploited, I will share my thoughts with the general manager. If I am served in a shop by a grumpy member of staff or a disinterested cashier, I will tell them in a friendly manner that their behaviour is having an effect on me and that they might be prompting similar negative reactions in those they meet. I can't help doing this. It is just in me. It is simply my way.

Putting things in perspective

The kidnapping also taught me how to put things in perspective. After what I had experienced, I immediately began to look at Life and live my Life in a different way. If you go through this kind of traumatic experience, it gives you a new focus on things. Your priorities are turned upside down. What was important before is suddenly no longer important. And the things you hardly ever thought about before are now constantly at the forefront of your mind.

I now view the outside world with a certain detachment. I first distance myself from what is happening before reacting or taking up a position. Distance is not the same as indifference. But I have learnt that what must happen, will happen. What is not possible right now, no longer merits attention at the moment. Whoever does not want to do something, notwithstanding his or her potential and no matter how regrettable it might be, has the right not to do it. Whoever refuses to see, misses a part of the big picture. So be it!

In the past, for example, I used to attach great importance to details, almost for the sake of it. Nowadays, I will only do this if the details fit in with the overall holistic view I have of things and contribute towards an increase in harmony, beauty and joy. When I can see possibilities in an organisation, but the leaders of that organisation are not ready or not interested in exploiting them, that is their truth, and not mine. I will do everything I can to try and bring them new insight that might persuade them to change their minds. But if I have done everything I can and they still persist in their stubbornness, then that, for me, is where the story ends.

Being able to assess where and on what I can best spend my time is part of this ability to put things in their proper perspective. There are things I can influence and change. There are many other things I cannot influence and change. For this reason, I focus on the former and ignore the latter. And if my efforts do not bring about the breakthrough I was hoping for, even though I have tried everything I know, then that is just the way it is. This is also part of the beauty of Life: learning to accept what is.

Connecting people with their potential

What my Life has given me in abundance, is the art and the ability to connect people, both with themselves and with each other. It often happens that I see potential in people that others do not see. Connectedness is the essence of our growth as interactive beings, who need others in order to evolve as individuals.

By looking at human beings as a source of potential and by connecting those different sources together, I am contributing directly and indirectly to Life. There is nothing more beautiful than to see positive things develop and unfold in others. Or to see things in them that they have not (yet) seen or felt themselves. I think that this is a gift. It is a gift I learnt when I was a young co-divisional leader at Belgacom; when I was CEO at ORMIT; when I founded Young Leaders-Inspiring Mentors in 2010; when I set up Wisdom Encounters; or when I proposed to transform our systemic constellation learning group into CoBrAS, and every time when I accepted a position on a board of directors or agreed to take on a new project with a client. On each occasion, my ability to connect people was the key. And you can only do this if you love Life, and if you allow Life to love you.

Connecting people is something that we will look at again in a later chapter.

Fully self-confident

My busy Life is both fascinating and challenging: travelling from one new destination to another, often up to three times a week, moving from one customer project to another, switching from one activity to another, and always with the same deep focus. Trying to bring correct, sustainable and impactful insights to leaders of many different kinds and many different personalities demands a huge amount of personal alignment and inner calm. I have this calm. I have found this serenity. Thanks to the path through Life that I have so far followed and thanks to my noble purpose, I have never before had such clarity of vision and sharpness of focus as I do today. In the past, all kinds of new opportunities also came my way. But I can now see how much time I wasted in meetings, discussions and conversations that led to nothing, except perhaps to heighten my own awareness that they were of no benefit to me or anyone else and had not allowed me to create the added value I so crave. Nowadays, that has all changed! My noble purpose helps me to have confidence in myself and in the things for which I stand, so that these things are now my absolute priority at all times. If I look at myself in the mirror, I want to be sure that I am doing what for me is the right thing to do. In part, this focus on my noble purpose has developed out of and been strengthened by my self-confidence. And my self-confidence has developed out of and been strengthened by having and living my own noble purpose. This is the remarkable special power of a noble purpose.

Whoever has an authentic and genuine noble purpose is connected with their true self. This brings with it a focus on living a 'correct' and coherently authentic Life. A deeply inspired and value-driven Life. A Life governed by strong Life principles and the right positive convictions. It is through the proper alignment of values, Life principles and convictions, united in a noble purpose, that you will be able to create a strong and powerful force – a force for good. This force will give you the self-confidence you need to succeed. Or to put it differently: your levels of self-confidence will increase dramatically when you live in accordance with the precepts of a noble purpose that is yours. The uniqueness of your noble purpose will drive you ever onwards and ever upwards. And that does something to a person!

3

A force for good

'Hide not your talents. They for use were made.
What's a sundial in the shade?' (Benjamin Franklin)

This chapter is about what noble purpose actually is and how important I think it is for humankind, society and the world. It is only by living for a noble purpose that people can be happy and fulfilled. It is the power of their noble purpose that makes human beings do things that are unique, special and beautiful in the service of others and of society as a whole. It is only because of noble purposes that remarkable things, products and services are invented and made.

When people are able to live their noble purpose, when societies are founded on a noble purpose and when societal awareness is developed through a noble purpose, it is only then that we will be able to create a worthier humankind, a better society, a fairer economy and a more beautiful world.

This wonderful potential of noble purpose, which reveals itself as a clear force for good, is by definition dependent on the way it is given shape and form by people. It is only through people and their desire to pursue a noble purpose that noble purpose acquires its justification and its reason for being. And this releases an immense power.

Mark Twain

'Logic will get you from A to B. Imagination will take you everywhere.' (Albert Einstein)

Samuel Langhorne Clemens[2], better known under his author's name of Mark Twain, was an American writer and humorist. Although nowadays best known for his novels *The Adventures of Tom Sawyer* and *The Adventures of Huckleberry Finn*, Twain also made important contributions in the fields of philosophy and social development. He once said: 'The two most important days in your Life are the day you are born and the day you find out why'. For me, this is the essence of human Life and of crucial importance within the framework of my reflection about noble purpose. The first of those two days, the day on which you were born, is the day on which you are given your physical existence. Body and soul come together and are united in a physical 'shell'. This fusion of egg and seed creates an embryo. That embryo becomes a baby. The baby becomes a child and the child becomes an adult. It is during this evolution from baby to adult that our Life emerges: we discover, explore, grow and flourish, but also encounter opposition, setbacks and problems. Most people regard this Life as something self-evident and very few take the time to stop and look at it. Certainly not when things are going well. There is no search for Life's meaning. The 'why' question is never asked. Disappointments, difficult moments and even severe trials are all blamed on the fickle finger of fate. 'That's Life!' people say and shrug their shoulders. However, this determinist view of Life ignores and even invalidates the intrinsic potential of human beings. It suggests a form of predestation, in which our Lives are 'programmed' to follow a set course.

When an individual, at some point during the evolution from infancy to adulthood, spontaneously starts to ask questions about the reasons for his or her existence, a magical turning point in that person's Life is reached. This is the moment of deepening awareness that can heighten our consciousness and bring us to great insight. At the same time, it can also be a moment of great confusion and doubt. Why? Because it is the moment when we leave behind what was and bid welcome to what will be. Those who have the courage to follow this path will take their Life into their own hands and begin a fascinating voyage of self-discovery. From that moment on, they will determine the direction of their journey through Life. Their soul becomes free to fulfil its potential in and through the body in which it is housed. As a result, Life is given a new meaning. A powerful feeling of freedom, strength and a sense of purpose is developed, leading ultimately to true self-re-alisation. This awakening allows us to see that we are more than just a body with arms and legs, with a heart and a stomach. We are not simply a lump of flesh that has certain randomly allocated strengths and weaknesses. It is at this moment of awakening that we are truly born, or perhaps it is better to say reborn to who and what we were meant to be in our Life. This is our second birth, our spiritual birth. The birth when we become our true self, our authentic self, when we are finally confronted for the first time in our Life with our divine 'I'. This is a self that has its own values, own convictions, own Life principles and own needs. This new voyage of self-discovery must continue until we have been able to identify and explore all the deeper and often hidden aspects of our own being. What's more, it is a voyage that can sometimes last a whole Life long. But every step forward brings us a step closer to the essence of who we are.

Sadly, this search for the real self seldom happens spontaneously. During periods of material success, few people are prepared to stop and reflect seriously on questions like 'Am I on the right track?' or

'Am I really leading my own Life?' Or is it perhaps a Life dictated by their parents and teachers? Or a Life that slavishly follows the conventions of the social environment in which they grew up or of the professional environment whose expectations they feel obliged to meet? In most cases, people only start asking questions about the meaning of Life once they have experienced some kind of unexpected setback or crisis, which finally forces them to confront themselves and the superficiality of their existence. This catalyst might be the loss of a loved one, or a failure to gain promotion, or being sacked, or being left by your partner, or the discovery that your child has a drugs problem, or any of a thousand and one other things that force us to face up to an unknown situation for which we were not prepared and which reveals our limitations, confused convictions, unfulfilled needs, forgotten or suppressed emotional pain and deepest fears.

In my opinion, the true power of Life is best developed by starting from an early age, stimulated by our upbringing and education, to reflect consciously and critically on the reasons for our existence. This is what I call our noble purpose, our higher goal. It is a goal that involves much more than leading a Life that simply drifts from one phase of that Life to another, without pausing to consider the implications of these crucial transitions and their potentially transformative effect. This exploration of who we are and how we can best make use of our uniqueness is the essence of humankind.

By this, I mean a humankind formed by people who are much more than big, small, black, white, red, yellow, perfect or imperfect physical bodies. And certainly not a humankind formed by people who are only concerned in one way or another with the rat race that is slowly bringing our species to destruction.

The four bodies

'One's first step to wisdom is to question everything and
one's last is to accept everything.' (Georg C. Lichtenberg)

As people, we do indeed have different bodies. In the philosophy
of yoga, we speak of the unity between body (our physicality),
mind (our rationality) and soul (our spirituality). By keeping these
three elements in balance through a form of meditation, prayer
or mindfulness, we are able to create energy in the body, strength
in the mind and purity in the soul. This finds its expression in a
further balance between the power of the energy and an absolute
clarity of vision. In an advanced stage, this even makes it possible
to move to a higher state of consciousness, so that we can perceive,
sense and intuit things that cannot be perceived, sensed or intuited
by others who vibrate on a lower consciousness level.

As a result of my deep reflections, intense observations and years
of study following my kidnapping and subsequent rehabilitation,
I now look at humankind and people in a subtle way that allows
me to identify and reveal all their separate 'layers'. I see much more
than just a powerful body or a strong mind. I have also learnt how
to connect with people's depths and sources, with their potential
and their beauty, with their positive forces but also their fears. I
can sense things before they have been spoken. I can feel things
that others cannot feel.

Put simply, we are so much more than just a physical body. We
are also a mental body. And an emotional body. And a spiritual
body. In fact, we are an inseparable combination of all four of
these bodies, which live together as a coherent and complementary
quartet. People often speak of the physical body as 'the' body,
but this is a reducing perspective that entirely misses the point.

When I interact with people, I use my four bodies to come into contact with their four bodies. It is through this complex yet subtle 'four-body' interaction that I am able to glean more information about others than if I were to simply look at their physical body. In view of this, it is perhaps worth taking a closer look at each of these four bodies separately.

The physical body is our envelope. It is the part of other people (and yourself) that you can see, with which you feel, act and interact. Our physical bodies, which are the amalgamated sum of our bones, skin, organs and limbs, are the means by which we are recognisable as individuals to the outside world. It is through our physical body that we learn to experience, by receiving both exterior and interior signals and impulses. In this sense, I regard the physical body as a cross between an antenna and a barometer. It is also our energetic or light body, of which our fundamentally important aura and our energy centres (or chakras) are integral elements.

The body as antenna makes it possible for us to position all our interactions. In this way, for example, we meet people to whom we feel attracted and to whom we would like to develop greater physical nearness. This happens more or less automatically. For example, you might be talking to someone during a reception and suddenly conclude that the conversation is gradually becoming more pleasant, almost intimate. You feel 'something' that you find attractive in the other person. This phenomenon can even occur with people who you have never previously met or even, in extreme cases, with strangers we pass on the street. Your eyes meet and when the person has walked past you, you turn to watch them go. And then you notice that they have done precisely the same! Of course, the opposite can also happen: there are some people for whom we feel not the slightest attraction; rather the reverse. With these people, we prefer to put physical distance between us and them. For example, when you are introduced to this kind of person at a reception, you often find that your body recoils at the first glance or handshake. You break off this handshake as soon as you can and perhaps even take a step back. You can also feel much the same reaction when someone leans with both his hands on your desk while speaking to you, so that you feel a need to sink deeper into your chair or push it backwards to create a 'safer' space between you and your 'assailant'.

In other words, our antenna also teaches us how to react to what we see, hear and feel. If we see a couple in love or a beautiful winter landscape, this gives us a good feeling. If we witness a drowned migrant baby, or the consequences of a terrorist attack or an environmental disaster, even if only on the television, our body reacts with a shudder. If someone tells us that they admire or appreciate us, it makes us feel warm inside. If someone criticises us unfairly or says bad things about us, it feels like a smack in the face. In all these instances, the body produces its own appropriate reaction.

The body as a barometer allows us to remain in contact with our feelings and emotions. When you are in love, you have butterflies in your stomach. When you are frightened, you have a knot in your stomach. When you need to take an important decision, you often rely on your 'gut' feeling. When you are stressed out by work or by a difficult situation at home, you feel it in your body as well as in your mind. In other words, your body warns you both physically and psychologically when something is not right, like when you feel hungry, too cold, too hot or too overworked. Consequently, it is important to listen to your physical body, because its antenna and barometer are picking up and transmitting signals that are essential for your well-being. Unfortunately, as I have seen increasingly in recent years, particularly in business environments, people are losing this all-essential contact with their physical body. Instead, their focus has switched to the mental body, so that this now receives a disproportionate amount of their attention.

This mental body deals with what you think and therefore operates outside the range of what you can perceive with your senses. Since the French philosopher Descartes[3] first put forward his famous dictum '*Cogito ergo sum*' – I think, therefore I am – far too much weight has been given to the importance of reason. In science, it is often said that something can only exist if it can somehow be measured. Of course, this definition is much too limited, since phenomena like love, compassion and determination clearly exist, but cannot be directly measured. At the same time, it must be recognised that consciousness and unconsciousness, conceptualisation, knowledge and intellect are all located in our mental body. Or rather our awareness of these things is located there. We need our mental body in order to understand what happens in, with and through our physical body. I am, therefore I think!

The emotional body is the sum of all our emotions, such as fear, anger, disgust, happiness, sadness, amazement, concern, love, depression, contempt, pride, shame, envy, etc., to name but a few! The basic universal emotions that are shared by everyone throughout the world are happiness, sadness, anger, amazement, disgust and fear. This last emotion – fear – is sometimes known as the mother of all emotions. Emotions and feelings result from our interaction with the exterior world and are (of course) discernable in the physical body. Emotions can move within the body from place to place and assume a succession of different physical forms. For example, you can sometimes be so angry that you can feel it in the pit of your stomach, but sometimes the same feeling can make you cry. Or you can be so happy that your face glows with pleasure, but it can also make you cry tears of joy, because you feel an even deeper happiness in your heart.

In one sense, the spiritual body is the most subtle body, since it represents our higher, pure (in the sense of not reduced or prejudiced) or 'divine' self. This is the body we often call the 'soul'. It is not 'divine' in a religious sense, but in a mystical and transcendental sense. To connect with our soul, we need to learn how to enter deep into our own inner being and observe with a greater consciousness than ever before the things that are. It is through the spiritual body that we can influence the mental body to have an impact on the physical body. Sounds complex? Let me explain with an example. Whenever I have to give a lecture, it is essential for me to feel calm, focused and empowered. Through a short meditation, I make connection with my spiritual body and become aware – through my mental body – of my impact on my physical body. In other words, my meditation induces calm and focus in my physical body, but this has to happen via my mental body, where my consciousness resides, otherwise I would not be able to perceive that the desired effect had been achieved.

It is through being connected with the spiritual body that we come into contact with the reason for our existence. This requires us, throughout the process of our personal evolution from baby to child to adult, to peel off the successive layers of our symbolic human 'onion', until we finally arrive at the core, where the softest, most succulent and most perfumed part of that onion of the soul is to be found. This is only possible if you have huge amounts of self-awareness, self-respect, self-confidence and self-leadership. Put simply, a noble purpose is very much a matter of the soul, and not of the head!

I also use this same 'four-bodies' theory in relation to organisations. Every organisation has a physical body: offices, factories, buildings, a network infrastructure, etc. Its mental body is its accumulated knowledge and know-how, its competencies and its innovations. The emotional body consists of all its interactions between people within the organisation and between the organisation and the outside world, while its spiritual body is its soul or noble purpose, its reason for existence as outlined in its vision and mission statements. The spiritual body forms the basis for the organisation's raison d'être, as a result of which the physical, mental and emotional bodies are developed.

Why have I chosen to discuss these four bodies in this book? Because we, as human beings, and even more so if we are also a leader, must learn how to deal with each other in a purer, deeper, more correct and more meaningful way. We owe this not only to ourselves, as creatures of value, but also to society, which is constantly in search of new meaning, and to our children and the generations of the future, for whom we also bear a responsibility. In my view of the world, I take as my starting point the belief that every person has all four bodies, including the spiritual one. Therefore, I also assume in principle – in other words, once all the basic material needs are satisfied – that every person is capable of connecting with their noble purpose. For me, the way forward for humankind is to be found by building a society in which everyone can live in a sufficiently dignified manner, so that it becomes possible for them to enter into contact with their spiritual body, and, by extension, their noble purpose. That not everyone can or will want to do this is self-evident; but it is equally self-evident that everyone does nonetheless have a specific reason for their existence. It is up to them to decide whether they make use of it or not. We will look at this more closely in the chapter entitled 'The beast is dying'.

How noble is noble?

'Not all of us can do great things. But we can do small things with great love.' (Mother Theresa)

The word 'noble' in noble purpose has, of course, nothing to do with 'the nobility', in the sense of the aristocracy. 'Noble' in the context of a noble purpose means 'possessing outstanding or admirable qualities'. Or you might even say 'nobility of spirit'. In other words, 'noble' refers to the good side of the reason for our existence, which implies that it is to the benefit of others, society and humankind. This can cover an enormous range of possibilities. The focus of noble purpose in question might be small and local, but they can also be huge and global. When Anna, our cleaning lady, goes about her weekly task in our home, smiling and whistling as she does so, and when I tell her that she is a joy to watch, she answers that she feels privileged to be able to play her part in keeping our beautiful 1850s house in tip-top condition. Consequently, she is not focused on her dusting, polishing and scrubbing, but on something that is of a higher and nobler order. When Eric, a transformation manager at the Swiss Straumann company, the world reference for tooth implants, says that he feels honoured, as a result of my coaching, that he is now better able to contribute to Straumann's noble purpose – summarised in the motto 'More than restoring smiles, restoring confidence' – you can feel that the man is passionate about his job. Or what to think of the Belgian Herman Van Rompuy, the first President of Europe, who at a much higher level but in all humility and with great erudition and simplicity, asked the nations of Europe to display increased solidarity and fellow-feeling for all the continent's citizens? This is a noble purpose that had impact equivalent in scope to that of former President Barack Obama in the United States. There is also noble purpose in the work of Bill and Melinda Gates with their Bill & Melinda Gates Foundation, who are using their fortune to do so many amazing things for humankind and society. Or what Bob Geldof did with Live Aid, or what Simone Veil achieved as a stateswoman and philosopher are more examples of noble purpose driven leaders.

The examples are legion.

Of course, there are just as many examples of purposes that were anything but noble. Adolf Hitler had a very clear purpose when he founded the Third Reich, but millions of lives were lost as result of his efforts to realise that purpose. There is nothing noble about that. At a different level, the same can be said about a company like British Petroleum, who made a series of grave strategic errors, simply to save time and money, which led to the explosion of the Deepwater Horizon drilling platform, one of the greatest ecological disasters in history. This is hardly consistent with the noble concept of socially responsible entrepreneurship, about which we hear so much today. Even religiously-inspired purposes are sometimes far from noble, as was clearly the case with the so-called People's Temple sect, whose leader Jim Jones orchestrated the mass-suicide of 909 of his followers – a third of them children – in Guyana in 1978.

In fact, I refuse to recognise these latter examples as instances of purpose without nobility, preferring to see them simply as 'objectives' – no more and no less – that the leaders in question wished to fulfil. This means that we need to make a fundamental distinction between an objective and a purpose. Both of them are necessary, but their meaning is very different. The impact and resonations of a noble purpose are of a totally different order to what can be achieved by reaching an objective.

Noble Purpose	Material objective
Noble / At service	Not necesarily noble / Maybe at service
Timeless / Permanent	Time bound / Limited in time
External Focus (others)	Internal Focus (self)
Fully Passionate	Transactional
No direct reward focus But very rewarding	(Direct) reward focus
Focus & clear priorities	Ad hoc 'priorities'
Internal Stimulus	External Stimulus
Serendipity & quietness	Excitement & constant movement

Noble Purpose compared to material objective

A noble purpose places itself exclusively at the service of others. It therefore goes beyond or is outside our own person. This is also true of our intrinsic motivation to have and achieve a noble purpose. We do not do it for ourselves. We are simply the transmitter of a higher idea or ideal.

A material objective is not intrinsically noble. It is rooted in something that we want to achieve for our own purposes. Objectives are fundamentally inward-looking, focused on ourselves and not on the wider world outside.

If my objective is to enjoy giving successful seminars and completing successful organisational transformations, this has nothing to do with nobility of spirit. My focus is then on my own success. This will probably also mean that I will want to reach that objective as quickly as possible, and as often as possible. But if I give those seminars and conduct those transformations for the purpose of helping others to achieve their own noble purpose and help organisations flourish and outperform at the service of something bigger than their own results, then my work becomes noble as well. And this will be noticeable to my public from the way I behave.

A noble purpose is for all time, in the sense that it is not limited in time. My noble purpose does not have to be achieved by a certain date. It cannot be quantified in numbers or volumes. A noble purpose emerges from your deepest being as a person and from the 'divine' meaning that you wish to give to your existence. It is this that makes a noble purpose something beyond time, something eternal. Once we have identified and defined our noble purpose, we can no longer live without it. We become our noble purpose. We achieve our own full realisation through the realisation of that noble purpose.

By contrast, an objective is subject to the limitations of time: 'I want to achieve it by that date'. If this happens, the objective has been successfully completed and you can move on to the next one. In this way, objectives tend to follow each other in succession, potentially without end. People sometimes say to me that their noble purpose is to be a good father or mother. But that is not a noble purpose! It is the duty of every parent to try and be a good father or mother. In other words, it is an objective, not in the least because the nature of 'being a good parent' changes as the children get older and grow into independent adulthood.

A noble purpose makes it possible for people to act with passion on a lasting basis. A noble purpose gives us so much energy, which flows from the connectedness we feel with our deepest inner self, that we never feel as though we are actually working. It is more like we are engaged in a passion. We are occupied with the realisation of our Life project, with the realisation of our own self. This self-realisation has great power and beauty.

An objective is only invested with transactional energy: we have to complete it by a particular date and then it is immediately over and done with. I am not saying that objectives cannot give you energy, but if those objectives are not related to a noble purpose, the energy dimension is of a less exalted and less resonating quality. When this happens, we will focus on the successful completion of the various elements of the objective. Leading a Life that consists of the need to complete a succession of arbitrary objectives, often imposed by others, is something very different from leading a Life that is driven by your unique noble purpose.

Having a noble purpose implies that you do not expect an immediate reward. You do not lead your Life according to a noble purpose with the intention of getting something directly in return. The recognition, appreciation and benefits you receive from following your noble purpose are to be found in the way you live your Life and what kind of person you become as a result. Viewed from this perspective, a Life lived for a noble purpose brings huge rewards.

An objective usually has a direct or indirect reward as its focus. Consider, for example, my noble purpose, which is to inspire influential leaders worldwide. This sometimes makes it possible for me to do remarkable things, which allows me to have a significant impact on these men and women. Sometimes I am so highly motivated to create this impact on specific people and in specific contexts that I am initially prepared to work free of charge. However, the appreciation people have for the impact I am able to create through my noble purpose means that I can always ask for very generous terms of remuneration later, or else I receive high levels of unanticipated rewards, either directly or indirectly. If, however, I were to concentrate instead on trying to get the largest possible amount on each of my invoices, this shift in focus would result in the creation of a very different kind of energy. Money would now become the objective, and a noble purpose cannot be expressed in euros, dollars and pounds. That being said, I have noticed over the years that most people and organisations who are driven by a noble purpose almost without exception still receive high levels of rewards (whether in the form of honoraria, prices for products and services or some other form of return). This is because of the special energy, power and radiance generated by the pursuit of a noble purpose, which people find both appealing and inspirational. This is simply not possible with the pursuit of objectives per se.

Living Life according to a noble purpose also helps you enormously to set the right priorities. This is because you are connected with the source of your true being, deep down inside of you. As a result, there is a direct link between who you are and what you do. The power of that link means that doubt and doing things that are no longer relevant for you are almost automatically left behind. Your noble purpose creates a clear framework of Life, which allows you to filter out everything that cannot contribute to the fulfilment of that purpose.

In contrast, everyone who lives for objectives is dependent on first getting and then achieving those objectives. And because objectives follow each other sequentially and are limited in time, and because we constantly need new ones, this means our focus is fixed on what I call 'ad hoc' priorities. These are priorities that are dependent on the moment. The constant scanning of our environment to see if this or that might be a potential objective means that we are constantly searching for something, so that the meaning of Life is measured in terms of having or not having objectives.

This leads on to a following difference between a noble purpose and objectives. In a Life driven by a noble purpose the stimulus for action comes from within ourselves. We are unconsciously fed and motivated by the conscious connection with the source of our being. This gives us the feeling of having a healthy and balanced control over our Life.

A Life driven by objectives requires us to have a far more opportunistic approach to the things we do, because we need to be constantly on the look-out for new objectives that might be interesting for us. This is the scanning process already mentioned, which means that our stimulus for action comes from outside ourselves.

This in turn leads to a great deal of zen in the Lives of those who follow their noble purpose. It creates serendipity. In contrast, people who live only for objectives have less peace of mind, because of their need to constantly be looking for new opportunities, which can be very tiring.

The third day

Mark Twain talked about the two most important days in our Lives: the day we are physically born and the day we discover why we were born. But for me there is a third and even more important day: the day we take action. The third day is the turning point, the moment when we decide to take that deep descent into our own being, so that we can fully connect with who we really are and, as a result, make contact with our noble purpose. In this sense, the third day is the 'call to action', the impetus to take the first step towards real self-realisation.

I always advise people to make the third day a matter of conscious choice rather than a consequence of necessity. For example, because we have reached out limits, or because we have flirted too long with a possible burn-out or bore-out, or because we risk losing an intimate relationship, or because our child is following the wrong path as a result of our never being there to offer guidance. It is much better to allow your turning point to occur when you are able to distance yourself from what is happening around you, so that you can fully focus on the moment without other distractions. Unfortunately, for many people nowadays this is not always easy, since they no longer know or feel what is important for them: career or health, success or relationship, reputation or family, money and power or peace of mind and zen, a busy Life or the right Life…

Every day I see men and women who are not living consciously and pay little or no attention to the essence. People spend more time each year planning their holidays than they are prepared to spend planning the all-important deep dive into their unknown self, which will allow them to live consciously for the rest of their days. This says much about where we human beings choose to place our priorities. Almost in spite of ourselves, we throw ourselves headlong into an idiotic rat race to achieve externally triggered objectives, in the hope that we can earn even more money, so that we can acquire even more often irrelevant material possessions, which we seldom have time to use or enjoy.

There is a huge misconception that it is not possible to gain much of what we want in Life by living in a way that is coherent and holistic. You don't have to stop being professionally busy to have a good relationship. It is perfectly possible to be successful and still have a fascinating social Life. Making time for yourself and your own self-deepening is not incompatible with achieving outstanding business results. In fact, living in accordance with a noble purpose, as we have already seen, actually makes all aspects of our Life easier, by allowing us to spend less time on what is irrelevant and focusing instead on the things that are right for us.

In other words, people need to have more belief in their ability to shape their own destiny and find their own balance. They need to learn how they can activate the 'right things'. This requires depth and self-reflection. How can this be achieved? By distancing ourselves from the grind and routine of everyday Life, by embracing the peace and the calm, by seeking connection with our true self, perhaps through prayer, meditation or some other spiritual exercise, by having sufficient contact with nature. These are all methods that can help us to acquire the essential information and insights we need of our 'divine' self. It is there – and there only – that the source of our noble purpose is to be found. But for people who are always busy, who have an endless list of objectives to meet, who never have time for anything (and certainly not for something as 'woolly' in their eyes as self-reflection and spirituality), it is a huge step and demands great self-discipline to make the switch that leads to greater depth and self-understanding. As the Swedish diplomat and former UN Secretary-General Dag Hammarskjöld[4] once commented: 'The longest journey is the journey inwards'. Alexander the Great[5] expressed much the same sentiments when he said that the longest journey he had ever made was between his head and his heart – and that says a lot, coming from a man who had conquered more than half of the then known world by the age of thirty! Perhaps the difficulty of this journey explains why nowadays fewer and fewer people seem to be reaching their third day. Far too few for what is good for humankind and necessary for society. We keep on struggling forward as fast as we can, until one day we suddenly and unexpectedly run into a brick wall. It is only then, often too late, that we realise just how disoriented we have become.

I would urge everyone to build sufficient time into their Life to feed and nourish their spiritual body. In much the same way that we all feed and nourish our physical body. After all, we all find the time to take a shower or clean our teeth at least once each day! So why can't we do something similar to maintain our spiritual health? Despite my packed agenda and my sometimes crazy travel schedule, I always keep a moment free each day, ideally morning and evening, for yoga and meditation. I also read inspiring texts, magazines and books. I listen to deepening music, often sitting in a train or plane. I spend 'quality time' with my friends, family and business relations. I make time for myself to be myself and for the things that uplift me, make me feel good, like my regular excursions into nature. I don't have the feeling that I am getting ahead of myself, or that I am constantly stressed, or that I don't have the time for my relationship, my essential friendships and my social activities (which I select carefully). In short, I think that I am strongly connected to my sources of inspiration, as I discussed in the previous chapter of that name.

When we focus on the right things and the right actions, a new dimension opens up for us, allowing us to see the world in a different light. We gradually get into a flow, we have new-found energy and strength that attracts what is good for us, we meet all kinds of new opportunities and we live with more joy and less drudgery.

Exceptional achievements

'What is worth doing is worth doing well.' (Gilbert Cesbron)

It is thanks to this flow, attractive power, energy and joy that remarkable things can happen. I firmly believe, both on the basis of my own experiences and my observation of others, that we as human beings are capable of achieving exceptional outcomes simply by pausing at a certain conscious moment to reflect on our Life and do the things that are right for us and for others. In other words, the things that emerge naturally from our noble purpose.

Countless men and women throughout history have booked outstanding achievements in numerous fields of endeavour (business, social, artistic, scientific, spiritual, ethical, economic, societal, literary, etc.). These are achievements that were once considered impossible but have since had a huge impact on the world. And they were all made possible by people connecting with the deeper meaning of their Life. These are the men and women who today still inspire us to explore new paths and follow new ideas. What can be more socially relevant than human beings who inspire other human beings to give the best of themselves in the service of humankind?

There are dozens of people I could name who have inspired me over the years, because of what they were able to achieve through their noble purpose and because of what these achievements have meant for people and society. I have even been fortunate enough to meet some of them during my research into inspiration and societal impact.

My list includes: Marie Curie[6] (for her work on radio-activity), Alfred Nobel (the inventor of dynamite), Samuel Beckett (author and playwright), Tenzin Gyatso or the 14th Dalai Lama (Nobel Prize for Peace), Amartya Sen (inventor of the Human Development Index), the previously mentioned Dag Hammarskjöld (UN Secretary-General), Nelson Mandela (freedom fighter), Richard Branson (serial entrepreneur), Anita Roddick (The Body Shop), Barbara Streisand (singer with a social message), Mathieu Ricard (a scientist who became a monk, philosopher and photographer), Al Gore (who opened our eyes to climate change), Muhammad Yunus (Grameen Bank & micro-credits), Armand Peugeot (Peugeot cars, forerunner of the current PSA group), Patrice Chéreau (director, theatre maker, author, philosopher and so much more), Dora Janssen (art collector and patron), Jacques Rogge (honorary chairman of the IOC), Luc Tuymans (painter and artist), Axel Vervoordt (art collector, curator and interior designer), Oprah Winfrey (radio and TV maker of talk shows), Toots Thielemans (musician), Alexandre Mars (businessman and philanthropist), Ellen MacArthur (the fastest solo sailor to complete the circum-navigation of the world and a pioneer with her foundation for promoting the circular economy), Dadi Janki (the spiritual head of the India based but operating globally Brahma Kumaris). These are all inspirational examples of wonderful people who have achieved wonderful things with and through their noble purpose.

In the next chapter I will discuss in detail how I see the connection between working with a noble purpose and the joy that this creates. Or to put it in slightly different terms: it will be about how we can achieve our own self-fulfilment by living our noble purpose to the full.

4

Joy through noble purpose

'People think too much about what they must do
and not enough about who they should be.'
(Meister Eckhart)

Why are we alive?

'The one who follows the crowd will usually get no further than the crowd. The one who walks alone is likely to find himself in places no one has ever been.' (Albert Einstein)

As a result of my near-death experience, it has become clearer than ever for me that Life is a precious gift. As human beings, we have been set on this earth with the opportunity to live Life to the full and to do remarkable things with that Life. But only if we want to and learn how to. Life is a non-stop journey in search of deepening and contact with our true self. It is a voyage of discovery to explore our full potential. This voyage is sometimes pleasant, sometimes difficult, but always fascinating, as we make our way slowly but surely towards connectedness with our deep, pure and divine self. Life is much more than the treadmill of 'eat-work-sleep-repeat' that we hear so much about today. Life is primarily what you make of it yourself, regardless of the cards fate dealt you when you were born.

In this chapter, I will focus on every human being who is interested in significantly improving the quality of his/her Life. I will speak to you directly, dear reader, in the hope that you will be inspired to follow the example that I will share with you in the coming pages. The content of these pages has been written for everyone, with no distinctions in mind. It is equally valid for employees and employers; for women at the top of the career ladder and men at the bottom; for new generation professionals and those approaching the autumn of their career. What I want to share with you here is about the essence of Life. It answers the key Life questions: why are we alive and how can we increase the amount of joy in our Lives?

I believe that all people have three universal needs, which I define as our three fundamental Life energies: love, interaction and creation. I have reached this conclusion based on my own Life experience and the conversations I have had with many thousands of different people at my conferences and workshops on the theme of 'what is the absolute essence of Life?'. And what are the most frequent answers I hear? 'Giving and receiving love', 'interacting with others', and 'doing something with your talents'.

'Love' is the thing that people usually mention first. Everyone wants to be loved. Everybody wants to love someone else. The feeling of strength, warmth and security that love gives us is massive. Take away a mother's love from a newborn baby and it will pine away, and probably even die. Why? Because we are born as dependent and vulnerable creatures, who need love to survive. Our love for our Life partner, our children, our parents, our friends, for what we do in and with our Life are all ways to find the deep emotional connection with the things that allow us to live truly and prosper. A Life that is deprived of love, or of giving love, is a sad and sombre Life, a Life not worthy of the term 'human'. When I ask people what constitutes the essence of Life, the most common (almost universal) response is to talk about love, specifically the love between partners and between parents and children. These relationships form the basis for our existence. In the chapter entitled 'Calculating the cost and paying the price' we will be looking more closely at this nucleus as part of the '3-sphere' model.

Notwithstanding our need for love, there are two other surprising aspects that I have observed over the years that also need to be mentioned: we often fail to have sufficient love for ourselves and we often fail to be lovingly available for those who love us. The latter means that we are not able to give to others what they are able to give to us. And the former means that we cannot expect others to give their love to us, if we are not first able to give love to ourselves.

I regard loving yourself as being, without doubt, the most fundamental basis for a happy and balanced Life. It is only by learning to appreciate and respect ourselves, by giving ourselves the right attention and the right place in Life, that it becomes possible to connect with our deeper self, our inner strength, our human richness and our talents. It is these things that then give us the energy and the desire to love others. As a result, we then find that we have love in excess, so that we can also give some to ourselves, without the need to be dependent on the love of others. Such dependence only occurs when we feel empty because we are unable to tap into our own reserves of love. For this reason, I do not regard loving yourself as a form of egotism. On the contrary, it is an indispensible condition for developing as a balanced human being.

In my philosophy, loving someone is not something that is confined to our Life partner, our family, our friends and our other close relatives and acquaintances. As leaders, we must also love our colleagues and the people who work for us, even if some out-of-date management training courses and business books advise against it. Our role as an impactful leader obliges us to do this. It is only by loving the people in your professional environment, by valuing them and cherishing them, that they will be able to give more of themselves and show greater commitment to you and your organisation. However, because many leaders do not like themselves and have an internal vacuum in their consciousness about love, they either attempt to show their love for others in a flawed manner or else go to the opposite extreme, so that they are as hard on others as they are on themselves. The lack of self-love among leaders is one of the most frequent causes of faulty or even disastrous collaborations. Because these leaders make a wrong connection between the exalted form of love (sometimes referred to by the Greek word *agapé*) and their own leadership, organisations and societies develop that are cold, distant, arrogant and even authoritarian. In other words, they are loveless – even though love is unquestionably an essential need for everyone, and therefore needs to be cherished and used in all our environments: personal, social and professional.

Carl Gustav Jung[7] was an Austrian psychologist-psychiatrist and a pioneer in the field of the collective unconscious and human archetypes, in which context he also developed the principles of synchronicity.[8] It was his work that inspired my belief that interaction is our second essential source of Life energy. Each time that we interact with someone, there is always an opportunity to improve ourselves. For example, when we unintentionally keep coming across the same kind of people, who we do not really like. Or when we constantly find ourselves in the same kind of situations that we would rather avoid, because they are not really in our best interests (often quite the reverse). These meetings and situations will continue to occur until at a certain moment we become consciously aware of what they actually mean for us. In this way, we reach a higher state of consciousness about ourselves and have therefore evolved positively as a result, allowing us to take another step forwards in Life. By working on these 'old' interactions and interpreting them correctly before moving on, space is created for new situations and new interactions, which can hold up a new mirror to a different aspect of our deeper self. This process is repeated until every essential aspect of our Life has been experienced and 'reviewed' in this manner, so that we finally become a complete human being, capable of living in harmony with ourselves.

In other words, it is by being able to interact with others that we are given repeated opportunities to become more of our true self and more fully human. We need our fellow human beings to be able to position ourselves against our feelings, thoughts, convictions, interests, fears, etc. Although some people might dream of living on a desert island, research has shown that this dream would soon evaporate when faced with the reality. We need the mirror provided by interaction in order to discover ourselves, learn from others, and grow as a person. Attempting to live alone in the world is a prelude to psychological deterioration, decline and death. We can also refer to this mirror as *karma*,[9] a concept from Hinduism and Buddhism that can literally be translated as meaning 'act, action or deed'. In both Hinduism and Buddhism, *karma* embraces both the physical and mental actions of the individual that have an impact on that individual's Life and his subsequent reincarnations. Everything that we do, think or say comes back to us in the end. *Karma* is therefore not only about the deed, but also about the consequences of the deed. It is through *karma*, the mirror of interaction, that I am able to learn about myself; about what I like and what I don't like; about what is important to me and what is not; about what makes me happy and what annoys me. It is by entering into interaction with others that we are able to experience and obtain approval and opposition, praise and criticism, appreciation and envy, etc. These are all different situations and they prompt in us a reaction of some kind. We are challenged and learn to face up to these challenges. We are 'provoked' into revealing more of our true self. This is how we make progress in Life.

The third essential type of Life energy is creation: as Human beings, we have a need to be creative, to do things with our talents, to generate added value in some form or other. It makes no difference whether we are a train driver, cleaning lady, inventor, chemist, manager, politician or entrepreneur. It is not what we do that gives us Life energy; it is why we do it and how we do it that makes all the difference. It is the noble act of doing something with our hands, our head, our body, our talents, our potential, our strength and our effort as a contribution to something greater than ourselves that makes us happy. Creation does not mean simply being creative in the sense of 'making something'. Creation is also about being actively engaged with your talent. Creation is, therefore, making things shimmer and sparkle for a cleaning lady, unconditional love for a child by its parents, service to the community for a politician, etc. This kind of creation can have an impact that is small and local or huge and global. It is not the scale of the impact that is important, but the fact that you have an impact. For this reason, I sometimes describe this third source of Life energy as the leaving of a trace or a legacy. We all wish to be remembered for who and what we were in this Life. During farewell speeches and funeral orations, reference is almost always made to what a wonderful person he/she was, what warmth and strength they exuded, how deeply they moved, touched and inspired the people around them. Nothing is ever said about how poor or rich they were, or how many people worked for them, or what jobs they had or what roles they played. The remembrance of a person, their legacy, is all about how they lived their Life.

From work pressure to work pleasure

'Appearing satisfied is a great art. Being satisfied is an ever greater art. Becoming satisfied is a work of genius. But remaining satisfied is the true masterpiece.' (Anonymous)

In this chapter, I want to look more closely at the third form of essential Life energy: the creation of impact in the service of others. In our world – where nowadays, to my irritation, everything is reduced to material and economic parameters – this energy can play an important role in helping to make people more fully and completely human and to make society more humane and respectful. To achieve this, however, will require us to adopt a radically different view about why, as people, we do what we do.

The best way to realise ourselves

It is my strong conviction – in fact, my philosophy of Life – that we achieve our self-realisation as human beings through work. By which I mean it is through creating 'things'[10] and making a specific contribution, which we then call 'work', that we become more of a complete person. Of course, this is not possible by performing this or that transactional job for a few hours each day to earn your income and secure your safety, comfort and perhaps even reputation. Nor will it be possible through jobs where we have little or no connectedness with the organisation and where our engagement is limited or totally absent. Hundreds of millions of people spend a third or more of their day working at jobs against their will, where they feel out of place, have distant relationships with their bosses, and would like nothing better than to be able to do something different with their Lives.

Real work and, consequently, self-realisation involves creating added value for the benefit of the noble purpose of your organisation. In these circumstances, work becomes a combination of your passion, your talents, your Life and work experience, your enthusiasm, your uniqueness, your convictions and your manner of being and looking at the world. When this happens, people fulfil their role in a unique way, through this combination of their own highly individual passion, talents and experience. In my philosophy, every role of meaning is performed by people who are fully themselves, and not just a fraction of who they are, perhaps because they are attempting to comply with their own or someone else's pattern of expectation about how they should be.

Searching for meaning

It is also my deep conviction that we are better and more quickly able to achieve self-realisation by performing meaningful work, work with a purpose. For me, this is the essence of people's happiness: living a purposeful Life. We can only become complete human beings when we feel and know that what we are doing is what we were put on this earth to do. What could be more special than getting out of bed each morning, relaxed after a good night's sleep and full of energy to face the new day, safe in the knowledge that you are a satisfied human being, because you are leading a meaningful Life. The strength and energy generated by people who have meaningful work in a meaningful organisation is truly remarkable. At the same time, this also brings a sense of calm, because meaningful work gives us flow. And being in flow helps us to set the right priorities and make the right choices. As a result, meaningful work also brings us harmony

In his inspirational and pragmatic book 'Why employees don't do what they're supposed to do and what to do about it', Ferdinand

Fourniès contends that a lack of meaning in their work is the main reason why people in organisations 'don't do what they are supposed to do'. People want to feel that their work has purpose and provides meaning. If that is not the case, their thoughts and feelings become unsettled. When this happens, people work more slowly and with less motivation. They also ask more questions about the value and point of what they are doing, until there comes a moment when they slowly begin to lose interest altogether.

Research has shown that when people are asked what is most likely to persuade them to give 100 percent effort at work – the total available energy that each of us has to offer – 98 percent of the respondents answer that they will only make this maximum effort when they think that their work gives added meaning to their Life. Ninety-eight percent! In other words, almost everyone who works is willing in one way or another, in an ideal world, to commit themselves fully to what they are doing when this coincides with their understanding of why they are doing it. And the other two percent? They are mainly prepared to make use of their maximum energy for material reasons: better turnover, results, financial performance, market share, share price, KPI's, etc. Two percent might be a very small minority, but it mainly includes many of the people who have the most direct interest in and the most direct impact on the material value of the organisation. This is where you will find nearly all the top managers and executives, the men and women who are responsible for results and who nearly all have a significant stake of some kind in driving the organisation's success. It is this prospect of material success that gives this group its drive. I am not saying that they are not interested in work that gives meaning to their Life, but I am saying that their prime focus, when it comes to their willingness to release their energy, is fixed firmly on the material side of the equation. And because this group also leads the organisation, they create an organisational culture based on their own narrow world view, in which KPIs, turnover, bottom line, market share and other parameters are the drivers. However, by developing a culture of this kind, the two percent ensures, whether consciously or unconsciously, that the 98 percent slowly but surely make less use of the energy that is at their disposal.

Ending transactional relationships

These statistics show that it makes sense for the leaders of organisations to think carefully about the question of meaning and to ensure that their people are triggered into action by meaningful work. Meaningful work transcends the purely transactional level and connects people within the organisation in a pleasant and productive manner that allows much more to be achieved. In contrast, the transactional level is based on an illogical paradigm. The employer wants to get as much as he can out of the employee in the shortest possible time and at the lowest possible cost. Employees are therefore regarded as a cost element rather than as a value creation element. On the other side of the equation, the employee wants to get as much out of the employer as he can by doing the least possible work. This is a contradictory situation that can never work well. Even so, it has been firmly anchored for decades in an economy of imbalances and a society of frustrations, but we have now reached the point – thankfully! – that this system is about to explode.

These kinds of transactional relationships must be brought to an end and replaced by sustainable, positive relationships in which employers can attract people who wish to take part with them in a meaningful project based on a noble purpose. By bringing together the (financial) resources of the employer and the human energy of the employees and by devoting them to a noble purpose, a new organisational dynamic with far better results will be created.

Ending transactional relationships also means that the outdated economic logic that can be seen in the film *Modern Times* by Charlie Chaplin will become less attractive, certainly for the coming generations, who will increasingly opt for organisations where they can be and become their true selves.

From doing to being

In order to find purpose in what we are doing and to evolve from work pressure to work pleasure, we must be able to be fully ourselves. Being ourselves allows us to bring out the best in us.

I like to put it this way: what I do does not define who I am, but who I am guides me to do what I do. What do I mean by this? For example, it is not because you are a taxi driver, auditor or CEO that you only possess the specific and typical characteristics of a taxi driver, auditor or CEO. You are a much more complex and much richer person than the limiting and defining characteristics of your job or role in Life. Moreover, you are not predestined to remain in that job or role for ever – although this is still what often happens in the majority of cases. As human beings, we have almost limitless possibilities that we can choose to activate or not. Sadly, in most cases, we do nothing.

It is who we are, as a person, that defines what we do. In most cases, it does not happen by sheer coincidence and without any element of choice that you become a taxi driver, auditor or CEO. By being in a particular phase of your Life, where certain convictions, needs, wishes, ambitions and situations influence your thinking, you look at the world at that moment through a very specific and personal lens. It is your situation, your Life at that time, which prompts you to become a taxi driver, auditor or CEO. But you are free to decide to change this job or role whenever a new challenge emerges that more closely matches the path you want to or need to follow. Of course, this is once again the ideal of what should happen, but for the majority of the world's population – even in the 'civilised' western world – this is not yet a reality. There is still a long way to go before we can all be who we are and translate that meaningfully into the job that we do. Even so, that is the direction in which we must travel.

It is for this reason that I advise organisations to develop a culture that focuses on the 'being' level ('who are we as an organisation and what do we stand for?') rather than on the 'doing' level. Or to put it in other words: who we are determines what we do. And what we do leads to what we have, and not the other way around: what we have can never make us what we are.

The deranging truth

'If you make a mistake and do not correct it, you make a second mistake.' (Confucius)

Notwithstanding my strong conviction that we can achieve our self-realisation as human beings through our work and our non-stop search for meaning in Life, the reality of our modern world is often painfully different. There are still hundreds of millions of actively working people who have been kidnapped and are being held hostage by a perverse economic system.

The first explanation for this painful reality can be found in the origin and evolution of the word 'work'. The Latin *tripalium*, from which the French word *travailler* is derived, refers to a kind of instrument of torture, consisting of three beams lashed together in a star-shape, which was used to restrain animals and in some cases even people, as a painful punishment. Until roughly the 18th century, work was seen as something denigrating, because it was largely carried out by slaves and serfs on behalf of their owners and masters. Even those who tilled the land – historically, agriculture remained the most important economic activity until well into the 20th century – were regarded by the social elite, by the clergy (with the exception of a number of scholastic orders like the Cistercians, who worked the land themselves) and by the military as a subordinate population group. These agricultural labourers also performed a number of 'corvees', tasks that they did for their lords and masters without pay or reward. Hence the negative connotation that the word 'corvee' still has today: an undesired or unpleasant obligatory job.

It was only from the beginning of the 18th century that work came to be linked with production, but the major change came with the advent of the Industrial Revolution. Work was now seen as a source of creative liberation from the idea of the corvee. Or so it was thought. But what did people now get as their reward in exchange for their work? Throughout the centuries, we can see that slaves were customarily given food, serfs were given protection from the elite and the new industrial labourers were paid a pittance. What these slaves, serfs and labourers received was actually a form of compensation for the misery associated with their work. This compensation bore no relation to the added value they created, nor to the effort it took. In other words, throughout history the prevailing economic systems have been built on injustice and inequality. That is still the case today and it is a shame to our society, a shame which can no longer be explained or justified from a humane and humanist perspective.

For example, people working in the textile industry in Bangladesh still receive a starvation wage. Moreover, they are obliged to work in terrible conditions, for no other purpose than to maximise the profits of a fortunate few. Much the same is true in Africa. The continent is one of the richest in the world in terms of its abundant natural resources, yet millions of people die there each year from hunger and disease, while in the West we continue to live Lives of wasteful overconsumption, based in part on products and materials coming from that same African continent. But this is not the only form of injustice. In many countries, in Europe and elsewhere, well-educated women often earn substantially less than less well-educated men for doing exactly the same work, while in some public services officials in secure, permanent posts are paid according to their grade and seniority, and not according to the contribution they make. Are all these things 'fair'? No, they are not.

In other words, throughout history, in my opinion, there has been a distortion in the way we look at work and how the time and effort it involves are rewarded.

And it is with us still. In modern economic thinking, there is a logic which persists in arguing that everything in a company must be done with the interests of the shareholders in mind. This means that inequalities are perpetuated, leading in turn to social tensions. It was the winner of the Nobel Prize for Economics and champion of the free-market economy, Milton Friedman,[11] who once argued: 'There is one and only one social responsibility of business – to use its resources and engage in activities designed to increase its profits, so long as it stays within the rules of the game, which is to say, engages in open and free competition without deception or fraud.' In the latter part of the 20th century, this philosophy led to the development of an unhealthy mentality in which 'shareholders' – both in the sense of the owners of companies and in the sense of the administrative leaders of public organisations at national, international and even supranational levels – focused purely on economic return and optimal performance. Of course, this focus was also largely (if not completely) in their own interests. Human beings, society, the environment and so much more were made subordinate to economic mechanisms and the needs of the state. As a result, ordinary men and women in their tens of millions were once again kidnapped by a largely selfish elite of entrepreneurs and public leaders.

Disconnection and disengagement

Happily, since I set up the Global Inspiration and Noble Purpose Institute (GINPI) in 2010, I have noticed an important change in the thinking of an increasing number of these entrepreneurs and public leaders. That being said, the distortion of the working environment as I have described it above still has a massive impact on both people and society.

While there has been an almost exponential growth in universal GDP since the start of the Industrial Revolution, and even though this has gone hand in hand with the material progress of large sections of the world's population (although there are still huge imbalances between the North and the South), it is alarming to note that these developments have also gone hand in hand with a massive increase in the use of medicines and anti-depressants. In other words, it is not because we are richer that we are happier! Or rather, that we feel happier.

Steven Pinker[12], a Harvard professor and author of the hyped book *Enlightenment Now* does not agree with my point of view on this matter, even though we otherwise have much in common. We both share the values of the Enlightenment and we both agree with the proposition that science and humanism should be applied to the solving of humankind's problems. And we both believe in the ultimate progress of that humankind. Where we differ is that I see a major disconnection between, on one hand, effective progress in fields such as prosperity, security, human rights, health, peace, etc., and, on the other hand, people's experience and appreciation of that progress. I attribute this disconnection to the fact that people no longer feel sufficiently connected with their own selves, with their inner motivations, with their strength and their abilities. Because they are insufficiently aware of their place in the world and have little contact with the things that are truly important to them and bring meaning into their Life, they enter into working relationships that make them materially richer but spiritually poorer.

Thankfully, direct forms of slavery have been more or less abolished. I say 'more or less' because there are still some forms of hidden slavery, such as indirect slavery and, in particular, child slavery. These are despicable practices that should no longer be tolerated in the 21st century.

That being said, nowadays most people are assumed to work of their own free will and receive rewards that are commensurate with the time and effort they give. Yet even though this work is performed voluntarily, there is still a huge part of the active working population that feels little or no sense of engagement with their work. According to a poll carried out by the American Gallup[13] research bureau in 2017, a staggering 85 percent of respondents in 142 countries said that they felt no real connection with their job. In other words, only a paltry 15 percent are enthused by their work and feel committed to it. 15 percent against 85 percent... The cost of this widespread indifference towards work in terms of unused human potential and lost performance runs into billions of euros. Each week!

How is it possible that we, as human beings, continue to make progress in terms of prosperity, humane values and scientific advancement – in other words, in the terms of Steven Pinker – while at the same time 85 percent of the world's active working population are not motivated by their work? It is possible precisely because people are disconnected from themselves and from the things that give them a real purpose! As a result, they fail to see – or if they see, they fail to experience – that in nearly every domain we are better off than we have ever been before. Instead, all they see is what they do not have, what is not getting better and what still makes them afraid. As a result, they become trapped in purely transactional and disinterested relationships with the people who give them work. They do jobs which, for them, seem to have no point. They occupy themselves for hours each day with things that they are unable to place within the frame of a wider and more meaningful context. They lose themselves in disconnected activities that are far removed from the concept of a noble purpose.

Modern slavery

Because people want to achieve a certain standard of material prosperity and/or wish to climb higher up the social ladder, they allow themselves to be kidnapped by a false economic logic, so that they lose all connectedness with their own selves. This lack of self-connectedness results in the total absence of a noble purpose, so that they become trapped, largely without realising it, in a form of modern slavery. This new form of slavery is a highly perverse and immoral way to ensnare people by tying them to a series of material rewards, such as a function, a title (which is often meaningless), a salary, bonuses (for the elite, at least), a car (sometimes), a smartphone (often), a computer, a hip place to work, etc. Thanks to all these presents from the Father Christmases in the HR department, people become addicted to the comfort they bring, to their reputation, their position in the organisational pecking order, their material wealth... People often only see this material side of things, which, it has to be admitted, does have great pulling power. However, at some point they become so used to all this material excess that they suddenly realise something else is missing. At first, they find it difficult to put their finger precisely on what this 'something else' is. Quite often, they put the blame for what is missing on the boss, the organisation or the system. Or on the role that no longer interests them. They feel that something is not right and, in fact, that they are not happy. What they fail to understand is that this 'not being happy' is the result of their no longer being connected with their own inner drivers, which can only be triggered by serving a noble purpose. They now have power and wealth, in whatever form these come, but no real strength and energy. They even lack the strength to question themselves or the energy to break out of the system. Because one of the conditions for breaking out of the system is that you have to give up all that nice material comfort and even nicer material prosperity... And so people stay where they are, kidnapped and trapped in the proverbial golden cage.

I regularly meet managers, politicians, public figures and leaders at the top of important organisations who are all trapped in this way. Sometimes it amazes me just how deeply they embrace their own kidnapping. Take Irene,[14] for example. She is the top woman in a London-based holding that is responsible for managing several other companies. I first got to know her through a mutual business friend, who as CEO of his own organisation had made use of our services for three years and now felt that Irene might benefit from them as well. During my first conversation with her, I asked what she was searching for in Life. 'Nothing, really,' she answered. 'Everything is just fine.' She had a stable relationship with a loving partner. She had a wonderful family and all the children were doing well. She was at the top of a highly prestigious organisation and sat on a number of even more prestigious boards. Our dialogue was all very easy-going, more like a polite conversation than a professional consultation. Until I suddenly asked her: 'Why do you get out of bed in the morning, Irene?' She was unable to give an immediate answer. 'I'll have to think about that,' she said. She was the woman who had it all worked out, the woman who was responsible for tens of thousands of employees – but she couldn't answer the simple question of why she got out of bed each morning. Amazing – but sadly all too common! By the time we met for our second session a week later, she had had the opportunity to think about her answer more deeply. But all she could come up with was: 'to earn a living'. I could hardly believe it. Irene received an extremely generous salary that gave her, in material terms, everything she could possibly ever want, yet what made her get out of bed in the morning was the desire to earn even more money! I told her that instead of being concerned about 'earning a living', it was perhaps time to think more about 'getting a Life'. At first, she was surprised, but gradually she began to understand that I was holding up a mirror to her soul. And the reflection told her that even though she had everything that most people could ever dream of, it was not enough. It was at that moment that she saw that 'something' was indeed missing and that she needed to go in search of what it was… If this kind of thing can happen with people right at the very top of organisations (and I could quote you dozens of other examples from my own business experience), how much more likely is to happen with the people who have to report to those at the top? Or those who have to report to the sub-top? And so it continues as you move further and further down the hierarchy, getting worse all the time.

The work-Life balance is not a balance!

Because people are trapped in modern slavery, which means that their work is purposeless, they develop an understandable but nonetheless unhealthy way of functioning. This involves them searching for a balance. A balance between working and not working. Between transactionality, modern slavery and a lack of freedom on the one hand, and free will and pleasure on the other hand.

For me, this so-called 'work-Life balance' is a construction devised by HR gurus to justify what is seen as an unnatural balance between 'giving your all' – work – and 'being who you are' – Life. This construction attempts to explain that we actually have two lives: a work life, where you are not really living, because your working life is not compatible with real Life; and a real Life, which you can only live outside of work. The French are experts at this artificial and almost obsessive separation of *la vie professionnelle et la vie privée*. It implies that the way someone is at home is different from the way they are at work. In other words, you behave differently, think differently and act differently at the two different places. As a result, people develop a kind of double personality: a work personality and a home personality. No wonder so many people seem confused nowadays!

This is why I regard the work-Life balance as complete nonsense. You are a complete, integrated person, with a single set of convictions, values, Life principles, needs and fears. And these govern your behaviour at all times, whether you are at work with your colleagues, at home with your family or out and about with your friends. In my vision for the society and organisations of the future, which I call Houses of Noble Purpose, it will not be possible or acceptable to make a distinction between who you are in your different capacities. People must be allowed to come fully and integrally into their own by also being themselves in their place of work. When people are truly themselves, they are imbued with a new strength and energy, are connected with what is essential and important, and learn how to stand up for themselves and for what they believe. It will be the task of organisations to encourage these self-aware and free human beings to work in this manner, the manner they need in order to become who they must be.

But sadly, oh so sadly, people are all too often content to remain in modern slavery, so that they do not feel real – in other words, do not feel how they really are. As a result, they accept things and do things and say things that they do not believe, with which they do not agree, and whose relevance and meaning they cannot see (because, for them, there is none). This often happens because they fail to learn during their adolescence how to make contact with their noble purpose within the context of an economy that is still based on scarcity and an unequal distribution of wealth and power. They are deceived into believing that they must live to work, rather than work to live!

In short, then, work is experienced far too much by far too many people as an obligation, as nothing more than a means to meet their material needs and the expectations placed on them by society. In other words, they see work as a necessary evil, something they don't particularly want but must have if they wish to 'make something' of their Life. It is the price they have to pay to be 'free', although this freedom, as we have seen, is often nothing more than a purposeless existence in a golden cage.

The call for action

'If you want to see the valley, climb to the mountain top.
If you want to see the mountain top, rise into heaven.
If you want to see heaven, close your eyes and be still.'
(Kahlil Gibran)

To break out of this golden cage, to be become truly free and to live a worthwhile Life, the kind of Life to which everyone on this planet is entitled, many things will first need to change. As an individual, you might decide to wait until 'something' happens – although you may find out that this no more than 'Waiting for Godot' – or else you can take the initiative into your own hands. In the first instance, it will be up to you to decide how urgent it is to take action to change your situation and how much energy and effort you are willing to make.

In this chapter, I will explore 'depth' more deeply – by which I mean we will be looking at the more psychological and spiritual matters that you will need to confront and master on your journey towards freedom. I have made this journey myself and am delighted to share my experiences with you.

Waiting for the tipping point

The easiest but also by far the most inefficient, undesirable and most psychologically draining way to break out of your golden cage is to wait until something dramatic occurs, a Life-changing event that affects you or one of your loved ones, so that its impact on your Life is earth-shaking. Waiting until you have an accident, for example. Or until you have a burn-out. Or you until you become seriously ill. Or until you lose your job. Or until you buckle under the weight of the expectations of society, your shareholders, your colleagues or your family. Or until someone close to you dies. Or until your house burns down. Or until you are declared *persona non grata* by the media. Until, until, until... These are just a few examples of situations with which people are confronted, situations that can lead to their Life being turned upside down almost overnight.

Don't you find it strange that so many of us prefer to wait until this kind of dramatic event occurs before we finally take action to improve our unsatisfactory Life, rather than taking the bull by the horns and doing something about it ourselves? How can we explain that even the most mature, experienced and well-informed leaders – never mind those who they lead – fall victim to this same kind of indecision and inertia? The answer is, in fact, quite simple – which is what makes it so insidious. We humans are creatures of habit, conditioned into acceptance by our reputation, status and material well-being. This makes it difficult for us to throw off the chains of modern slavery, because it will require us to step out of our comfort zones and into unknown territory, the only place where we can find freedom but one where the outcome is always uncertain. In short, there are plenty of reasons for doing nothing, for leaving that part of Life with which we are dissatisfied undisturbed. We hope that things will one day get better, that someone else will do something to improve our fate, that something unexpected will fall from the sky to save us. Of course, these are no more than excuses for our own immobility and inaction. But if all you can do is live in the hope that someone or something else will miraculous get you out of the mess in which you find yourself, there is a very real chance that you will miss Life's train altogether. And where would you be then? Delaying or avoiding the essential decisions in Life is seldom good for our motivation, our energy and our joy of living.

The stress caused by this delaying and avoiding gradually builds up like a pressure cooker, so that we become physically, mentally, emotionally and psychologically fatigued, or even exhausted. This can have serious and unpleasant consequences. We are no longer able to see things in their proper perspective. We become obsessed with minor and essentially irrelevant matters. We become irritated by details but miss the big picture. We lose control over our reactions. We lose our normal energy, find it harder to get out of bed in the morning and fall asleep in the afternoon. We have even less desire than before to take the initiative, or to talk with others, or to spend some quiet time with colleagues and friends. We are eaten away by doubt and feel suffocated by the same specific and often recurring thoughts about our own weakness and inability to act.

In these circumstances, it is hardly surprising that people feel less happy about what they are doing and how they (should) do it, so that their sense of alienation towards their working environment continues to grow. Too much valuable time is wasted on complaining about others, our situation and the fact that we no longer find people and things as fun, fascinating or inspirational as they used to be. I have met thousands of different people with the most wide-ranging responsibilities in many different kinds of organisations whose gaze was blank and where no spark of their soul was to be seen. If you ask them how things are going, they tell you that they are drowning in work, stressed by the need to meet their KPIs, worried about their next promotion, irritated by their unhelpful colleagues, etc. They exude an air of superficiality, negativity, passivity and, worst of all, indifference.

Instead of being aware that things cannot carry on in this manner and then actually doing something about it, they continue to tread water in their existing state of confusion, tiredness, boredom and disillusionment. The strength that these people need to take a major step forward in their Life has become so weak that they are no longer able or brave enough to act. And this often happens precisely at the moment when they have planned that oh so important and significant meeting with their business partner, manager, customer, shareholder, etc., or, in a different context, with their Life partner, child, parent or that old friend with whom relations have become strained recently. Or else when you are just on the point of taking an important decision about whether to stay or to go; to accept the inevitable or to fight against it; to accept or reject that promotion, knowing that it will mean more money but also more of the same old routine…

Since my kidnapping, I look at Life in a totally different way. I am now convinced that Life in general – for all of us – is put together in such a complex and subtle way that it is not possible for our human species to cope with negative energy or self-destructive thoughts indefinitely. This explains why Life has the ability to give us a kick up the backside. In fact, it is such a hefty (and often unexpected) kick, that we have no option but to do something about it. When you are shot to pieces during a kidnapping, when one of your children survives a serious accident, when your Life partner arrives home with the dramatic news that he or she has cancer, when the organisation decides there may no longer be a place for you after the forthcoming reorganisation, when the fantastic project you were hoping to win is awarded to your biggest competitor, when your own company goes bust or falls victim to an aggressive takeover, when the results booked by your division are so disappointing that the shareholders decide to sell… These are all examples of unanticipated and irreversible moments that have a huge impact on our lives. These turning-point moments confront us so starkly with the realities of our existing Life that we are shaken out of our lethargy. We begin to question our 'old' routine and our old unaware approach to Life. The cards of our Life are reshuffled and our priorities rearranged. What seemed so certain in the past is now no longer certain at all. Spending time with your badly injured child or sick partner; learning to deal with major disappointments, loss of reputation, dismissal from your work or even, in a worst case scenario, the death of a loved one; being forced to realise that Life is finite and that, once it is over, there will be no coming back; having to live with a body that has been seriously damaged by an accident or a kidnapping… These are all seminal events that were not in the original script of your Life, events so dramatic that they compel you to question everything that has gone before. This is the moment when all the 'why' questions come to the forefront. Why did I not spend more time with him or her? Why did I not listen more to him or her? Why did I not give a greater priority to this or that? Why have I never asked all these 'why' questions until now?

If that bombshell moment had never occurred, all these crucial questions would probably have remained unasked, and you would have continued to struggle your way through Life, your lips barely above the water, so that you would almost certainly never had made the right Life choices.

Making conscious choices

Life is therefore all about making the right conscious choices. By which I mean the Life in which we are free. In this sense, I am wholly convinced that having the courage and the ability to make conscious choices is our passport to true freedom. Or perhaps I should say to our psychological feeling of being free. Because being able to make conscious decisions about our destination in Life is of Life-changing importance. Whoever is able to decide about the most crucial things in his or her Life, based on their own free will and without losing sight of the consequences and the qualities of those choices, is, in my opinion at least, a free person.

The way in which I make my own personal choices is based on a philosophy that I developed during two different but equally vital stages of my Life: just after my kidnapping and when I began to give keynote speeches.

During those keynotes, I was asked time and time again to explain why people so often fail to do the things or take the decisions that are right for them. The fact that this question seemed to be so important for so many people persuaded to me to work pro-actively around the notion of free choice in obstructive working environments.

My philosophy is rooted in my firm belief that people strive both consciously and unconsciously to achieve harmony in their Lives. The majority of the human race wishes to live in connectedness with the basic needs we discussed earlier: love, interaction and creation. For this reason, viewed from my humanist and positiv-ist perspective, I further believe in the power of human beings, through their experience of situations, even the most dramatic, to become more fundamentally human, because those situations help to make them more self-aware. I also believe that the desire to be free is built into each of our genes. In normal circumstances, we need others, but this need stops when our feeling of freedom is lost. At the same time, we have often been over-conditioned by our familial and social environments to make conventional choices that satisfy the highest common denominator, which is the prevailing norm. Colouring outside the lines is therefore seen as inappropriate, pretentious or abnormal.

Freedom comes from our capacity and our will to make conscious choices that move us forward through Life, in one direction or another. In most cases, we want to and are able to predict the impact of these choices in advance. By contrast, people who fail to take decisions, for whatever reason, move backwards in Life.

Our failure to make essential Life-choices is like allowing ourselves to be kidnapped by our own fears and obstructive feelings. If we don't make a conscious choice, our fears and feelings will do it for us. But the very worst form of this self-kidnapping is when, as a result of our indecision, other people make choices on our behalf, choices that we then criticise, even though we had the opportunity to do something about it ourselves! The Life of people who find themselves trapped in this unenviable situation is often one of constant complaint, not only about those who made the choices, but also about the mediocrity of those choices and the reasons behind them. But taking action on their own initiative...? No, sadly not.

In order to help you to make conscious choices, I have created the '3-spheres' model, which you can read about below. The three essential Life components are the nucleus, the social sphere and the professional sphere. The nucleus is the core of our Lives: us as individuals, in our interaction with others, with our partner (if we have one) and with our child or children (if we have them). If you do not have a partner, the nucleus can also include that one special friend, the one you can always turn to for help and guidance. For people who are religiously inclined, their relationship with God can also be included in the nucleus. In other words, the nucleus (in one sense, at least) is the basis of our Lives. At the same time, the social sphere is also important, including as it does our parents, our brothers and sisters, our close family, our friends and our interactions with all these loved ones, as well as our social non-professional activities. Finally, there is the third and equally important sphere: our professional sphere. This embraces all our professional activities, our different business and societal roles and responsibilities, our various mandates, our investments, and our *pro bono* and philanthropic activities. Below, you can find a diagram that illustrates this '3-spheres' model.

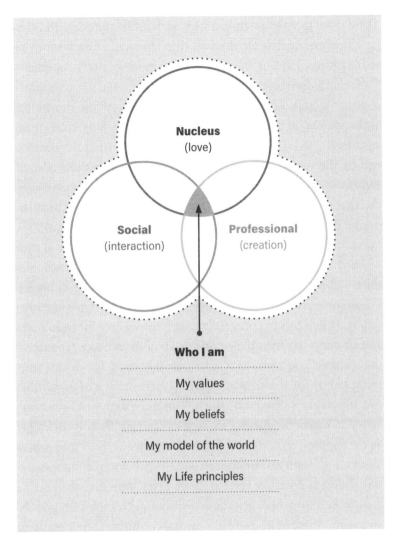

The three spheres model

The nucleus is connected with our need for love. The social sphere is connected with our need for interaction. The professional sphere is connected with our need for creation.

These three spheres are linked with each other and partially over-lap. This means that we need all three spheres, if we wish to be stable people. Finding the right balance between the three spheres is of vital importance. They are never static, but are constantly moving in relation to each other, in keeping with the things that are happening in our Lives at any given moment. Sometimes more attention will be devoted to our nucleus; on other occasions it will be the social or professional spheres that takes precedence. But if we want to be and remain a fully developed human being, the three spheres must remain in contact with each other. The degree of contact will vary during different periods of your Life. Sometimes they will be more widely spread from the central zone where they intersect, so that the zone becomes smaller. Sometimes they will be closer together, so that the zone becomes bigger. What you must avoid is that the three spheres overlap each other totally. When this happens, it becomes impossible for us to make a distinction between the priorities we need to make for each of the spheres. You can't, as it were, see the wood (or in this case, the spheres) for the trees. Everything gets on top of each other and the result is chaos. Of course, you must also avoid the other extreme, where the spheres are so far apart that there is no longer an overlapping central zone. When this happens, each sphere lives its own Life, with no connection with its two companion spheres. It is almost as if we live three separate Lives, with no coherence or complementarity between them. Symbolically, each Life 'goes its own way'. This can lead to great mental confusion, often resulting in energy drain, burn-out, depression and, in extreme cases, even suicide. In order to preserve the connectedness between our three spheres – nucleus, social and professional – there is a symbolic supra-sphere around the inter-connection of the three spheres. This is the sphere of harmony, the harmony which (as I have previously mentioned) every human being is seeking. It is thanks to this harmony sphere that the other three spheres remain in coherent contact, even if the degree of that contact continues to fluctuate. I regard this harmony concept as a fantastic way to give us insight into the 'makeability' of the human species and our resilience.

In Life, there are numerous moments when our harmony can be temporarily disturbed. This is a normal part of our day-to-day existence and there is nothing wrong with it. On the contrary, these are moments of development when we, as human beings, stand in front of our mirror of Life. When we try to recover our harmony, we are continually challenged to take decisions that are coherent with who we are. These numerous moments of disturbance are caused when one of our spheres demands a disproportionate amount of attention. This can be either a reactive process, when we are confronted with a situation that we had not foreseen, such as an illness or a dismissal, or a proactive process, where we think about an important decision we need to take and then act accordingly, so that we can keep control of the situation. This might be the case, for example, when you decide to make a career switch (professional sphere), or to spend more time with the children (nucleus), or when you decide to move to a foreign country (social sphere).

How exactly should we deal with those reactive situations and pro-active decisions? How should we react to the things that happen to us and how should we make our essential choices? (Of course, I assume you already understand that I am not talking here about the choice between an Italian or Chinese restaurant or a decision about which film to see!) What are the mechanisms that make it possible for us as human beings to make choices?

The core of our being is symbolically represented by the central zone of our '3-spheres' diagram, the zone where all three spheres partially overlap. Every time that we need to make an important choice, we make an appeal, either consciously or unconsciously, to the elements contained in that central zone. These are the things that make us what we are as human beings. This includes, amongst other things, our convictions (both positive/supportive and negative/weakening), our values (which direct our behaviour), our Life principles (the essential drivers of our Life), our model of the world (how we look at things from the perspective of good or bad, acceptable or unacceptable, beautiful or ugly, yes or no, etc.) and, last but not least, our needs (what is important to us?). Every time that Life confronts us with the disruption of our harmony, or if we disturb that harmony ourselves by the need to take an important decision, we have to make a choice that will lead us in one direction or another. For example, we can decide to do something or do nothing. We can decide not to decide. We can decide to act later, when the moment is right. We can decide to let others decide in our place. And so on. In other words, we have a very wide range of things we can choose and decide.

Whether we decide and what we decide during these moments of confrontation with Life is determined by the connections we make with that intersecting central zone. With our level of being. Who we are will decide what we do. We will be led by our convictions, our values, our Life principles, our model of the world and our needs. If you believe this, then you also believe in the enlightened and humanist view that each of us, as individuals, is free or at least has the liberty to make free choices. Nobody else can make those choices for you. Nobody! Unless, of course, someone forces you at gunpoint to make a decision against your will. But then this kind of kidnapping is obviously not a free choice! To avoid being forced to live this kind of kidnapped Life, where we are constantly thrown from left to right and back again by the decisions of our bosses, our Life partner, our parents, our friends, our children, our business relations, etc., we must believe that we, and we alone, will make the choices that affect our Lives. Just as importantly, we must live out that belief. Even when we are confronted with the most dramatic of human situations (and I realise I am pushing things far here), we always have the choice to decide between doing something or doing nothing.

It was Viktor Frankl,[15] the Austrian neurologist and psychiatrist, the founder of speech therapy, Holocaust survivor and, above all, author of *Man's Search for Meaning*, who first helped me to see that we always have a choice. His story about some of his fellow prisoners in the camps, who even in their hopeless position were prepared to share their last piece of bread with others who had none, made a huge impression on me. At the same time, he makes the comparison with other prisoners, who did nothing but complain about their terrible situation and how they arrived there. In his most crucial insight, Frankl points out that the Nazis were able to take almost everything from the captive Jews. But there were some things they could never take: the prisoners' human dignity and self-respect, and the choices they were able to make.

So how free are we today to make our own choices? Well, we are as free as we want to be and are able to be. But we need to be aware that there is one ultra-important condition attached to the making of free choices…

Calculating the cost & paying the price

This one condition is a willingness to pay the price attached to our choice. Because each choice always has a cost. Sometimes this cost can be immeasurably high; sometimes it can be insignificantly small. The cost can be emotional, material, spiritual, financial, physical, mental, or a combination of any and all of these. For example, there will be an emotional price to pay in terms of sadness when you decide to leave the organisation where you have worked happily for many years, but whose future you will henceforth no longer be able to shape. There might be a material cost to pay if you decide to delocalise a division in order to increase its return or opt to move from a smaller to a larger main office. The same is true if you decide to live a more ecological Life, so that you exchange the comfort and convenience of your own car for the vagaries of public transport and car pooling. You may have to pay a spiritual cost if you decide to do something that goes against your own self-interest, but serves a higher purpose than your own welfare and well-being. A financial cost will be incurred if you decide not to go through with a transaction in which you have already invested, because you need to rediscover your focus and calm. And a mental price may be due if you decide not to accompany your friends on that once-in-a-lifetime world tour, but then can't get the thought of what you are missing out of your head.

These are just a few examples. There are many, many more prices that you will potentially need to pay as a consequence of the choices you make.

You can take it from me that for every essential choice, where you temporarily give priority to one of the three spheres, there is always a price to pay. You are the only person who can calculate the level of the cost and I would advise you to do this in advance whenever you make an important Life decision. You can do this as follows. Take a sheet of paper and draw a line down the middle. Note down in the left column all the advantages of taking the decision. Note down all the disadvantages in the right column. By making a balance sheet in this way, you will find connection with the things that are essential for you and so gain insight into what is the best thing for you to do. I have often seen people with a positive balance of as much as 75 percent on the left still decide not to do anything. Just as I have seen people decide to act when there is a negative balance of 75 percent on the right. As long as we are fully aware of the choice and stand behind it, the choice we are making is a real one. And then we are truly free.

Making choices therefore involves looking at the price it will cost and then deciding whether or not we are willing to pay. Because I fully understand this and prepare well for the choices I need to make – some of which have an important impact on me, my relationship, my family and my business – I live with a deep and intense feeling of freedom and control over my Life. Sometimes I later regret making a particular choice, but by quickly connecting with my sense of responsibility and my awareness of the temporality of things – after all, it is just one choice in a lifetime of choices – I soon return to the essence of Life.

When we need to make important decisions in Life, it is crucial to look at ourselves and our situation honestly. We must have the courage to decide whether or not the things we currently possess (personal, social, professional) are sufficient and adequately satisfy the ambitions we have in Life, just as we must decide whether or not the price to perpetuate this situation is too high. If the current situation is better than the alternative and if the price for maintaining this situation is 'affordable', then it makes sense to stick with what you have. But if the price of holding what you have is significantly higher than the price of change, then I would advise you to make the switch – and make it quickly.

So why do we so often fail to do this? We know that we should do something different – that we should face up to that difficult conversation; that we should have the courage to make that major investment; that we should spend more 'quality time' with our partner; that we need a change of course to bring more balance into our Life – but somehow nothing ever comes of it. The reason for this is that we are often kidnapped by our own comfort zone and don't know how to escape from it.

We all have a comfort zone. It is our safe haven, the place from where we normally function. When we are there, we know what we are doing. We are familiar with the environment. We have control. We understand how the people and things around us will react, so that we can predict what will happen. As a result, we don't have to think and feel no stress. It is like being on automatic pilot.

If, however, we remain in our comfort zone for too long, we will eventually get bored. We learn nothing new, approach things smugly, routinely and uncritically, and miss out on new information and new insights. As a result, we become increasingly irritated by 'more of the same' and the lack of anything new, leading to laziness, complacency and an inability to spot new opportunities.

A huge amount of research has been done into the learning dynamic of adults. Its conclusion, in a nutshell, is that grown men and women can only learn, and therefore make progress, if they are prepared to leave their comfort zone. Whoever wishes to evolve and grow, whoever wants to acquire new expertise, whoever wishes to breathe new Life into a relationship that is flagging, whoever wants to get on the same wavelength as his/her children, whoever wants to tackle that difficult conversation with his/her parents, or an obstructive colleague, or an impossibly demanding customer… will only be able to do so if they have the guts to leave behind the things that are familiar and make us feel safe. If we are looking for a change of responsibilities or are anxious to start a major transformation or to push through an ambitious new project, it will not be possible for us to achieve these milestones in our Life from within the limiting confines of our zone of comfort. As Albert Einstein once put it: 'It is insanity to do the same thing over and over again, and expect different results'. If we want to welcome something new into our Life, we must consciously connect with our inner self to learn what things make us feel comfortable and what things make us feel less secure. It is only when you know where your comfort zone is and what it contains – and, by extension, where it isn't and what it doesn't – that your learning process can begin.

Even so, stepping outside of your comfort zone is never easy. It has both a positive and a negative side. Among the positives, you gain new insights, acquire a wider scope and a broader vision, discover new energy (or re-discover the old), feel healthy stress, find renewed motivation and refine/extend your competencies. This expresses itself in a renewed sense of optimism, because you are at last making progress again. Among the negatives, you feel uncertain about what might happen, worried about how to best use your new skills and best deal with your new contacts, unsure about the parameters of your new context, frightened by the prospect of failure… This expresses itself in a less healthy form of stress and self-doubt about your ability to control the situation. At the end of the day, the positive reasons for leaving your comfort zone transform it into a fascinating challenge, and one that can bring you great satisfaction. And this notwithstanding the negative aspects, which are usually far less numerous than the positive ones.

Even so, many people are far too often reluctant to accept this challenge. When they are asked to enter into a new relationship, or take on a new role, or invest in a new project, or move to another country, or reorganise their company,… they suddenly freeze and pull full back. Instead of seizing the opportunity and taking the step they should take, they either postpone the decision or decide not to do it at all.

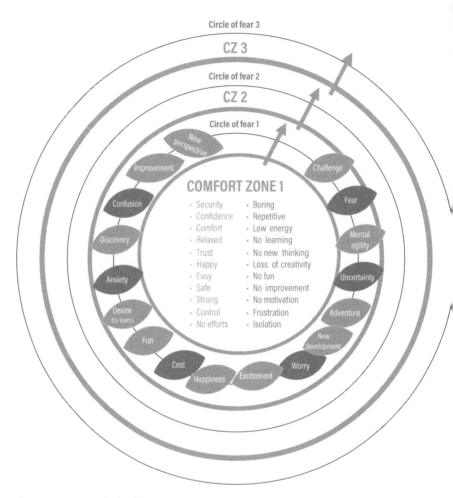

Comfort zone and circle of fear

For me, the most fundamental cause of this indecision is that people are kidnapped by what I call the 'circle of fear' that surrounds our comfort zone. Without exception, we all have such a circle. For some the fear will be situated at the emotional level, while others might be more concerned by mental aspects. Some will be worried by the possible risk to their reputation posed by a lack of control or impact; others will be afraid that they will not receive the recognition they hope for and may become just an anonymous cog in the huge organisational machine. There will be those who feel that their freedom of choice and action may be limited or that their knowledge and competencies will be lost, at least in part. There are as many different kinds of fear circles as there are people on earth! We have each constructed our own circle, entirely unconsciously, during our childhood and adolescence, often under the well-meaning influence of parents, teachers, youth movements, etc. The circle also has a positive side, of course, because it prevents us from taking reckless decisions. But it must not gain so much power in our Life that we become afraid to make any decisions, especially the essential Life decisions that we need to take if we are to develop and progress. If we can learn at an early age to try new things and take reasonable risks, there is a good chance that we will feel comfortable doing the same in later Life. It will feel 'natural' to us, because we often did it as a child, and so we know that an occasional failure is part of the learning process. If, however, we were 'over-protected' in our early years, so that we were constantly being warned about potential dangers and never encouraged to test out new things, there is a strong likelihood that as adults we will also be reluctant to 'colour outside the lines'.

This early pre-programming of our approach to the comfort zone and the circle of fear can be a serious problem when we reach adulthood. In some cases, it can hold us back in all spheres of Life. In fact, it can often be difficult to know which of the spheres to prioritise, if two or three of them are conflicting. When this happens, it is essential, no matter how hard it is, to break out of your comfort zone. You must first search consciously within the zone, to identify the elements that are preventing you from taking a decision. What deep needs or fears is the zone trying to protect? What do you need to break free from, if you wish to escape and evolve? After all, as the old adage puts it: 'You can't make an omelette without breaking eggs'.

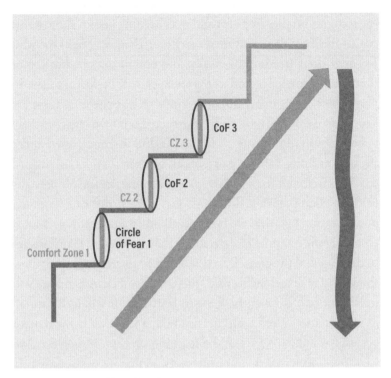

Human progress and learning phases

It is possible to expand our comfort zone, so that we can break the circle of fear that surrounds it. This is something that we must do in three repeated stages: preparation, effort and consolidation. At the moment we acquire new competencies (this can be in any field: emotional, mental, technical, physical, etc.), we will have a desire and a need to consolidate them. Consequently, around this expanded comfort zone – let's call it comfort zone 2 – a second circle of fear – circle of fear 2 – will develop, as a result of which we learn how to deal with our newly acquired knowledge, skills, courage, etc. This is the point at which we prepare ourselves to make a new effort, so that we can expand our comfort zone again and break through circle of fear 2. This leads to the creation of comfort zone 3 and circle of fear 3. This process is then repeated until we no longer wish to or are no longer able to repeat it. It is, in fact, a normal process of developing awareness about our own self: our evolution and the development of our competencies in the broadest sense.

The way in which we can break through the circle of fear and move out of our comfort zone has much in common with what we discussed previously about taking matters into your own hands – instead of waiting until some dramatic tipping point occurs, both processes require us to adopt a new form of behaviour, so that we can discover the boundaries of our abilities. To do this, the best method I know and the one I continually use in transformation processes for our clients is the 'iceberg' method.

Dive deep into the iceberg

It is always important to look at your behaviour. What is stopping you from becoming what you want to become? What is hampering your evolution? What is limiting your well-being? What things are you doing, or not doing, or doing wrong, so that you allow yourself to be kidnapped and held hostage in an unsatisfactory situation, making it impossible for you – for now – to live the Life to want to lead?

To answer these questions, we need to explore our own individual iceberg, which I see in a symbolic way as comparable with our being human.

As you probably know, only 15 percent of an iceberg is visible above the water. This 15 percent is held above the waterline by the 85 percent that you cannot see below the water line. People's behaviour – the behaviour that we see – is comparable with that 15 percent. This is what we do and don't do, and what we say and don't say: in other words, our complete communication with others, which determines how these others look at us. However, it is the remaining 85 percent of who we are – the 85 percent that people cannot see – that governs our behaviour.

I am a great believer that people who are constantly in interaction with each other, as we all are, should make an effort to plumb the depths of the iceberg, to learn what they can about the hidden 85 percent of those with whom they interact. This investigative process, which demands both time and effort, is the only way to really get to know other people and to discover what is truly important for them. We can only work together, live together and create together effectively if we understand each other – and that means understanding what is under the waterline.

But before we attempt to explore the depths of others, it is first necessary to explore our own depths. What exactly are the constituent elements of your own hidden 85 percent? This is where you will find your convictions, values, needs and fears. You also need to be aware that the deepest elements in the iceberg are also the elements that have the most impact on the elements above them. If, for example, your deepest element is your fears – for example, the fear of being excluded or of not being good enough – this will have an influence on your needs (the need for recognition, to belong, to be seen, to do better than the rest, etc.). This will then, in turn, play a role in the formation of your values, such as authenticity, excellence and resilience. Last but not least, these fears, needs and values will then have a combined impact on the formulation of your convictions ('everyone should learn to fend for themselves' or 'the welfare state will take care of us').

Our fears, which are well hidden from the outside world, therefore dictate our behaviour. If we are afraid to stand up for ourselves, or if we constantly want to be in the picture, or if we have a need to

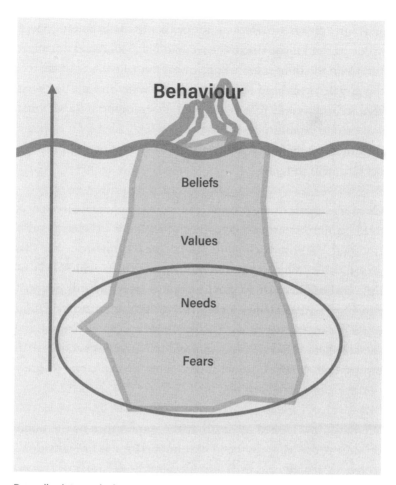

Deep dive into our iceberg

work in total transparency, or if we prefer to have a secret agenda, or if we are a control freak, or if we must always involve others for fear of seeming dictatorial… all these things are related to the way in which our iceberg is built up.

So, looking at and analysing our behaviour is important – and it is particularly important when we need to make important choices. Our general behaviour (what we do and don't do, what we say and don't say) is a perfect indicator of what is happening deep inside us. And if you discover that your behaviour does not allow you to do the things that will help you to make the right choice, this is when you need to dive under the waterline and see what your iceberg is really telling you. And, more importantly, see what you can do about it. To make this possible, I have developed a methodology that is included in my 'Joy through noble purpose' development program.

Of course, this learning process is far from easy, because it requires us to learn from our mistakes. Yet although it is a cliché, it is also true that 'every setback is the set-up for a comeback'. For this reason, I see Life as a continuum of experiences, which help us little by little to move forward on our journey towards personal enlightenment and self-awareness; towards the ultimate realisation of the balance between the nucleus (how we can be loving), the social sphere (how we can achieve qualitative interaction with others) and the professional sphere (how we can create a legacy through our noble purpose).

We have now looked in detail at the importance of the noble purpose per se (chapter 5) and how important it is for individuals to live in accordance with a noble purpose (chapter 6). I have also explained how we can achieve our 'being human' through meaningful work. That is the point at which the paths between noble purpose and work intersect.

The time has now come to see how the paths of the individual and the organisation also intersect. Because it is in organisations, whether great or small, that people actually work. In chapter 7, I will make clear why organisations need to develop and operate through their own noble purpose philosophy. This will transform them into systems in which people can be truly themselves, because they are contributing to the noble purpose of the organisation.

5

Houses of Noble Purpose

'Higher values create higher energy levels in people.'

(Gerrit Broekstra in *The Spirit Driven Organization*)

For me, organisations need to become ecosystems in which people can realise themselves through their meaningful contribution to the noble purpose of the organisation. In organisations with a short-term vision, where financial results are the only yardstick for success, this is simply not possible, because these organisations take no account of the personal development needs of their personnel. On the contrary, people are held firmly in check and trapped in a modern form of slavery by a leadership based on command and control. Values are at best theoretical concepts to hang on the wall in the HQ entrance hall, but no-one experiences them as a real compass for their behaviour.

Society is evolving so quickly that organisations, like snakes, must shed their old skin to become integrated systems that seek to serve that society through a clear noble purpose. This noble purpose must be visibly embraced by the leaders, who must be genuinely concerned to make a positive impact and find ways to achieve this through the people in their organisation. Those same leaders must further build and perpetuate a culture in which values and principles are the foundation for everything that the organisation does, giving direction for what is acceptable and appropriate, and what not.

By combining a noble purpose, loving leadership, a correct strategy and a value-based culture in a holistic approach, organisations gain in strength and become what I call 'Houses of Noble Purpose'. And that is the subject of this chapter: how we can build Houses of Noble Purpose, directed by loving leaders who develop a clear

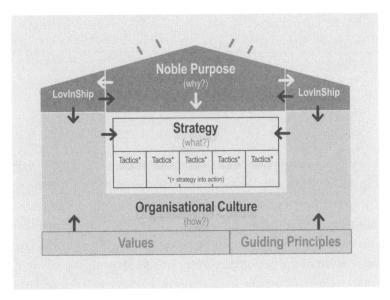

The House of Noble Purpose

and powerful organisational culture with strong and lived values and principles, on which the business strategy is based.

Put simply, the 'why' of an organisation is its noble purpose. That is the roof of the organisation's house. The 'how' of the organisation is the leadership and the organisational culture, with honest values and guiding principles as the most important elements. They form the walls and foundations of the house. The 'what' of the organisation is its strategy and tactics in practice. They form the rooms of the house. And you can see, in this model the strategy and tactics are embedded within the noble purpose and the culture, just as in a house the rooms are protected by the roof and walls. In other words, to allow the strategy and tactics to have the right impact, they must be geared to the things for which the organisation stands – its noble purpose – and to the manner in which the company behaves, both internally and externally – its leadership and culture (with its values and principles).

This is far from easy, which perhaps explains why, sadly, it currently happens so little. Far too often strategy is still regarded as being the key factor in 'success', so that there is no real noble purpose, leading to a weak or ill-adjusted organisational culture that is unable to get the strategy properly on the rails.

The theory that encourages organisations to develop into Houses of Noble Purpose is revolutionary and for the time being has only been adopted by a handful of visionary leaders. Most of the clients of GINPI (the Global Inspiration and Noble Purpose Institute) fall into this small category: based on strong convictions, they want their organisation to make a strong and sustainable impact on people and society in a new way. In fact, I see this evolution as the only way to create a sustainable economic future and a happier society. The era when organisations were dominated by a short-term perspective focused exclusively on their own interests, with little respect for people, society and the world, is rapidly coming to an end – in a positive sense. I see more and more often that entrepreneurs and organisational leaders are starting to ask questions about the reasons for their organisational existence, as a result of which they are more frequently seeking to strike a balance between the short term and the long term, and between all their stakeholders.

The key question then becomes: what needs to happen to persuade organisational leaders to follow the path that leads to the House of Noble Purpose model? Does their organisation first need to be 'kidnapped' before they can start to question themselves? This might be a kidnapping that occurs because a business model collapses (as was the case with the once dominant retailer Sears). Or because customers turn their back on the organisation in huge numbers (as was the case with Ryanair, when it became known how they treat their staff). Or because its personnel is demotivated, with many of them in burn-out (as was the case with France Telecom, where several employees committed suicide). Or by continuing to offer products, services and solutions that no longer meet the needs of the market (as was the case with numerous once famous names, including Nokia, Kodak and Marks & Spencers). Or because there has been too little innovation, as a result of which an important part of market share has been lost to competitors (as was the case with Blokker, Carrefour and Saab). Or because there has been a clear lack of respect for people and society (as was the case with BP, Enron, Ryanair and the blood diamond industry). Or because of decisions that were totally irrelevant and diametrically opposed to what the citizens of the 21st century want and need (as, sadly, is still the case with many European institutions and possibly even more national governments and authorities).

In the deep discussions I have with the shareholders, CEOs and leaders of not-for-profit organisations, such as public institutions, parliaments or international authorities, I am afraid there is often still clear evidence of kidnapping in one form or another. Many of the top people have doubts whether they and their organisations can carry on for much longer, given the way things are currently organised and run. Many of them are already looking for 'something else', something that gives their organisation more purpose and offers an answer to the question that is being asked with increasing urgency and frequency: why in god's name do we do what we do?

The time has arrived for organisations to start thinking about how they can evolve to become ecosystems, which can combine economics and ecology, humanism and performance, short-term actions and long-term purpose, and respect for themselves and respect for all stakeholders in a clear and transparent manner. This is the combination that is included in my House of Noble Purpose concept, and I will now explain how this new organisational model works.

In doing so, I wish to address in particular those leaders and entrepreneurs who are interested in new forms of balanced leadership and balanced entrepreneurship, through which their organisations can evolve into meaningful ecosystems.

I will make clear why the old paradigm, in which financial performance was the only measure of success, is finished. This paradigm is anchored in a particular form of leadership that I refer to as 'BlooderShip'. In order to evolve into a House of Noble Purpose, this BlooderShip will need to be replaced by what I call 'LovInShip'. This means that from now on the organisation will need to be inspired by its noble purpose – and not by its quarterly results.

The balance sheet revisited

'We are accountable not only for the evil that we do, but also for the good that we do not do.' (Elisabeth Laseur)

If I ask CEOs what the ultimate purpose of their organisation is and what they regard as the absolute proof that the organisation is performing well, by far the most common answer I receive is: the financial results that the organisation generates, with the pleasing side effect of being able to pay dividends to its shareholders – although they forget, of course, that these results are not generated by the organisation itself, but by the people who work for it.

As a multiple entrepreneur, who believes in a balanced capitalist logic, I freely admit that results and dividends are important, even essential. But there needs to be much more than that. As the car-building pioneer Henry Ford once said: 'A business that makes nothing but money is a poor business!' If we can learn to see results as the outcome of working together in pursuit of the noble purpose for which an organisation stands, this gives a totally new dynamic to the question: how will we ensure that we, as an organisation, are able to make a relevant societal contribution in which all our stakeholders are involved, about which they feel proud, and as a result of which they become better people?

This brings us back, of course, to the essential 'why' question: why do we do as an organisation what we do? Why do we do as a team what we do? Why do I do as a leader what I do? But this leads on to a second important question that also needs to be considered: how do we generate our results? Whoever focuses exclusively on generating results, without stopping to think about how they do it, effectively creates a system where the ends justify the means and everything is subordinated to the bottom line. This immediately makes us think of companies like the Enrons, Deepwater Horizons/BPs and Lehman Brothers of the world, where profit was king. But it can just as easily make us think of phenomena such as environmental damage, catastrophic global warming, record levels of burn-out, increasing alienation and loneliness, and this notwithstanding our ever-increasing material prosperity.

In France, for example, there was the case of France Telecom, where almost 30 employees took their own lives during the period 2008-2009. In Bangladesh, there was the collapse of the Rana Plaza, a human death trap where thousands of people died as a result of working in appalling conditions in an unsafe building, and all to meet the demands of well-known fashion brands in the West. In the Gulf of Mexico, there was the disastrous oil spillage from the Deepwater Horizon platform, a clear instance of failed management by the BP Company. Until then, BP had been regarded as a responsible organisation, but its flagrant breach of its own safety regulations (as detailed in its charter!) soon changed public perception for the worse. In Switzerland during the past decade, the CFO of insurer Zurich and the CEO of Swisscom have both committed suicide. In Germany and Japan, the top men of various famous car companies have spent time in prison for fraud and corruption. These are all examples of how seemingly successful organisations and their leaders can fall from grace as a result of being metaphorically kidnapped by the materialist system that they themselves had helped to build.

Nor should it be forgotten that the 'collateral damage' of this obsessive focus on financial results as the only measure for success is massive. This impact is often hugely underestimated when organisations get themselves into trouble through their own short-sightedness and stupidity.

Via the 'balance sheet revisited', I have developed a simple methodology to reduce the negative impact of this exclusive focus on profit. It is an approach that still recognises certain financial imperatives, but also takes account of humane, ecological and societal aspects.

To begin with, it will be useful if I explain how I first came to use my 'balance sheet revisited' arguments and why it is now often the basis of my efforts to persuade entrepreneurs and leaders to think more deeply about what they and their organisations are doing.

In the spring of 2013, I was asked by a number of members of the Belgium government to give my opinion about the way the state-owned Belgacom telecommunications company was being run.[16] The question was whether or not the organisation's CEO, Didier Bellens, should be allowed to remain in post. Both the business and the political world had praised Bellens for the fantastic financial results he had achieved and one group of politicians in particular was delighted with the generous dividend that had been paid out to the shareholders (which included the Belgian state).[17] However, another group of politicians and their cabinet staffs had a major problem with Bellens's almost dictatorial way of working, which was reported on at length in the press. They openly questioned whether or not he should be allowed to keep his job. Those who were tired of his arrogance and the general air of controversy surrounding the organisation wanted him to go. But for others, the impact of his financial success was an important reason to let him stay, under the motto of 'never change a winning team'. The problem was, however, that Belgacom was no longer a winning team, because dozens of its best and most respected managers had already left (or been forced out) and the general atmosphere was corrupted by suspicion and fear.

To illustrate my arguments, I drew a balance sheet on a flip chart. On the one side – the assets side – I noted down the dividends that flowed to the Belgian state, amounting to hundreds of millions of euros in just a few years' time. This money made it possible for the politicians to invest in other fields or to fill up the gaps in their budgets. On the other side – the liabilities side – I noted down the impact of the conflict with the social partners and the increasing threat of strikes, the cost of recruiting new top executives to replace those who had left (because they couldn't work any longer with the CEO), the estimated cost of lost performance by a demotivated workforce, the huge increase in sickness leave and the incidence of burn-out, the decline in customer-orientation with a rise in complaints as a result, the direct and indirect damage to the organisation's reputation, the loss of confidence in the customer-supplier relationship, etc. Alongside all these items I placed an actual or accurately estimated cost.

This made it possible to do a quick and easy calculation, which showed that the gains on the assets side from the dividends were far outweighed by the cost of the losses on the liabilities side from

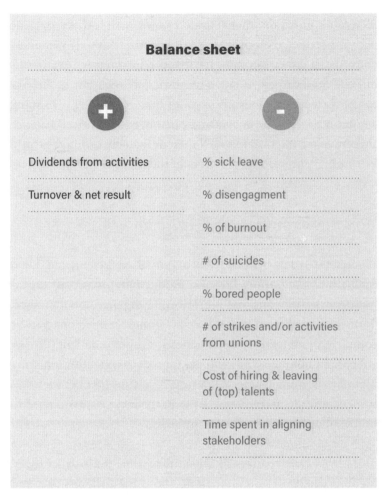

Balance sheet

+	-
Dividends from activities	% sick leave
Turnover & net result	% disengagment
	% of burnout
	# of suicides
	% bored people
	# of strikes and/or activities from unions
	Cost of hiring & leaving of (top) talents
	Time spent in aligning stakeholders

The balance sheet revisited

a whole range of factors. You didn't need to be a genius to draw the obvious conclusion. A few weeks later, the council of ministers announced the departure of CEO Bellens.

By shifting the focus from financial results to the indirect costs of a particular leadership style, situations that are initially regarded as 'positive' can be seen in a more realistic light.

As a result, if organisational leaders nowadays try to impress me with the scale of their profits and dividends, I am only genuinely enthusiastic if they can show me that this has been achieved without collateral damage and at a minimal liabilities cost. If they try to use their financial results as proof that 'everything is running smoothly', I respond by getting out my metaphorical 'balance sheet revisited' flipchart to see if they are actually telling the truth, by putting all the relevant factors in their proper perspective.

The operation succeeded but the patient died

In short, it is not because your organisation is achieving good results (i.e., the bottom line and productivity) that your organisation is healthy and has a motivating organisational culture. To make a medical comparison: sometimes an operation can be completed with total technical perfection, but the patient still dies afterwards. For me – and certainly for the patient – this is not my idea of a successful surgery! If a surgeon claims his operation was successful while his patient is lying in the mortuary, you need to think about finding a different surgeon!

This is why I am a passionate advocate of using the 'balance sheet' method whenever you are talking about results, both past and future. If the actual level of the measured and quantified liabilities is outstripped by the level of the anticipated assets, you can safely conclude that the company is doing well. But the opposite is also true. If the liabilities are outstripping the assets...

BlooderShip

Leaders who focus exclusively on results, who think only about
the short term, who install a culture where command and control
and financial performance are the sole measures for the 'desired'
behaviour, and who devote little attention to the creativity and
intrinsic strengths of their people are, in my opinion, trapped in
what I call 'old paradigm leadership'. I have even coined a new
word to describe it: BlooderShip.

Blood Leadership

This kind of old paradigm leadership, with its obsessive focus on
results, was developed and later promoted for a number of reasons,
not least because of the spirit of the times, in which companies,
organisations and even the business schools for the training of
future leaders were all steeped for more than 40 years.

During the period in question, which ran roughly from 1970 to
2010, the economy enjoyed a period of unbridled growth, based
on improving performance and productivity, achieving maximum
profitability 'at all costs', and serving the interests of shareholders,
with little account for the possible impact on people, the environment and society. According to this extreme form of capitalist
logic, it was the role of people, the environment and society to
serve these results-based interests and objectives – and not the
other way around. This trio of players was not seen as allies in the
generation of added value or as partners in the creative process.
Instead, they were more often seen as a hindrance and a burden,

ones that you could not do without but against which organisations and their shareholders needed to protect themselves. The need to survive, thrive and grow persuaded many leaders to adopt this very narrow and restrictive form of leadership.

To make matters worse, the business schools also continued to promote this style of pure results-oriented leadership for many years. New leaders were trained in the vital importance of measuring things, KPIs, turnover growth and net profit. The entire creative process was reduced to facts and figures. Command and control were put forward as the only way to deal with personnel if you wanted to achieve financial success. This was the kind of indoctrination that was rammed down the throat of every MBA student and it produced a generation of leaders who kidnapped every form of humanity in business and entrepreneurship for almost 40 years.

Their lack of interest for, amongst other things, consultation, involvement, self-guidance, collective intelligence and creativity led in most circumstances to leadership that lacked empathy, human feeling and concern for the person behind the performance. Not surprisingly, it was leadership without any hint of meaning or purpose.

These leaders – who in most cases were men, with everything 'macho' this implies – thought of their jobs in terms of 'hard competition', 'beating the rest', 'conquering the market', etc. They needed to win the largest slice of a cake that – in their eyes – was getting smaller all the time. The idea of working together to increase the size of the cake never occurred to them. Instead, they concentrated on eliminating their rivals, milking their suppliers, deceiving their customers and exploiting their staff, all for the 'purpose' of maximising their return. There was nothing humane about it. Humanity was regarded as something that was too imprecise and unmeasureable to fit into this new concept of leadership. To most of these managers, it was unknown and therefore unloved.

This gradually led to the evolution of a standard style of management that was similar to that of an army at war, where generals in battle need to be able to rely on the immediate and unquestioning fulfilment of orders by their subordinates. This is the so-called 'command, execute and don't ask' principle. Of course, most organisations are not at war and are staffed by people who are presumed to work together to achieve a common objective. This requires a totally different kind of logic to the 'shoot everything' philosophy of the turn of the century, in the hope of becoming the winner who could take all.

You can still find this kind of leader today. I call them 'warlords', managers who still run their organisation as though they were at war with the rest of the market and the world. They are typified by an aggressive mindset, use of language and behaviour that hark back to the old style 'military' leadership of the past. Unfortunately, this is the kind of leadership that, certainly in psychological terms but sometimes also in real terms, can lead to bloodshed. I call it 'Blood Leadership' or 'BlooderShip' for short, a leadership that follows a war-like logic based on 'attack, overcome, destroy and conquer!'. It is dog eat dog. 'Us against the rest', and often 'me against you' as well. Everything that does not contribute towards the organisation's chance of winning the battle for financial profit is deemed to 'stand in the way of success' and, as such, is mercilessly eliminated.

One of our clients is a reputable company with a history going back more than 150 years. The CEO, who is highly intelligent and an engineer by training, had a tendency to use this kind of 'fighting talk', and often at the most unexpected moments. An example? I was invited to attend a two-day brainstorming session that he organised for his entire senior management team at a pleasant location in the country. During an excellent dinner on the first evening, the CEO gave a fine speech in which he expressed his full confidence in his team and even suggested that between them they should think about organising a management buy-out of the company. Not surprisingly, the team members felt flattered and were full of enthusiasm the next morning, when the brainstorming was scheduled to start.

Unfortunately, the CEO's own attitude was now completely different from the evening before. He said that this was the worst offsite meeting ever, that he no longer wished to consider the buy-out option with the team, and that he even had serious doubts about the competence of several of them! It is difficult for me to say whether or not these comments were accurate and justified, but his approach and his use of language was completely wrong. He had the power to hire and fire all the members of the management team. So if some of them were incompetent, it was his responsibility to coach them up to the required standard or let them go. What's more, it is utterly illogical, unless for some bizarre tactical reason, to praise a group of people one evening and then brand them as idiots less than 24 hours later.

The use of this kind of BlooderShip in organisations has a damaging impact that is hard to overestimate. It creates a bad atmosphere, it disconnects and demotivates, and it generates uncertainty and distrust. To make matters worse, after his unexpected outburst the CEO calmly suggested that they should move on to the order of the day, as though nothing had happened! But this was an opportunity that I could not allow to pass by. The CEO had kidnapped the meeting with his intervention, but I now wanted to turn it into a learning moment. With this in mind, I invited all the members of the management team to say openly what they thought about what they had just heard. This led on to a morning-long discussion about the principles of trust, how trust can be built up, and, just as importantly, how it can easily be destroyed. So at least we all got something out of the meeting!

Authoritarian leaders often fall back on their rank, their title, their position in the hierarchy, their 'stars and stripes'. They take decisions in secure boardrooms, usually situated in some isolated and privileged location in the company's headquarters building. They build war rooms,[18] where (supposedly) the most vital strategic decisions of all are made. They love to hold 'kill-the-competition' brainstorming sessions. They have a permanent 'attack!' mindset, but are paranoid about being attacked themselves. They develop tunnel vision, as a result of which only their own ideas are deemed acceptable, so that there is no longer any time or space to listen to other insights, for fear of missing new opportunities or losing existing power. They become more and more isolated in their ivory war-tower and gradually lose contact with the workplace, their middle management and (worst of all) their own self-awareness and intuition.

But even that is not the end of it! I often observe in BlooderShip organisations that the top managers do not behave in keeping with the corporate values[19] that they themselves have introduced! If they respect them at all, it is only because of what they can achieve with them, and not because how they can achieve it. In this way, the values do not serve as an example to the organisation and its wider environment.

This kind of Janus-like leader frequently talks, often with great passion and skill, about exalted concepts such as collaboration and respect, or daring to take risks and show initiative, or searching for sustainable solutions in a complex world… But in spite of these fine words, they continue to act in accordance with their own warrior logic, where they seldom say what they are really thinking but prefer to maintain a hidden agenda that will allow them to 'divide and conquer', not only outside the organisation but also inside it as well. As a result, they lose their exemplary role and their capacity for empathy. They punish those who take but miscalculate risks and they interfere with work at all levels. Occasionally, they may try to give motivating speeches, but their words sound hollow and lacking in authenticity. They organise large personnel gatherings that are no more than staged PR events, in which they try to convince their people with rational arguments, instead of appealing to their deeper emotions. Memos and newsletters are full of the same meaningless messages, compiled by external agencies or 'disconnected' internal communications specialists, which have about as much charisma as a hospital bed pan. This 'information' is experienced by those for whom it is intended as non-credible and incoherent. In fact, that is their impression of the organisation as a whole – and its leader.

The disparity between what these leaders ask their people to be and do and how they behave themselves is staggering. They have a seemingly total inability to practice what they preach, because they no longer have any real contact with the person that they are supposed to be. This leads to situations where, even today, organisations are still trapped inside this kind of BlooderShip culture, where it is neither inspirational nor even pleasant to work. Employees need to be careful about what they say. Mistakes are not tolerated. Vulnerability is exposed and punished. Aggressive language, inconsistent behaviour and unpredictable management reactions are the norm. It is a situation that is both mentally and physically draining, which pushes people to their limits and, sometimes, even beyond ...

This is the exact opposite of what people really need in organisations: autonomy (to set their own objectives, to try out new things, to learn new competencies, etc.), coherent authenticity (to be who they really are and to live what they truly believe), harmony (in their interactions with others and in their way of working), acceptance (for who they are, as human beings, having a role) and joy (the deepest form of happiness in who you are, what you do and how you interact).

The 'shit' with which people are sometimes deluged as a result of their leaders' lack of honesty, courage and commitment is mind-boggling. The dumping of information, the forced acceptance of meaningless messages and the allocation of incomprehensible tasks without explanation are all symptoms of an organisation that has lost its way. Recently, I heard a friend say how fed up he is of the pointless team meetings in his company, a leading international bank, where 80 percent of the time is taken up discussing abstractions such as corporate rules and financial parameters at the group level, which have no meaning or purpose for him and his colleagues at their team level. Most of the remaining 20 percent of the time is spent talking about collaboration and the need for collegiality...

This is a common phenomenon. Leaders often overwhelm their people with speeches about market share, profit levels, organisational transformation, bottom line, double-digit growth, matrix organisations, change management, etc. These are all subjects that generate little enthusiasm and commitment among people in the workplace, who are more concerned with searching for connection, meaning and relevance in what they do and why they do it. In fact, during my keynotes I often say that the use of such language is the most irrelevant way to try to enthuse your people with your vision for the future. These are often matters that people lower down in the hierarchy find hard to place, because they have so little to do with them in their day to day work. In most cases, they won't even know what you are talking about. BlooderShip and the use of fine-sounding words and jargon will never – I repeat, never – be enough to persuade people to give 100 percent of their effort, so that they can perform to the best of their ability. On the contrary, you will force them to crawl deeper into their own shell, forcing levels of efficiency, effectiveness and results into a downward spiral.

LeadershiT

I wanted to understand why often even intelligent people use this BlooderShip way of working. And also how and when someone gets like that. For this reason, I have made a study of the patterns involved over many years, wherever I came into contact with them in my dealings with leaders all around the world. During our discussions, I tried to analyse the root cause of their behaviour. My conclusions were fascinating.

In my opinion, no-one, deep down in his true self, wants to follow the path of BlooderShip. I believe that only very few people – the pathological leaders among the leaders – consciously wish to behave in this way. I believe equally that many of those who use BlooderShip methods do so in spite of themselves. They have good intentions, but at a certain moment they fall back on a more primeval approach, which even they are not really happy with. But they often fail to see or understand what is happening. They are unaware that their leadership style is now out of date, even potentially harmful. They have been kidnapped during their journey towards true leadership by what I call their 'childhood shit'. By this I mean the painful and distressing things that occurred during their childhood and adolescence, which at some point and for some reason came to play a huge part in their leadership in later Life. This often results in leadership ideas and behaviour that lacks charisma and balance. Above all, it is not sustainable and leads to huge collateral damage.

What I am about to describe has deep psychological meaning. I am not a psychologist or psychiatrist by training, but through the years I have had thousands of conversations with leaders of many different types, from all social backgrounds and environments. This has allowed me to identify and analyse the psychological programming of leaders. It has also allowed me to develop a method to help these leaders to see how they have adopted styles of leadership that are a direct – although often unconscious – reflection of their own psychological programmes. If I am engaged in a confidential conversation with this kind of leader, which nearly always happens as part of the intimate relationship that grows when my teams and I take on an advisory role in an organisation, I can usually see quite quickly that the reason behind their behaviour is often of a psycho-dynamic order and has much less to do with rational business factors.

Things like being bullied as a child; having an emotionless, almost military upbringing; having a difficult relationship with a father or grandfather; coming from a problematical social background (which can range from very rich to very poor); the need to overcome physical limitations; having to come to terms with gender orientation: these and many other similar events from youth have an enormous impact on leaders and their leadership in adulthood. This is an impact which, if you have a little 'people knowledge' and an interest in your fellow human beings, it is hard to miss. Even so, it is often sublimated in the leader concerned, so that it is denied and/or not accepted as the reason for his/her BlooderShip. At some point during their leadership development, they have unconsciously learnt ways to compensate for the 'shit' under which they suffered during their youth. As a result, the leadership style that develops in this way has deep roots and is anchored in the limbic memory, where our emotions and memories are stored. The full development of that part of our memory occurs between the ages of 8 and 12 years; in other words, during the transition from child to young adolescent.

As a survival strategy, we have learnt unconsciously as a species to avoid the repetition of painful emotional moments. These moments are pushed away deep into our memory and we develop an unconscious form of compensatory behaviour to keep the pain at a safe distance. This is how BlooderShip is created. In fact, it is really LeadershiT: leadership that is driven by our personal childhood 'shit', which we are unable to process and for which we have no respect. In other words, our leadership style is derived directly from our childhood experiences and has a huge influence on how we live our Life. And because of the impact leaders have on others, this influence is multiplied exponentially, so that it can affect millions of people.

To give a clearer idea of what I mean, let's look at a number of concrete examples of how 'childhood shit' later led to BlooderShip. Out of respect for our customers, I will, of course, refrain from giving names and details.

The chairman of an Asian international industrial group, who was bullied during his childhood years because he was 'different from the others', developed a compensatory form of behaviour during adolescence to protect him from the 'big, bad world'. Many years and a number of important leadership roles later, he had become someone who never revealed fully what he was thinking/feeling, and always kept his cards very close to his chest. Over time, he had unconsciously developed a style of leadership that denied everyone access to the underlying reasons for his actions. As a result, people seldom knew why he did what he did. He made frequent use of intrigues and hidden agendas and manipulated decisions by only sharing bits and pieces of information to different people at different times, so that no-one other than himself could see the big picture. His colleagues, staff and business partners found it impossible to work out what was going on or why. People could only guess at the reasons behind what they increasingly saw as his illogical and irrational decisions. Everyone around him was aware of his manipulative leadership style, but few had the courage to challenge him on this sensitive matter. Those who did were soon sent packing. If you asked him why he decided to do this or that, he would give you a logical explanation for his actions. But it was perfectly possible that the very next day he would say something completely different and use his own arguments against you. This confused and worried other managers who needed to take decisions within their own fields of responsibility, so that they often made wrong and even contradictory choices. As a result of these 'bad' choices, which had actually been orchestrated by the chairman, the managers were then criticised, humiliated (often publically), or even downgraded. It was almost impossible to point out the folly of this way of working to him, since he immediately felt he was being attacked, like when he was a boy. By any normal standards, his behaviour was clearly irrational, but he refused to see it in that light, because he immediately linked any attempt to correct him to the bullying of his youth, a subject he was incapable of dealing with rationally. In other words, the 'shit' from the past, which he did not wish to be reminded of, triggered his actions in the present.

At certain key moments in his adolescence, the CEO of a non-stock-listed Belgian holding did not receive the attention he needed from his father. On the contrary, he was constantly being criticised for doing things that were irrelevant or not up to the standards that his father expected. Even so, he turned out to be a brilliant civil engineering student and quickly made an equally glittering career, at which he worked very hard. Unfortunately, he also felt the need to be a BlooderShip leader, to compensate for his need to be seen and to be regarded as important, which he had carried over from his youth. This manifested itself in a 'just-look-how-much-I-am-in-control' kind of leadership, in which he interfered with almost everything in the organisation, so that he could be valued by everyone for his foresight, thoroughness and ideas. Questioning those ideas was only possible if you first stressed how relevant and important they were. This meant that the people working around him had to be very subtle in their approach, taking sufficient care to first flatter him, so that they could then make more difficult topics discussable.

In similar cases, I have noticed that this kind of youth experience often results in a leader that has an assertive need to prove himself, and will seek to eliminate or at least restrict everyone and everything that gets in the way of his perception of his own self. I have seen instances of top leaders who have reduced the other members of their senior management team to a kind of subservient 'vassal' status, where all they were expected to do was carry out instructions from above. And I am talking here about vassal-managers who are jointly responsible for multi-nationals with 200,000 to 300,000 employees worldwide and a turnover in billions! But if they expressed a different opinion or rocked the boat too much, they were soon shown the door... This is, of course, the same phenomenon as the one I have outlined above: 'shit' from the past, rooted in a trauma of not being recognised, triggers action in the present that aims to ensure that you are now recognised and appreciated by everyone. As far as the Belgian manager in the above example was concerned – and he was a perfectly charming man when no hierarchical relationship was involved – it was sufficient for me to discuss with him his own views about the subject of his leadership and its impact. Once I was able to make clear to him the link between these views, BlooderShip and his own childhood, the scales quickly fell from his eyes, to be followed by a deep sense of awareness and catharsis.

I have huge respect for the chairman of a Swiss holding that has numerous important companies in its portfolio. The man comes from a wealthy and much-respected entrepreneurial family, whose fame stretches back for generations. In short, he is a member of the social elite. As a result of his background and education, he has learnt to be highly discreet, humane and respectful. But remarkably enough, these admirable qualities meant that, in his case, he was often unable to take decisive decisions when disputes arose among the top people in the holding or between the CEOs of the subsidiary companies about the best direction to follow. This lack of decisiveness resulted in a deterioration of the general atmosphere within the organisation, but the chairman still refused – or was unable – to make a final decision. Instead, he preferred to let things 'take their own course', with all the negative consequences you might expect. In the absence of a decision from the top, conflict broke out at the lower levels, first between the CEO's and then between the directors of the holding. It was frustrating to see how the chairman – officially because of 'a lack of time' – was unable to do what a chairman is supposed to do: namely, get everyone's noses pointing in the same direction, by appealing to their sense of trust, commitment and mutual respect. In this case, the 'shit' from the past might seem less obviously 'shit' than in the two instances previously quoted, but its negative effect on the chairman's leadership behaviour was no less dramatic, resulting in both direct and indirect forms of BlooderShip that influenced his entire environment.

Although 'childhood shit' is nearly always rooted in emotional trauma, this trauma sometimes has a physical cause. This was the case, for example, with the CEO of an important utilities company, who had had a visible physical scar since he was very young. As a result of this scar, he was often excluded by others as a child. The other children saw that he was different and thought this meant that he was 'odd', so that they didn't want him to join in. This exclusion taught him to rely on himself and to protect himself from an outside world that wanted nothing to do with him. The clarity of analysis and vision that he now has as a CEO is directly related to this 'childhood shit'.

In his role as a visionary leader, he has developed the habit of surrounding himself with a small elite of managers, whom he regards as his confidantes. In reality, however, these confidantes – as I once suggested to him in discussion – are more like followers than trusted advisers. He is very demanding in his dealings with them, but also correct and respectful. He gets a great deal of respect and buy-in from them in return, and also from his wider environment – but only up to a point. His initiatives often fail to get the full backing of the organisation as a whole; in part because his concentration on his elite means that he is simply too remote from the majority of people for whom he is responsible, but also in part because he focuses too much on the things in which he excels: creating clear visions and infallible strategies, which he then expects others to carry out to perfection. I have seen him address large meetings of his workforce and his organisation's AGM, and he always speaks well and answers questions clearly and intelligibly. But even if the content of his storytelling is strong and his logic impeccable, you still always have the feeling that he is doing something he does not like, as a result of which people fail to believe 100 percent in what he is saying. This relates to his dislike of 'standing in the spotlight', which in turn dates back to the physical scar and the mental scar from his childhood. In short, he has a certain problem with being seen.

In theory, this should not have the slightest impact on his behaviour: after all, he is a brilliant and visionary man (often light years ahead of his colleagues in the same market), shows respect to everyone he meets and is highly value-driven. But his focus on his elite and his tendency to keep in the shadows has unconsciously (and, since I met him, consciously) affected both his behaviour and his performance. He now knows that he functions in this manner and is working hard to come to terms with the roots of his leadership and what it implies. For example, his 'elitist' approach means that there is not really a good through-flow of information between himself and the rest of the organisation, which in turn means that people are reluctant to take risks, because they do not fully understand in which direction the organisation is travelling. For this reason, he is often criticised as a 'poor communicator', who is incapable of leading 'the way he should'. And so, once again, the 'shit' from the past – his fear of being excluded – triggers his behaviour in the present – his preference for working with an inner circle – even though in this way he perpetuates his exclusion from the majority of his people!

In summary, we can conclude that many leaders are kidnapped by their 'childhood shit', which they are unable to deal with in a healthy and healing manner.

When I arrive in organisations that are lead by leaders who have been kidnapped by BlooderShip, I usually discover that their organisational culture has been moulded in such a manner that it becomes an extension of the paradigm. There is either a strong 'command and control' culture; or else the organisation is para-lysed into inactivity by an indecisiveness that stifles initiative and risk-taking; or else there is a silo mentality, where everyone works against everyone else and there is no shared common purpose; or else everything is focused exclusively on production and perfor-mance, with little place for humanity, openness and trust. The atmosphere in these organisations is blighted, so that people no longer know (or care about) what to do.

It frequently happens that the leaders themselves suffer under this form of BlooderShip, but do not know how to escape from it. In these cases, I need to confront them subtly and skilfully with the negative implications that such BlooderShip has for themselves and others. I often start by asking them what kind of leader they would really like to be and how they would later like to be remembered. This gives a first insight into the leader's way of thinking and yields material for deeper exploration. In particular, I next ask what benefits their BlooderShip actually brings them. When I explain what the term actually means, this can be a highly confrontational question and the reactions are often fierce. In some cases, after further (often heated) discussion, this leads to awareness of the true situation. More commonly, it takes some additional time before realisation and acceptance finally dawns on them. When I can see that we are moving in the right direction, I then ask a third question, which is even more confrontational.

But before we move on to that, I would first like to share with you another of my personal convictions.

I assume that most leaders have a good sense of love and connectedness. When I speak of love, I do not mean carnal love (which the Greeks called *porneia*) or passionate love for your partner (which the Greeks called *eros*), but rather the holistic and universal form of love (which the Greeks called *agapé*). We experience this latter form, for example, through the all-embracing affection, esteem and deep respect we have for our children, parents, friends, religious community, societies, social organisations, nature, the environment, our fellow human beings, Life itself, etc. This *agapé* demands a high degree of self-knowledge and self-respect, openness and tolerance for the opinions of others, and a willingness to question yourself with the intention of evolving into a better person.

How is it possible that men or women who display this *agapé* in their private and social spheres suddenly switch to BlooderShip in their professional sphere? Why can they not also make use of *agapé* in their professional context? This is the basis of my third question, which simply asks leaders: at what point do you decide each day to switch from one mode of behaviour to another? When do you stop being *agapé* and become BlooderShip? In the car or train on your way to work? Once you reach the office? When you enter the special lift that leads up to 'your' floor? When you see the magnificent view from your office at the top? What is the mechanism that persuades someone temporarily (i.e. during office hours) to turn off his love for his fellow men and turn on an attitude that is filled with suspicion and hostility?

In the many hundreds of conversations that my team and I have had with leaders who find themselves trapped in BlooderShip, it is striking how often we find a lack of self-knowledge and self-esteem in the leaders concerned. All too often they have become disenchanted by what they do and no longer fully understand why they do it. They have lost their harmony between body, mind and spirit. They no longer have any real and deep contact with themselves, and none at all with nature. They are often highly driven, achieve excellent results and still have power and influence. But the price they pay, and also force their environment to pay, both privately and professionally, is huge.

Frequently, this kind of leader has lost all semblance of serenity, purpose and empathy. They take no account of the people they expect to 'fight battles' on their behalf. There is no place for feelings of collegiality and no tolerance of vulnerability. Their own opinion is the only correct and viable opinion. Any form of dissent is ruthlessly suppressed. Slowly but surely, these leaders find themselves isolated and alone, first at work and then in Life.

Is it really that lonely at the top?

You often hear it said that it is lonely at the top. And indeed, it can be, if you allow yourself to be kidnapped by BlooderShip, so that you push people away instead of drawing them closer to you, which gives you a reputation as a remote stifler of initiative, rather than as a charismatic discoverer of talent. I have coached dozens of leaders who were not aware of the damage they caused to others. As a result, they had no-one around them who could put forward new and different ideas, no-one in whom they could trust and confide, and, ultimately, no-one who wanted anything to do with them, because of who they were as a person. They could not understand why people failed to look them straight in the eye or tried to avoid them in the office corridor. There is a scene in the film *The Devil Wears Prada*, in which Meryl Streep, who plays the role of the tigerish editor-in-chief of *Runway Magazine*, arrives at the head office for the first time. The way in the whole organisation metaphorically convulses in fear and runs for cover speaks volumes about the impact of Bloodership. As the film progresses and we learn more about the main character, the clearer it becomes that she has been kidnapped by a style of leadership that she also finds abhorrent and from which she desperately wants to escape – but just doesn't know how.

I often hear from top managers that they feel weighed down by the loneliness of their position, because they lack the courage to discuss their uncertainties and doubts with the people who would normally report to them directly. They fear that they will be seen as 'incompetent' if they do not appear to be 100 percent in control at all times. Talking about your doubts with your subordinates, they feel, is simply 'not done', since this can be interpreted as a sign of 'weakness'. The same applies to shareholders, colleagues of an equivalent rank and also their own manager/leader (if they have one). Nor can they talk about these things at home, because they think that their partner is either not interested or – even worse – does not understand the context.

As a result, many top managers find themselves kidnapped by loneliness: they are controlled by a belief and a form of behaviour that keeps them separated from others. Often, unnecessarily so.

My conclusion? This belief and behaviour are frequently the result of an ever-growing series of disconnections: first from their own self, then from their environment, next from the organisation to which and for which they are responsible, and finally from nature, which they now ignore almost entirely, even though it can have a tremendous healing effect on the human species.

Leaders need to accept heavy responsibilities and are therefore expected to be confident, flexible and resilient at all times. But this is asking a lot of any human being! There are times when we all need a second opinion or could use a little friendly and impartial advice. However, to ask for guidance, or to have doubts about which approach is really best, or to question your own view of the world when the situation demands it: these are all things that require a great deal of self-leadership, coherence, and mental and physical strength.

One of my clients, the CEO of a stock-listed company, once said to me: 'I sometimes feel so lonely, in spite of my prestigious position, my impressive surroundings and my huge income. But I can't allow myself to discuss my uncertainty about some strategic decisions with the chairman of the board, because he will instantly regard me as a second-grade CEO. And I can't discuss these things in confidence with my own team, because they want to see a strong leader, a leader in keeping with our company culture, where doubts and vulnerability are never expressed openly.' To which I replied: 'But that is precisely the reason for your isolation and also explains why you no longer feel comfortable in yourself. You have asked yourself all these questions, but you haven't been able to provide all the answers. As a result, you continue to be plagued by your doubts. So it's time you found the courage to discuss these things with your chairman and even more so with your team. There is probably nothing they would like more!'

In general, leaders are reluctant to surround themselves with what I call 'wise guides' or an 'emotional advisory board'. Consequently, they all too easily get locked into their own mental model. They develop a fixed way of doing things, both in how they think and how they act, and as time passes they become less and less inclined to question it. Wise guides can break through these fossilised convictions and take the thinking of leaders to a high level. These guides might be inspirational people in their own right, who can heighten their leaders' awareness, or impartial experts who dare to offer alternative opinions, or more experienced colleagues who have walked many different pathways in their long careers. Sadly, leaders make too little use of all these options.

In conclusion, then, the proverbial 'loneliness at the top' is, in my opinion, a largely self-constructed obstacle based on a series of outdated ideas about how strong leadership is not compatible with any demonstration of vulnerability and a willingness to seek advice.

Fortunately, the world is currently evolving from the 'age of reason', in which the rationality of facts and figures were the driving force, to the 'age of purpose', in which relevance, meaning and sustainability in the broad sense will become the new essentials. Our society and our economy have both become extremely complex, and everything continues to change at lightning speed. This means that leader and other top people need to be able to cope with a new VUCA[20] (Volatile, Uncertain, Complex, Ambiguous) world, whether they like it or not. However, VUCA can no longer be properly understood simply by using logic and reason alone. Instead of trying to understand things exclusively with our mind, in the future we will need to understand things more with our instincts, our gut feelings. We will need to rely increasingly on our more subtle holistic insights. This will require us to look at organisations and the concept of leadership in an entirely different way.

It will only be the leaders and organisations who are empathetic and willing to question themselves who will be able to survive and make a contribution to our rapidly evolving new society. All the others will be consigned to the dustbin of history, having run lemming-like over the cliff in their blind attempts to deal with the complexities of the new paradigms.

Transform or die!

'Making mistakes is the privilege of the active. It is always the mediocre people who are negative, who spend their time proving that they were not wrong.' (Ingvar Kamprad)

The point that I want to make here is this: you can either swim along on the tide of the positive evolution of the times and be a leader who actively transforms your organisation for the better; or else you can stay stuck in the mud of the old short-term paradigm of the past, where everything had to serve the needs of the shareholders and your own power as leader. If you choose the latter option, you will soon find yourself passed and left behind, and your organisation will disappear within the next 10 to 15 years. Because organisations that do not transform are destined to die.

In ten years' time, the only leadership that leaders who remain locked in BlooderShip will be giving is to failing organisations, as they are swamped by the sands in a lonely desert of oblivion. No-one from the younger generations will want to work for this kind of organisation or this kind of authoritarian leader from the old paradigm. Organisations whose leadership and culture continue to focus on short-term financial results and who do not (or cannot) transform themselves into ecosystems that are capable of contributing sustainably to both the welfare of humankind and the evolution of society, will lose not only the respect of people the world over, but will also lose market share, their customers and the confidence of the financial markets. In short, they are doomed.

I have already mentioned the effects on humankind of this type of one-sided, short-term, results-oriented thinking. We saw that the percentages for burn-out, bore-out, disconnection, unease and lack of basic Life joy are higher – frighteningly higher – than ever before.

For this reason, organisations have an important role to play in improving both the physical and the mental well-being of society. It is only when organisations start to properly understand the impact of what they do on the social fabric and how essential they therefore are for shaping this fabric, that it will finally be possible to work towards a new societal model. Amongst other things, this means that organisations must be held accountable for increasing the work satisfaction of all their employees and for creating a positive balance for all their stakeholders.

The cost of factors such as demotivation, sickness, burn-out, suicide and other human dramas are far too often transferred to society, instead of being borne by the organisations responsible. This is antiquated economic logic! In the future, it must be the employers who bear these costs, based on the precepts of an updated paradigm that will make them liable for creating the workplace joy of their entire workforce. This will require organisational leaders to think very carefully about how they choose to obtain their financial results, how (and how hard) their people must perform, how these people can contribute sustainably to the success of the organisation, and, above all, how they can become better people because of the nature of the work they are doing. Put simply, work in the future must contribute towards human and societal evolution. The transactional work of the past that hindered this evolution must be abolished. Organisations that show a genuine concern for their people and work together with them in pursuit of a noble purpose are the best guarantee for a happier and better balanced society in the years ahead.

One of our customers, the then CEO of a large division of Arcelor Mittal, once asked my advice about the restructuring of the group. In order to survive, it would be necessary to fire tens of thousands of workers. I suggested to him that when he was drawing up the restructuring plan, he should first look at the tens of thousands of men and women who would be affected and not at the tens of thousands of savings that these people represented on the balance sheet. I also explained to him that he not only had a responsibility towards 'his' tens of thousands of employees, but also to the many tens of thousands of others, represented by their partners, children, loved ones, etc., who would also be hit equally hard. People build up their lives thanks to or in close connection with their work. If that work is taken away, so too for many of them is their Life. The impact of this can be catastrophic. Postponing the dismissals was not possible – this would have put the entire group and its more than 300,000 employees at risk – but by shifting the focus from the technical scrapping of tens of thousands of jobs to the best way to deal with the social impact of that scrapping on all the people affected, the CEO's awareness was awakened to the need to find the most humane way to deal with this unfortunate but necessary situation. He later told me that our conversation, in which he first recognised, both as a leader and as a human being, the responsibility he bore towards the lives of all those people, was one of the most consciousness-raising moments in his career and in his Life as a whole.

I urge every organisation to see the engagement of its people as the fundamental basis for its sustainable functioning. If a maximum percentage of the workforce is committed to the organisation and if there is real job satisfaction, if the burn-out and bore-out statistics are low or non-existent, if employees spontaneously take the initiative to work in self-steering groups or teams, these can all be seen as indications of a correct and respectful organisational culture, in which autonomy, self-development, growth and balance all have a place.

In the opposite scenario, where the social climate is sour and where levels of sickness, burn-out and even suicide are high, the leaders of such organisations need to ask themselves some serious questions. But this will not be possible as long as their BlooderShip focus continues to concentrate exclusively on 'results first'. Nor will it be possible until these BlooderShip leaders realise that they also have a social responsibility towards the welfare and joy of their people and, by extension, towards the well-being of society and the economy as a whole.

Fortunately, numerous initiatives are now being taken all around the world and in the most diverse sectors to look at society, the economy, organisations and leadership in a new light. I firmly believe that this new way of doing things must be holistic, in which all the key parameters – economy, ecology and welfare – are linked to each other. A healthy economy should take account of ecological aspects. Similarly, ecological measures should be framed as far as possible within an economic context. Organisations will only be successful if that success is based on its people's welfare. And people will only feel happy and purposeful if they can commit themselves to organisations that offer solutions for societal, social, cultural, ecological and other problems. We will look at this more closely in the following pages.

Short-term actions must always be framed in terms of long-term respect for humanity, nature and a sustainable economy in the service of society. More and more organisations and initiatives are applying this philosophy. With my annual 'Wisdom Encounters', a three-day summit meeting in the Swiss mountains, I bring together leaders who wish to focus on how to increase their sustainable societal impact. During these three days, men and women at the very top of their profession, and it really goes from high net worth entrepreneurs to leaders from politics, the arts and spiritual movements, over company CEO's, presidents from family trusts, social entrepreneurs and leaders from NGO's, reflect on how it is possible to develop concrete actions that can lead to a better society, economy and world.

It is my dream that Wisdom Encounters will one day grow into a kind of 'Davos' for wisdom and humanism, where each year inspiring and committed leaders from around the globe will assemble to exchange ideas about a world in transformation, developing specific and practical proposals to achieve sustainable impact on a large scale through their noble purpose driven actions. I want Wisdom Encounters to become a community that works for a noble purpose, in the service of humankind and the future of our upcoming generations and planet.

On the first day of the summit, we look at global transformations, the problems they raise, the solutions they require and the kind of leaders who can provide them. The second day focuses on the more individual level of self-leadership. We ask the leaders to reflect on their own noble purpose and how they wish to achieve it. This exercise is repeated on the third day, but then from the perspective of the organisations that the leaders run. How can these organisations be transformed into Houses of Noble Purpose and how can they install LovInShip to achieve that?

Wisdom Encounters is not about ego or power. Nor is it about titles, networks, products, services and sales. Wisdom Encounters is about authenticity and about leaders who wish to make progress in their own Life to the benefit of society. For the participants, these three days are a wonderfully inspiring and reinvigorating experience, a break-out from their day-to-day Life, to which they can then return with new insights and fresh ideas.

Since I started with Wisdom Encounters in 2014, I have seen more and more leaders who now understand the importance of having a noble purpose for their organisation and wish to begin the journey of transformation that this requires. I have also seen an increasing number of initiatives, new approaches and measures that help to strengthen the philosophy behind the idea of a noble purpose. These projects are developed by visionary men and women, and have already grown into a movement with a global impact.

Conscious Capitalism

Speaking for myself, I have been strongly influenced by the ideas of Professor Raj Sisodia,[21] co-founder of Conscious Capitalism.[22] He has conducted groundbreaking research into new and more aware forms of capitalism. This research formed the basis for his book *Firms of Endearment*,[23] which I read in 2006 and in which he promoted a new way of doing business.

The creed of Conscious Capitalism can be summarised as follows: 'We believe that business is good, because it creates value; it is ethical, because it is based on voluntary exchange; it is noble, because it can elevate our existence; and it is heroic, because it lifts people out of poverty and creates prosperity. Free enterprise capitalism is the most powerful system for social cooperation and human progress ever conceived. It is one of the most compelling ideas we humans have ever had. But we can aspire to even more.'

Conscious Capitalism argues that capitalism as we know it today needs to be elevated to a higher level. This new form must create value and connect people – employers, employees, stakeholders and, by extension, society – through a process of voluntary exchange that can raise people out of poverty. Conscious leaders must live and work in accordance with a noble purpose and must use their organisations to create financial, intellectual, social, cultural, emotional, spiritual, physical and ecological added value for all their stakeholders.

B Corporations

'B Corporations' are closely related to Conscious Capitalism, but the concept is slightly different. While Conscious Capitalism embraces a holistic approach to organisational design and the economy, B Corporations[24] are companies and organisations that have received an official certificate to show that they have satisfied a number of strict conditions.

B Corporations are able to meet various closely monitored standards in the fields of social and sustainable performance and public transparency. They also report on how they achieve an equitable balance between profit and noble purpose. In this manner, the B Corps accelerate the global cultural shift towards a new way of looking at success in business and they help to build a more inclusive and more sustainable society.

B Corps also offer solutions for the challenges society faces, which cannot be solved by non-profit organisations and government institutions alone. The B Corps are better placed to reduce poverty and inequality, make the environment healthier, and create high-quality jobs with a noble purpose.

Worldwide, the B Corps form a tight-knit community of leaders and managers who wish to use their companies and organisations to make positive contributions. Their values and intentions are recorded in their 'Declaration of Independence', which I would like to share with you: 'We envision a global economy that uses business as a force for good. This economy is comprised of a new type of corporation – the B Corporation – which is purpose-driven and creates benefit for all stakeholders, not just shareholders. As B Corporations and leaders of this emerging economy, we believe that we must be the change we seek in the world, that all business ought to be conducted as if people and place mattered, that, through their products, practices, and profits, businesses should aspire to do no harm and benefit all. To do so requires that we act with the understanding that we are dependent upon one another and thus responsible for each other and future generations.'

Both movements – Conscious Capitalism and B Corporations – have made a huge impression on me. They persuaded me to start thinking in a different way about leaders and organisations; about how they need to move beyond short term gain and focus on all their stakeholders; about how they can be an added value for society; about how they can create a new paradigm for social progress and greater well-being for everyone.

It was these ideas that eventually led me in 2012 to develop a new business and social model that I named 'The House of Noble Purpose'. In the following chapters, I will explain why I am convinced that noble purpose is the best way to secure all our futures.

The House of Noble Purpose model

'One tree falling makes more noise than a whole forest growing.' (African saying)

By combining noble purpose, Loving LeaderShip, a clear strategy and the right value-based culture in a holistic approach, organisations can become powerful Houses of Noble Purpose. How exactly can they do this? Read on!

In this chapter, I will argue in favour of making the transformation from transactional organisations to Houses of Noble Purpose. These houses are organisations that act from a strong sense of noble purpose (the 'why') in the service – in one way or another – of humankind, society and the world. They are led by inspirational leaders who develop *agapé*-based organisational cultures (the 'how'), built on strong values and principles which are capable of uniting all stakeholders behind the goal of realising the noble purpose. This purpose is then achieved through the implementation of a clearly defined and sustainable organisational strategy.

Houses of Noble Purpose are therefore characterised by their inspirational nature (the 'why') and a method of operating (the 'how') that makes them very different from most other organisations. They will help to transform people and society, and therefore also the economy, in a way that brings greater meaning, sustainability, harmony and joy.

It will take time to achieve this goal, because it will first take time for the owners and leaders of companies and organisations to transform themselves into a new kind of owner and leader, who are capable of acting in a new manner that is entirely different from what they have learnt and from what society currently expects.

Viewed from a purely economic perspective, the philosophy behind the Houses of Noble Purpose makes it necessary to look at organisational success in a new light. This success can no longer be achieved through BlooderShip: in other words, by leaders who have been kidnapped by their own LeadershiT and by a workforce that has been held, until now, in a new form of modern slavery. The focus must shift from profit and production to purpose and people. From now on, financial performance will be just one aspect of the general contribution made by the whole organisation. What's more, it will be a contribution generated by inspired and engaged employees, who, thanks to the work they do in an organisation with which they are now fully connected, will develop themselves to become better human beings. As a result, each of them, at whatever level they work, will represent an added value that assists in the realisation of the ultimate goal of their organisation: its noble purpose.

Money or meaning?

We have now reached the heart of the matter. It is time to look at the one question that must always be asked of every organisational leader who is interested in embracing this new paradigm: 'Are you prepared and ready to direct your organisation on the basis of a noble purpose approach or do you intend to keep running the organisation on the basis of existing financial principles?' Each leader must give a clear answer to this question. There is no room for ambiguity and uncertainty. Making the transformation into a House of Noble Purpose demands coherence, courage, strength and authenticity. There are no half-measures; only 100 percent commitment will work.

When asking this question, I also explain that having a noble purpose is by no means incompatible with the realisation of strong and sustainable business results. Quite the opposite! The existence of a noble purpose makes it possible to align all the positive forces within the organisation, so that efficiency is substantially increased. People are triggered, motivated, inspired and engaged by being able to work towards this purpose.

Playing the noble purpose card is an 'all-or-nothing' matter. You either play by the new rules of the game – all of them – or else you stick to the old game. It is one or the other. You can't have a foot in both camps. If you opt for a noble purpose, this implies that your organisation must be willing to make and accept important choices with far-reaching consequences. It will not be possible to make these crucial choices unless you are wholeheartedly committed. Your engagement must be total. If you have not thought properly about what you are doing and why, your transformation will never succeed.

The reasons and motives for starting out on this process are of major importance. That is why we at GINPI attach great weight to the discussions we have with owners, boards of directors, leaders, managers and the most important stakeholders. Our experience shows that motivation comes in many shapes and form. Here are a few examples.

The motivation of Bernard Gustin, who until April 2018 was the CEO of the Belgian Brussels Airlines, which was then a partial subsidiary[25] of the German Lufthansa, was clear from our very first conversation. On the one hand, he wanted to get his management committee all working in the same direction and on the other hand he wanted this direction to be based on a new organisational culture with a noble purpose to which they could all subscribe. At this time, Brussels Airlines had a complex mix of cultures that often focused on very different interests. This was a result of the various companies that had been amalgamated over the years to create Brussels Airlines. First, there was DAT, which was itself a successor to the defunct Belgian national airline SABENA;[26] second, there was Virgin Express, which had been taken over from Richard Branson; and, finally, there was the new Brussels Airlines itself. These cultures were not always compatible, which often led to internal conflicts and strikes. In a hyper-competitive market, it was becoming increasingly essential to find a way to differentiate the company from its rivals, not only by offering original products and services, but also by developing a new and more unified customer-oriented image. The reflection moments that we organised with the management committee involved discussions that went back as far as the origins of SABENA and tried to assess the extent to which Brussels Airlines was an extension of the old national airline. We came to the conclusion that the original noble purpose of SABENA – the opening of access to the African continent – was still present in the DNA of Brussels Airlines. By combining that DNA with an updated version of the noble purpose – 'to be the most personal airline company, to bring people together, and to make travel a pleasure again' – it was possible to breathe life into a new organisational culture based on strong values (human, enabling, pleasure and agile) and a highly motivated staff. Notwithstanding the relatively small scale of the company, this niche approach in combination with a clear image yielded very positive results, and this in a sector where the competition is fierce. Brussels Airlines had 'taken off', as it were, which persuaded Lufthansa to buy up the remaining 55 percent of the company's share at a good price in January 2017.

While the Lufthansa Group originally intended to integrate Brussels Airlines into German Wings, it was recently decided that the Belgian company should be allowed to continue steering its own course, which is so highly appreciated by its growing number of customers. This will, however, require a new cultural adjustment exercise to be carried out, since – as so frequently happens after an acquisition – nearly all of the original senior managers have now left.

In April 2014, I was invited for a preliminary conversation by Carlos Tavares, the chairman of the management board of vehicle constructor PSA[27] and previously the number two at Renault-Nissan. At that time, the financial situation at PSA was pretty grim, and there was even talk of possible bankruptcy. The group was responsible for some of the most legendary brands in French industrial history, but a series of bad decisions, failed strategies and an 'à *la papa*' company culture, which was little calculated to encourage either performance or results, had brought it to the brink of disaster. Before Carlos Tavares took over, there had been a number of CEOs in quick succession, each of whom had tried a different strategy to stop the rot, but without success. My conversation with Carlos was about the new direction he wanted to take to get the company out of the mess it was currently in (he called it his 'Back in the Race' strategy). I suggested that alongside this 'Back in the Race' strategy he should also think about revamping PSA's culture by linking it to a connective noble purpose based on strong and clearly identifiable values. The CEO, who combines great vision and pragmatism, was immediately enthusiastic about the prospect of reactivating the group's noble purpose, which in recent years had been pushed more and more into the background.

Carlos and his management team succeeded in successfully devising and launching a new organisational culture, founded on transparent values: agility, dare, demand, drive, respect and team spirit (although in 2019 this was simplified to win together, agility and efficiency). The culture was also inspired by a new noble purpose: 'We design unique automotive experiences, giving freedom and delight to people throughout the world'. At the same time, PSA is also placing an increasing focus on the principles of the new economy. Carlos expresses this as follows: 'Our role as a company is to create sustainable and shared value for our stakeholders. Our customers, employees, investors, suppliers, civil society and the environment expect us to make a positive contribution to the economy, society and the environment. To push forward the boundaries of environmental and societal innovation, we will not hesitate to shake up existing codes by engaging in partnerships with demanding players who question our practices and our missions, and so help us to advance.' In just five years, the group has undergone a huge transformation, almost unprecedented in the industrial world and certainly for an automobile constructor of the size of PSA. The organisational culture has been turned upside down. New values and principles have been introduced and, most importantly, its noble purpose has been rediscovered and implemented. The streamlining of processes, the reduction in the number of models, and the extremely fluid integration in 2017 of the GM subsidiaries Opel and Vauxhall were all direct consequences of this transformation. From being almost bankrupt in 2013, PSA has worked itself up through its own efforts to become the second-largest vehicle manufacturer in Europe in 2018, with a turnover of 74 billion euros and a record consolidated net profit of 3.3 billion euros. But don't be fooled: this was by no means easy to achieve and the present situation is still far from perfect. The transformation process is still very much a 'work in progress' and at times has been the cause of stress and even dissent within the organisation. But thanks to the pursuit of a common noble purpose, the general direction continues to be resolutely forward.

The German Maximilian Brönner is the fourth-generation family owner of the Swiss Heritage B holding.[28] I met Maximilian for the first time in Zurich in December 2016. During our warm and inspirational conversation, I heard all about his wish to involve the holding and its various participations in a noble purpose that would closely match but also enhance their existing purpose. In other words, this desire for transformation was not based on an urgent need to correct poor performance or improve bad results, but resulted from a positive ambition on the part of a value-driven entrepreneur to turn his vision of a better future into a reality. As is usual when embarking on this kind of trajectory, I had a number of in-depth discussions about the essential matters that are close an owner's, entrepreneur's, chairman's and/or CEO's heart, the things where he really wants to make a difference. This allows us to check to what extent the leader is serious about wanting to transform his organisation(s) by introducing new systems driven by a noble purpose.

It soon became clear to me that Maximilian's plans and intentions were coherent and that he was genuinely keen to push through a major transformation of his holding. We started by explaining the basic principles of a noble purpose to the Heritage B board of directors. After that, I was asked to address the annual meeting of the holding's top 100 managers and officials, with the aim of inspiring those present and making them more fully aware about the importance of a noble purpose, not only in business but also in Life. Thanks to this consciousness-raising process, a new wind was soon blowing through the holding and its participations worldwide, based on shared values, a more long-term perspective, and service for a higher goal.

The CEO of Heritage B's largest participation, the Spanish Teka,[29] is the German Stefan Hoetzl. He has long been a highly motivated advocate of the noble purpose concept and asked GINPI to guide his organisation through a much-needed transformation. The aim was to make possible the integration of a noble purpose throughout the entire organisational network, which has 33 active branches worldwide, as well as a further number of commercial subsidiaries. After a first offsite meeting with the Teka management team to discuss purpose-driven leadership, a second phase involved intense collaboration with the same team members to develop an organisation with the right values and a strong, noble purpose, which would be capable of uniting such a wide and varied operational structure. Our various in-depth reflections on what Teka should mean for society and the world finally led to the crystallisation of a striking and all-embracing noble purpose: 'Unconventionally caring for people and inspiring meaningful moments'. This noble purpose was then proposed for acceptance at the annual Teka leadership meeting, and it was wonderful to see how deeply the organisation's leaders were touched by the deep meaning and impact of the purpose. A number of people told me that it was the first time in their career that they felt proud to be so closely connected in spirit to the values for which their company stood. Until then, the company, which had been founded as long ago as 1924, had largely been driven by financial motives. It was only after the arrival of Stefan Hoetzl at Teka that the decision to play the transformation card was made. This transformation is still underway and is proving to be a fascinating journey for all those involved, including GINPI. The speed, determination and authenticity that Teka has shown in turning itself into a House of Noble Purpose have been nothing short of remarkable. At the same time, the implementation of the process has been coherent and efficient. The most recent step was the bringing together of senior Teka managers for an inspiring three-day seminar on leadership, where they could learn and experience what noble purpose-driven organisations are truly like and how they can be ambassadors for the further realisation of the transformation.

One of the most recent House of Noble Purpose transformations in which GINPI has advised and supported was at Almirall,[30] a family-owned pharmaceutical company based in Barcelona. Almirall's CEO, Peter Guenter, and I had what we both now like to describe as a 'surprisingly philosophical and unexpectedly penetrating business discussion' in April 2018. Peter, a former senior executive at Sanofi, was much inspired by our conversation and soon after expressed a desire to introduce a new culture at Almirall, which has just undergone a major scientific shift in focus, by moving out of the respiratory field and into dermatology. This change in focus, Peter felt, now needed to be underpinned by a revitalised culture and a unique noble purpose. The company, parts of which are stock-listed, has been largely in the hands of the Gallardo family since it was first founded in 1924. For most of that time, it was run along the lines of a financial logic, which was reflected in its leadership parameters. It was not until the arrival of Peter and the subsequent realignment of the senior management team that the company could undertake the purpose shift that would reinforce its earlier strategic shift.

During an intense offsite meeting with the management committee, the foundations were laid for the announcement at a major event on 4 April 2019 of the new noble purpose of Almirall: 'To transform the patients' world by helping them to realise their hopes and dreams for a healthy life'. This is clearly about much more than selling the maximum amount of pharmaceutical products, so that profits and the share value can also be maximised. It means that the lives of patients and others close to them will be improved to such an extent that they can live almost normally. In other words, a Life where they will have the courage to be seen, allowing them to be integrated into society in the manner they have long wished. It also means that Almirall was able to set its stamp on the market in a new way and will henceforth be valued not only for what they do, but also how they do it. In due course, this will lead to organisational performance characterised by greater customer orientation, more efficient R&D and increased motivation, which in turn will result in improved financial performance.

More and more organisations are making the choice to undergo a far-reaching transformation of their raison d'être. Some of them have already become true Houses of Noble Purpose. The faster this movement develops – and make no mistake, it is a movement – the sooner we will be able to evolve towards a new society and economy that will be better for us all.

In this context, I would also like to mention a number of other interesting cases of trendsetting leaders and organisations, who have shown the courage and the determination to follow the noble purpose pathway. For me, they are immense sources of human inspiration. I regard these entrepreneurs and leaders as remarkable human beings, who are fully aware of what humankind, society and the world really need, and who are prepared to go the extra mile to create a positive and sustainable impact. What's more, they do this out of respect for future generations.

One such outstanding example is Paul Polman, who until recently was the courageous and inspirational CEO of the Dutch-British Unilever group.[31] He was responsible for developing a total approach that combined facts, figures and results with societal relevance and human-driven values, all in the service of a noble purpose that was defined as: 'To make sustainable living common-place'. With this in mind, Unilever set five priorities: 'A better future for children, a healthier future, a more confident future, a better future for the planet, and a better future for farming and farmers'.

These sentiments would no doubt be shared by Yvon Chouinard, who in 1965 founded Patagonia,[32] an American reference in out-door wear. Its noble purpose is even simpler: 'We're in business to save our home planet'. Patagonia is a fine example of the coherence that should always exist between noble purpose, strategy and an organisational culture in the service of society, nature and the world. The company regards its good business results as no more than a secondary outcome of their far-reaching ecological-societal approach, from which nothing and nobody will ever deflect them.

Their statement to the world reads as follows: 'At Patagonia, we appreciate that all life on earth is under threat of extinction. We aim to use the resources we have – our business, our investments, our voice and our imaginations – to do something about it. Patagonia grew out of a small company that made tools for climbers. Alpinism remains at the heart of a worldwide business that still makes clothes for climbing, as well as for skiing, snowboarding, surfing, fly fishing, mountain biking and trail running. These are silent sports. None require an engine; rarely do they deliver the cheers of a crowd. In each, reward comes in the form of hard-won grace and moments of connection with nature. As the climate crisis deepens, we see a potential, even probable end to such moments, and so we are fighting to save them. We donate our time, services and at least 1 percent of our sales to help hundreds of grassroots organisations all over the world, so that they can remain vigilant and protect what is irreplaceable. At the same time, we know that we risk saving a tree only to lose the forest, a liveable planet. As the loss of biodiversity, arable soils, coral reefs and freshwater all accelerate, we are doing our best to address the causes, and not just symptoms, of global warming. Staying true to our core values during forty-plus years in business has helped us to create a company we are proud to run and work for.'

Even today, more than half a century after its foundation, the company remains true to its mission and coherent in the pursuit of its noble purpose, even if this has a negative effect on the bottom line. At the start of 2019, they refused to sign a lucrative contract with Wall Street for the supply of stock market coats, justifying this decision with the explanation: 'Because Patagonia is hoping to partner with more mission-driven companies that prioritise the planet and hopes to add more B Corp companies to its partnership list'.

The noble purpose of Nature & Decouvertes,[33] founded in France in 1994 by François and Françoise Lemarchand, is: '*Offrir le meilleur du monde pour un monde meilleur*' (Offer the best in the world for a better world). Their aim is to do business with respect for both man and nature, with a focus on engagement and knowledge transfer. With this in mind, they have launched numerous educational initiatives, and since the company's foundation 10 percent of its annual net profits each year have been channelled into the Nature & Découvertes Foundation, which finances projects to promote greater nature awareness. In 2011, this funding amounted to 11 million euros and funded no fewer than 2,100 projects. The company has some 80 shops and works with more than 1,000 partners. Antoine Lemarchand, who currently leads Nature & Découvertes, embodies the key values of the business world of tomorrow: respect for people and respect for the planet. He seeks to redistribute wealth through a responsible ecosystem.

Similar examples in Belgium include the Colruyt supermarket chain and Torfs Shoes, as well as EASI, founded by ex-football player Salvatore Curaba. All three have a people-based approach reinforced through a strong, respectful culture that emphasises each company's uniqueness. Their ability to combine excellent financial performance with a high degree of social relevance means that both have been regarded as references in Belgium for years. They are universally praised as excellent employers, have high scores for Corporal Social Responsibility and are deeply concerned about the environment and human rights.

Back in France, Emmanuel Faber, the inspirational CEO at Danone, has the ambition to gradually rescue this huge group from the hands of the financial analysts, so that it can be made more relevant for people and society. His aim is to move Danone away from a classic (and in my opinion outdated) business model and turn it into a B Corporation. As he himself puts it: 'Certified

B Corporations are leaders of a global movement of people using business as a force for good. They meet the highest standards of overall social and environmental performance, transparency and accountability, and aspire to use the power of business to solve social and environmental problems. Our ambition to obtain this certification is an expression of our long-time commitment to sustainable business and to Danone's dual project of economic success and social progress.'

If we view organisations from the perspective of the House of Noble Purpose model, having a clear and authentic noble purpose is that house's roof. This roof represents the image of the house to the outside world.

But organisations will never be able to accept the idea of a noble purpose until they are run by the right leaders, who attach over-riding importance to humankind, society and the world. This means that the type of leadership necessary to build a House of Noble Purpose is LovInShip – and this will be the subject of the next chapter.

LovInShip

I would now like to discuss a new form of leadership that will serve as a counterbalance or antidote to all the different variants of LeadershiT and BlooderShip. This form of leadership is one of the most crucial concepts within the House of Noble Purpose model, which we promote at GINPI. It is a form of leadership that allows you to like your employees, that encourages you to inspire them through your own positive ideas and behaviour, that replaces cold KPIs by warm CPIs (Caring for People Indicators), and in which authenticity and vulnerability are central.

'LovInShip' is much more than just the latest management hype (most of which disappear within a couple of years) but is a completely new approach to leadership based on a humane and holistic perspective. It will influence our way of looking at companies, organisations and work. Leaders who adopt this new style as their guideline will have a different and much greater impact on society than in the past. In fact, I hope that LovInShip will have an impact on humankind as a whole and on the manner in which entrepreneurs, politicians and stakeholders deal with each other.

If I talk about a new concept of leadership that is revolutionary, then I mean above all that it is revolutionary in relation to how leadership has for so long been used (or perhaps 'abused' would be more appropriate) in organisations to keep people in slavery. This new leadership is what true leadership should always have been, viewed from the perspective of the philosophical purity of the concept: namely, inspiring others within an agreed framework to pursue an ambitious objective by making use of their full potential as human beings. In other words, it is only in comparison with leadership as it has been practised in earlier (and also more recent) times that LovInShip is so different.

This is comparable with the way in which slavery in the past was seen as acceptable by large segments of society, and certainly the elite. Today, slavery in whatever form is morally repugnant and wholly intolerable, a practice from a more inhuman age. The fact that women were unable to vote and were regarded as subservient to men until deep in the 20th century is equally archaic and reprehensible. Fortunately, during the last 50 years, there has been a significant positive evolution, although in my opinion there is still much work to be done to achieve full equality between men and women, when viewed from a humane and humanist perspective. 'Command and control' leadership, which was once dominant in management circles, has lost much of its popularity and in the years ahead will disappear entirely, certainly in companies. It will be replaced by a new and more holistic form of leadership that is based on the authenticity of an inspirational leader and which finds its power in the self-awareness of the human-being-as-leader.

This new style of leadership, which I strongly advocate, is developed from a positive and harmonious view of the world. It is focused on encouraging people to free themselves from the obstructive conventions of the past and to liberate their full potential; on setting up an ecosystem in which collaboration, shared responsibilities and self-guidance replace remote systems, limiting processes and demotivating procedures that demand maximum performance at all times. It is a form of leadership where the leader seeks a balance between mind, body and soul, the wise and sacred 'trinity' that is found in yoga, which I value so highly and apply daily. This new kind of leader also ensures that his people can search for, find and maintain that same balance. In short, it is a leadership founded on the making of correct choices and acceptance of the price attached to those choices.

I refer to this new style of leadership as LovInShip: leadership based on love for your workforce, your colleagues, your stakeholders and your fellow man in general, rooted in deep self-awareness, self-respect and coherence with your own values and Life principles.

1. *Agapé* – The power of love versus the love for power

In the old leadership paradigm, having power over people was seen as the characteristic of the ultimate leader. How often in the past I have heard leaders boast to each other about the number of departments, factories, people, etc. they had under their control. According to this logic, the leader with the biggest number was the most powerful. These leaders talked about 'my' people, factories and departments, as though they were the owners of these things and could decide the fate of their 'possessions' and their 'subjects'. And indeed, throughout the history of leadership, there have been periods when leaders, owners, entrepreneurs and bosses did effectively have this kind of right of disposal. Happily, those days are long gone. It is just that some leaders don't yet realise it…

In this constellation, power is seen as the best way to get people to do what needs to be done. It is by exercising power on people that objectives can be reached, that new boundaries can be set, and that innovations can be made. And, in part, this is true – something that we will look at in more detail in the chapter on 'Liberating the organisational energy'.

However, a much more effective way to motivate people to take action in a work context is to use the power of love. This power of love replaces the BlooderShip-driven love of power. When I speak in this way of leadership based on love for others, I am referring to the Ancient Greek concept of *agapé*, which I mentioned earlier. This *agapé* is clearly very different from what we usually associate with the idea of love, which includes, for example, love in a loving partner relationship, love for our children, love for our parents, etc. *Agapé* also has a very different meaning from the many other forms of love that were identified and described by the Greeks, whose refined use of language made possible nuances that are lost on us today.

For instance, the word *eros*, derived from the name of the Greek god of fertility and sexual desire, refers to sexual passion and irrational physical attraction. *Eros* could make itself your master, so that you could lose your reason. In Ancient Greece, this was seen as dangerous, whereas nowadays it is regarded as a sign that you have found the person of your dreams.

Mania was a possessive and dependent form of love, obsessive and controlling, with a deep need to 'own' the other person. This is, of course, the origin of our word 'maniac'.

For the Greeks, *philia* or friendship was a deep feeling of comradeship between two people of equal standing, who would remain true to each other in all circumstances, making whatever sacrifices might be necessary. The basis for *philia* was loyalty, equality, honesty, the sharing of emotions and thoughts, and a willingness to surrender a part of your own well-being for the well-being of the other.

Storge was another form of *philia*; namely, the love of parents for their children. This is the bond or natural empathy that a parent has for its child. It is the love that makes you endure things, the caring love that can be found in most families. This presence of *storge* in a family context makes possible the development of *philautia*, which is a form of self-love and self-compassion, in the sense of a willingness to forgive.

The Greeks also made further distinctions between *ludus* (pleasure and playfulness, teasing, flirting) and *pragma* (the love between partners who had been together for a long time, resulting in the ability to make compromises – hence our word 'pragmatism').[34]

In Latin, *agapé* was translated as *caritas*, meaning 'charity' or 'willingness to help'. This can be further interpreted to mean love in the service of others, in order to fulfil a greater purpose than your own self-interest. It can even mean an all-embracing appreciation and deep respect for everyone (Life partner, children, parents, family, relatives, friends, acquaintances, colleagues, business partners, customers, suppliers, neighbours, etc.) and everything (including society, our environment, nature and Life). It is a holistic love for Life in all its aspects. Transposed to the concept of leadership,

I regard this *agapé* as the highest, most exalted form of being a leader. It demands a high degree of awareness, respect for yourself and others, tolerance, an open approach to diversity, commitment, nearness, an ability to listen, a willingness to see all others as equals, etc. This kind of love in leadership focuses on the needs of others: colleagues, subordinates, and the workforce as a whole. For the Greeks, *agapé* was actually a radical ideal, embracing unselfish love. For me, it is the basis for a new form of leadership: LovInShip or Loving LeaderShip, the leadership in which love – the *agapé* form of love – is central.

Viewed from a philosophical perspective, I assume that every free person goes in search of – or, at least, can go in search of, if he or she so wishes – some form, to a greater or lesser degree, of *agapé*. I believe that people wish to live in harmony, so that chaos can be avoided. And so we look for *agapé*. Sometimes early in Life, sometimes only at the very end, when we are staring death in the face.

Connectedness with a deep form of internal and external beauty, respect and harmony can do wonders for we humans. This *agapé* is an important basis for harmony in ourselves, in our interactions with others, and in all other aspects of our existence. We can experience this at home, in the intimacy of our family. We can experience it at work, in our dealings with our colleagues. We can experience it in connectedness with our own self or in our contact with our closest friends. It relates to the moments when people are amazed by the simple but beautiful things of Life: art, music, nature, conversation, etc. For this reason, we can reasonably assume that all people – and therefore also the leaders of teams and organisations – regularly experience moments of this kind, moments of deep connectedness and beauty. In short, moments of *agapé*.

LeadershiT

In the new leadership paradigm, LovInShip will form the basis for strong organisations, balanced collaboration, sustainable realisation, long-term success, human well-being and the prosperity of the economic system. LovInShip is a powerful expression of being yourself in respectful interaction with others. It is only by being able to be fully yourself in your interactions with colleagues, superiors, subordinates and all other stakeholders, both inside and outside your organisation, that you can blossom and flourish, allowing you to create the balance in your relationships from which harmony and joy result. And more joy leads to better results, greater achievements and more innovative solutions.

This LovInShip demands sacrifices and hard work from the leaders who wish to pursue it. However, for the few leaders who have so far been able to distance themselves entirely from their own ego, this *agapé* love eventually becomes a living source of inspiration, which requires no further conscious effort, but comes perfectly naturally, making it possible for them to energise their people and organisations to previously unseen heights of success. In order to evolve into a state of LovInShip, it will be necessary for the human-behind-the-leader to allow himself or herself to be inspired by the things that bring calm, give strength and allow Life to be lived in full coherence with who he/she truly is. This deep inspiration is the basis for the self-awareness and self-development of every leader who wishes to play an essential and exemplary role in the new paradigm.

So let's now take a look at what inspiration means and involves.

2. Inspiration to inspire

'Would the child you once were be inspired by the adult you now are?' Nic Askew once asked. For me, this is an essential question that all leaders must ask themselves, ideally at different moments throughout their leadership career.

In all the years that I have had the good fortune to be able to interact with many thousands of people, I have often seen how little real inspiration there is in the world. And also how disastrous the effects could sometimes be. This lack of inspiration results primarily – if not completely – from people being engaged in tasks that are totally devoid of any form of inspiration; tasks that (for them) are without interest or meaning, serving only to further erode the inherent beauty of people, rather than stimulating their uniqueness, joy and progress as human beings. Too many leaders focus on a soulless and task-oriented operationality, where the only so-called 'inspiration' for the workforce is to be found in the doubtful forms of Excel spreadsheets, KPIs, management cockpits, to-do lists, closed meetings, overflowing mailboxes, and boring or difficult conversations with people about whom they care little (or not at all). The epitome of non-inspiration is when people are required to work their fingers to the bone in roles that they do not enjoy and which give them no satisfaction, often in working environments that offer no real stimulation or encouragement. Why do they do it? All so that they can earn a higher salary that will allow them to buy more things they don't really need or don't have the time to enjoy!

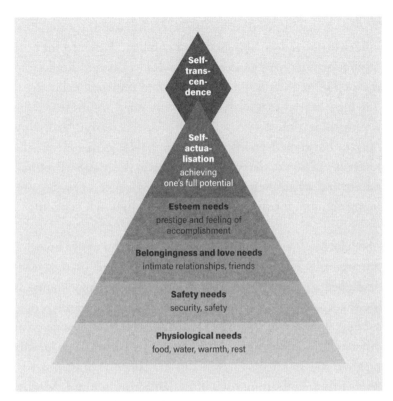

Maslow's pyramid re-interpreted

In my experience, most leaders occupy themselves first and foremost with the mathematical, 'ugly' side of leadership, and not enough with the inspiring and 'beautiful' side. Yet curiously enough, when I ask leaders – even leaders who have been successful in business terms and occupy positions near or at the top of the hierarchy – what is the thing they most need to run their organisations effectively, the most common answer is: people, moments, conversations and meaning that can inspire them and connect them with their deeply human, beautiful and amazing inner-self. The power of this connection with 'the beautiful' seems to be very important to these leaders, which makes it all the more remarkable that it is so often absent from their behaviour.

The things that inspire us as human beings will colour our thinking, influence our action, and guide our conduct. The need for pure inspiration is perhaps greatest of all for leaders, because leadership is much more than just a straightforward transactional activity. The huge impact that leadership has on others means that there is something almost sacred about it. For this reason, leadership must be based on deep inspiration, on the things that elevate the leader as a person to the two highest levels in the Maslow Pyramid: esteem and self-realisation. I like to use Maslow's work, because in my opinion, it contains lots of directly applicable wisdom.

Abraham Maslow,[35] a 20th-century American clinical psychologist, was originally an advocate of behaviourism, but later (in the 1960s) developed a most humanist-based form of psychology known as the theory of increasing needs. Maslow's theory regards people as being unique and motivated individuals, with a huge range of different drivers. In order to develop healthy personalities, people must be able to satisfy a number of fundamental human needs, needs that are inborn in each of us. With this in mind, Maslow devised a pyramid model to classify these needs. The base level of the model contains the most basic of physiological and survival needs, such as air, water, food, shelter, sleep, clothing, movement and sex. The second level contains safety needs, such as personal security, law and order, health, stability and work. The middle level of the five-level pyramid is the level of love and belonging, containing needs that relate to friendship, intimacy, family and a sense of connection. These first three levels are all within the reasonable reach of most people, but in order to rise to the fourth level of esteem (the need for status, prestige, appreciation, success, self-worth, respect from and for others) and the fifth level of self-realisation (the need for self-development, study, creativity, problem solving, ethics, self-awareness: in short, the desire to become the best you can possibly be), it is necessary for people to have a higher than normal level of self-knowledge and self-respect. It is between the first three and the final two levels of the pyramid that individuals experience tipping-point moments, which are generally of defining importance for the future evolution of their Life.

If, as a leader, you wish to be inspirational for others, it is essential to be fully aware of where you are positioned on the Maslow Pyramid. If you are still occupied with the needs in the lower part of the pyramid, there is a good chance that you will develop a type of leadership that is more akin to BlooderShip than LovInShip. Your lack of self-esteem and lack of respect for yourself and others will make it impossible for you to transcend your own needs in the interests of those you lead. Your attempts to put yourself in the position of the other (assessing his needs, expectations, fears and his image of interaction with the leader) will at best be strongly coloured by your own needs – in other words, your own position on the pyramid – and at worst will be impossible.

In other words, a leader who wishes to make an essential contribution to building a House of Noble Purpose must first, in my opinion, climb up to the fifth or preferably even the sixth level of Maslow's Pyramid. This evolution is necessary in order to be able to activate and convey the deep meaning contained within the noble purpose. Or to put it another way: a leader who does not vibrate with inspirational energy in the higher echelons of Maslow's 'being human' pyramid will never be able to make a real difference to the noble purpose transformation of his organisation, which is only possible with the injection of large amounts of rigour, coherence and, above all, strength and authenticity.

For this reason, I attach huge importance to the level of personal development of the leaders who ask us at GINPI to guide them through their organisational transformation trajectory, so that they can evolve into Houses of Noble Purpose. This is why the conversations that my team and I have with these leaders seek to address their deeper insights into Life. Even though most of our assignments are concerned with optimising management teams and organisations, which means that there are always plenty of facts, figures, balance sheets and measurable indicators to deal with, our conversations with leaders sooner or later – and usually sooner – revolve around the true nature of the man or woman behind the leadership role. What is it that motivates him or her? I want to find out if our clients really understand the depth of a noble purpose transformation and are fully committed to the process, or are they only doing it for marketing and PR purposes. If the latter is the case, we will try to show them that that is not a long-term solution after which we'll quickly pull out. GINPI only wishes to play a role if we are able to work with the psychological and spiritual foundations of our clients, because they are fundamental in how they lead and build organisations.

For a successful transformation based on this GINPI philosophy – which is largely humanist-inspired and believes in the makeability of human beings and the development of the potential that is intrinsically present in each person –inspiration is essential. By this, I mean that deep kind of inspiration that provides men and women each day with greater insight, originality and authenticity. These are the spiritual components of Life, which ensure that each day we are mentally, emotionally and spiritually fed, enriched and enhanced. Time after time. It is this ever-present inspiration that allows us to progressively become more and more human and more and more connected with Life. Being human and connectedness are crucial elements in LovInShip, and they go hand in hand with a sense of perspective and a high degree of self-awareness, self-knowledge, and self-leadership: in short, everything that gives Life colour, fragrance and flavour. To find inspiration, you don't need to be in a new town every weekend, or be on holiday in some exotic and exclusive resort, or wear fancy designer clothes, or drive a flashy car. Inspiration is an energy of a deeper order, but one that is present in our Life every day. It is to be found in our amazement at the exceptional deeds of ordinary people; in the meaningful gestures made by colleagues, friends, our children or our partner; in real conversations about things that really matter; in comments and kind words that pleasantly surprise us; in unexpected meetings with unique people; in places that are beautiful and harmonious; in moments that mean a lot to us; in nature and the flora and fauna that surround us.

Inspiration is a highly powerful and infectious form of energy. It is essential for leaders in general, but particularly for those in a noble purpose environment. Inspiration is about beauty, harmony and joy. And about radiating these things, so that others can see them. People want to work for men and women who are inspired, and not for boring leaders who are only concerned with transactional processes. People want to be stimulated by men and women who are capable of speaking about the wonder of Life, who show appreciation for others and have a huge amount of charisma. Nobody warms emotionally to leaders who reduce people to the mere implementers of tasks, who are not capable of developing and sharing a powerful story, and who are never satisfied with Life in general and performance (their own and others') in particular. People want to follow men and women who motivate them to give the best of themselves and connect them with their deepest sources of potential, strength and desire. Nobody wants to work for slave drivers or 'command and control' leaders who make increasingly unrealistic demands and are stupid enough to assume that these demands are achievable. No, the leadership paradigm that I advocate is LovInShip. And LovInShip is both deeply inspired and deeply inspirational.

As my good friend, the perspectivist and auteur Guibert del Marmol,[36] puts it: 'To be able to inspire, we must be inspired'. As a result, it is vital for all leaders to ask and to be able to answer the following questions: What inspires me? What and who are my sources of inspiration that encourage me to see things positively and do remarkable things? Which people, conversations, moments, places and event are essential to my inspiration and how can I use them to further cultivate that inspiration?

Speaking personally, I also often find inspiration in the 'little things' in Life: the peace of the morning, the power of the night, the rising or setting sun, a cornfield blowing in the wind, unexpected conversations, chance meetings, the tolling of a church bell, the call to prayer in a sultry Arab town, gazing at the sea or the mountains, the endless horizon during a long flight… Everything that fills us with deep beauty and joy has the ability to inspire us and make a positive mark on our physical and emotional systems.

One thing in particular is crucial for being inspired: contact with nature. As human beings, we each have a unique DNA,[37] our own personal 'programming', which can be activated in many remarkable ways but always vibrates when we are surrounded by nature. DNA (deoxyribonucleic acid) is the molecule employed by all living organisms to store and transmit hereditary information. It contains the genetic instructions that are essential for the development and functioning of all living creatures, including humans. It has been scientifically demonstrated that nature can have a huge positive effect on our mood, health and inspiration. That is why, at GINPI, we always prefer to organise our residential interventions at special places in or close to nature, places that consequently often contain a subtle but powerful flow of energy. Difficult conversations conducted in a natural setting very quickly acquire a different dimension to conversations conducted in an office. Walking with colleagues through a forest or along a beach, all heading in the same direction, brings so much more to discussions than sitting around a table indoors or, worse still, video-conferencing. I have no doubts on this score: wherever possible, you should seek inspiration in the power and beauty of nature.

By finding the right inspiration and, as a result, by developing greater self-awareness, you will also gain more insight into your ego and its place in your Life. In other words, you become more aware of what you regard as your ego and how that ego becomes less important the more you are inspired. It goes without saying that the 'wrong' ego – one that lacks inspiration – is a bad companion on your journey through Life and, as a leader, can be a serious obstacle to LovInShip. But is ego really as bad as many people seem to think? Or is there perhaps a way we can use our ego positively?

3. What about my ego?

'When the battle is over, arrogance is the new enemy.'
(Tao te Ching)

Whoever leads others carries a heavy responsibility. Everything that a leader – and by this, I mean leaders at all levels of an organisation and in all walks of Life – does and fails to do has a huge impact on his environment. This impact can be both direct and indirect.

Direct impact is when people are influenced in their thoughts, words and deeds by what you say and do. For example, if you have a conversation with a junior colleague about how you see the future, this will have a direct impact on that colleague's own ideas about that future and the role that he/she is able to play in it. Similarly, if during your speech at the annual New Year reception you launch a new product or announce a restructuring, you will have a direct (but more varied) impact on everyone present.

The way you speak, what you say, the level of coherence between your words and your gestures, your behaviour and your actions: these are all factors that influence people immediately, because of the person you are and your position in the hierarchy.

Indirect impact is when people are influenced by the behaviour of others who themselves have first been influenced by your behaviour. For example, if you announce a cost-cutting exercise in a meeting of the management committee, this will affect how the members of the committee subsequently interact with their teams. Or if you praise someone for their outstanding courage and sense of responsibility, this will not only motivate them further but also encourage them to share your comments with those around them, who will in turn be affected and/or inspired.

Of course, the same principles apply with negative impact. Imagine, for instance, if you speak denigratingly about the role that some people are required to play within your organisation. This will have a direct negative impact on those with whom you communicate directly and an indirect negative impact on those who learn about your comments from others. As always, everything depends on the quality and nature of your leadership. Do you tend towards BlooderShip or LovInShip? It goes without saying that LovInShip will have a very different (and much more positive) impact than BlooderShip.

The manner in which you have an impact on others is therefore a direct consequence of the manner in which way you communicate. Are you calm, affected, aggressive, agitated, disinterested, rambling, to the point, supportive, etc.? Do you look at people when you are talking to them or do you avert your gaze? Is your handshake weak or firm? I regard communication in general and for leaders in particular as the most direct and purest way to show who you are as a person. Who you are determines what you do. And how you do it. Sometimes consciously, sometimes unconsciously.

For this reason, it is essential for leaders to know exactly who they are, as human beings. By being aware of who they are as a person, they also become aware of why they do and don't do (or say and don't say) certain things.

The key question for a leader is then as follows: Are you communicating as your pure, real and authentic self, a self that is not defined by or has not been kidnapped by your leadership role? Or do you, in fact, communicate from within the context of specific roles, depending on the circumstances? If the latter is the case, do you behave and communicate differently in each of the specific roles you have? We all have many different roles in Life: as employer, boss, owner, entrepreneur, risk-taker, CEO, chairman, vice-president, minister, premier, son or daughter of, brother or sister of, father or mother of, friend of, member of this or that club, stakeholder in this or that organisation, etc. Who is the real you in your communication in each of these specific roles? Is there a difference in each case? It is perhaps interesting at this point to ask yourself this question, dear reader, and note down all the different roles you have and how you fulfil them. You will be amazed by just how many of them there are! We switch almost without knowing it from one to the other and, correspondingly, we jump from one communication style to another. In this way, on each occasion we only allow a limited number of our many facets to be seen, and never our totality.

I have developed a rather philosophical approach to the question of ego and leadership, in which I make the connection with authenticity and LovInShip. My ideas owe something to the teachings of Swami Bodhananda,[38] a Hindu monk who is famed for his knowledge of Vedanta texts and in whose ashram[39]

I received enlightenment in the summer of 2017, before inviting him to Belgium in the summer of 2019 to deepen my knowledge and understanding.

His fundamental position is that we can all act as free people from within different levels of our consciousness. It is from within these levels that we look (consciously or not) at ourselves and interact with the outside world. Our position in relation to our consciousness as a human being therefore influences what we do every day as a leader.

There are three main levels of consciousness, ranging from the most developed and most exalted to the least developed and least exalted. At the top, there is the pure or 'divine' self; in the middle, there is the interactive or surface self; and at the bottom, there is the material or object-related self. In an ideal world, we would function all the time from within our divine self. However, as a result of our material and risk-averse upbringing and our experiences in a competitive world, with its patterns of social expectation relating to 'success' and the excessive importance it attaches to doing and having, instead of being, we generally function from within one of the two lower levels of consciousness. In other words, we are captured by our ego or small self, or else we become enslaved to our material self.

The highest level – known as *sukha* in Hinduism or sometimes as the big self – is the most developed and most exalted level of consciousness. At this *sukha* level, our relations with the outside world are translogical or theological. Translogical means that these relations transcend pure logic; theological means that we are connected in these relations with our divine or spiritual self, our most beautiful and most complete self, which, in spite of the name, has nothing to do with any god or specific religion. The divine self is a-religious, a-political and a-philosophical. This

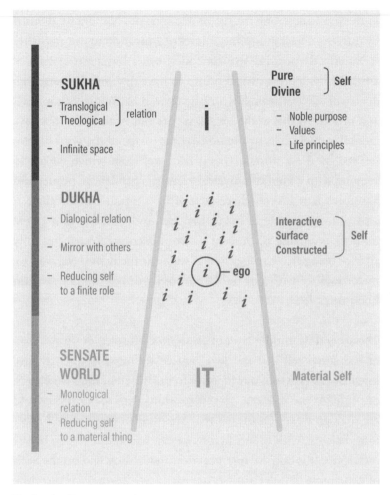

The levels of human consciousness

means that at the *sukha* level we are the best possible version of ourselves that we can be. We are at our most pure, most authentic, most detached and least subject to influence. This state has been reached through deep reflection about who we really are and what we want to do, rather than what we are expected to do as a result of our upbringing, experiences and interactions. We are no longer identified through the various roles in our Life, or our position in the professional hierarchy, or our income. Nor are we defined by our social background, our level of education or our network. It is perfectly possible for someone from a lower social class or a materially deprived background to have developed a very high degree of *sukha*, through which he lives in harmony with himself and others. At this exalted level, we are not troubled by negative mental models, bias or prejudice. Our image of the world is not limited by these things. This is the level from which we act in keeping with a kind of universal veracity, correctness, beauty and harmony. It is a level where each of us is unique, where there is a place for everyone in his or her total individuality and where nothing is lacking to prevent us from becoming ourselves fully and for being freely recognised as such. At the *sukha* level, we live in accordance with our noble purpose, our core values and out Life principles.

The second or middle level of awareness – known as *dukha, thou* or the small self – is the level where we most frequently and unconsciously attach our identity to the different roles we play in our Life. At the *dukha* level, our relations with the outside world are dialogical, which means that we need to interact and enter into dialogue with others before we can become someone in our own right. It is how we interact with these others and on the basis of which role that determines our identity. The *dukha* is therefore the level of our interpersonal self.

This brings me back once again to the previously mentioned Carl Gustav Jung,[40] the Austrian psychiatrist-psychologist, creator of the concept of the collective unconscious, human archetypes and the principles of synchronicity.[41] Jung explained that as humans, we become more human through our interactions with others. The interpretation that I give to Jung's work is that we can only develop our full self as a human being through this interaction, by virtue of the fact that it works as a mirror. Another word for 'mirror' is *karma*,[42] a concept from Hinduism and Buddhism that can literally be translated as meaning 'act, action or deed'. In both Hinduism and Buddhism, *karma* embraces both the physical and mental actions of the individual that have an impact on that individual's Life and his subsequent reincarnations. Everything that we do, think or say comes back to us in the end. *Karma* is therefore not only about the deed, but also about the consequences of the deed. It is through *karma*, the mirror of interaction, that I am able to learn about myself; about what I like and what I don't like; about what is important for me and what isn't; about what makes me happy and what annoys me. It was in this context that Jung developed the concept of synchronicity. Every time that we interact with others, we have the opportunity to learn something about and improve ourselves. For example, when we unintentionally keep coming across the same kind of people, who we do not really like. Or when we constantly find ourselves in the same kind of situation that we would rather avoid, because they are not really in our best interests (often quite the reverse). These meetings and situations will continue to occur until, at a certain momen, we become consciously aware of our role and place in the interactions, and what they actually mean for us. In this way, we reach a higher state of consciousness about ourselves and have therefore evolved positively as a result, allowing us to take another step forward in Life, making it possible to hold up a new mirror to a different aspect of our deeper self. This process is repeated until every essential aspect of our Life has been experienced and 'reviewed' in this manner, so that we finally become a complete and 'pure' human being, with the power to make our own authentic choices, ideally free from every form of kidnapping and in total coherence without own noble purpose.

Because of this process, the *dukha* or *thou* level is therefore the level where our ego comes into the foreground. But how exactly? The most common definition of the ego is the identification of the self with an incorrect self-image. People often say, for example, that someone has a big ego when he acts as though he is more important than he actually is. Based on this kind of analysis, our ego is the gap between who we think we are and who we really are. We see that we have different roles in our Life, which by definition involve interaction with others: son/daughter, Life partner, father/mother, customer, business partner, investor, entrepreneur, supplier, employee or employer, friend, acquaintance, neighbour, writer, conference organiser, hobby cook, etc. We can describe these roles as a series of little selves, in contrast to the big self of the *sukha* level. True, we often link our divine identity, and often quite consciously, to our rank, position, income, impact, etc., but without ever losing our authentic self. Or to put it in slightly different terms, some leaders – usually unconsciously – develop a dominant ego around one of their various roles, because, through their connection with their own LeadershiT, that is where they feel safest. From this comfortable but inauthentic position, it is easier for a role-related ego to connect with others and communicate. This reduction of the divine self occurs because they are not sufficiently aware of their real leadership, LovInShip and impact. As a result, out of all the small selves or egos they have acquired over the years, they choose one specific ego to which they attach a disproportionate importance. When that happens, they are kidnapped by this single ego. Kidnapped, because they are not conscious of how and why that ego has developed to become so strong. Kidnapped, because that single ego will now largely determine their communication (style), their interaction, and their manner of being. And when they are criticised because of that ego, they feel that they are being attacked in their deepest essence, whereas in reality it is their false self-image and the ego role with which they identify that are under attack. At that moment, although they don't realise it, they are unconsciously protecting themselves against their own weaknesses and needs. Not surprisingly, the people around them find it hard to understand why this huge ego is seemingly blind to those weaknesses and needs. This is a situation that can lead to great frustration.

The third and lowest level of our consciousness is the material world, also sometimes known as the sensate world. This is the level where we link our identity to matter, to the things that we have or want to have: a title, a job, a house, a type of car, the number of holidays we can take, an art collection, the kind of friends we have, the restaurants where we eat, the hotels where we stay, the amount of money we have in our wallet, the clubs to which we belong, the events we attend and where we want to be seen, etc. These material things define how we identify ourselves. The logic of this belief is that we can only become or be, by virtue of the amount of matter we can acquire. The more we possess, irrespective of what it is, the more we become. As a result, losing matter means that we also lose a part of our identity, of who we are. At this level, we therefore become our car, our house, our title, our company, our role, or any of a thousand and one other material things.

At the material level, our relations with the outside world are monological: it is a one-sided and one-directional relationship between ourselves and matter. There is no reciprocity. For example, I can have a relationship with the chair on which I sit, but the chair cannot have a relationship with me. I need the chair to be able to rest, work, sit, etc. But the chair does not need me. It does not even know that I exist. Even so, I can still attach great importance to this chair, especially if it is a fine Paul Kjaerhölm design chair. This means, of course, that the problems associated with this level are obvious. If someone is identified with their company, so that the company is their Life, and if that company then goes bust, the person in question will also be made emotionally and psychologically bankrupt. This material bankruptcy, in combination with the mixing of human consciousness and matter, means that it is no longer possible to be a real human being. I have seen many leaders who have been kidnapped in this way by their role, their power and their wealth, and have had to pay an enormous emotional and physical price as a result. It is only when they are confronted with their limits and with their own finiteness, often after deep discussion in which they finally identify their position in my consciousness model (the divine self, the ego or the material self), that it becomes possible to initiate a turning point moment, which allows them to live in accordance with a different and healthier self-image. This material level of our existence, in which so many people are trapped, is therefore the least exalted level, because this is the level where we are furthest away from our divine self. In our materialist society, it is a human drama of immense proportions that so many people attach so much value to material things at the expense of their own authenticity. This is a theme to which I will return in the chapter entitled 'The beast is dying'.

Within the logic of LovInShip, it is self-evident that the leaders of the future will need to act within the highest level of development, the *sukha* level. Why? Because of the great impact leaders have on others, it is vital that they become fully aware of that impact. And given their ability to influence the shaping of society, it is also necessary for them to be guided by a single but genuine exemplary function, rather than half a dozen false ones. At the same time, I also believe people want to be led by leaders who know themselves fully, who act on the basis of great authenticity and inner connectedness. Organisations must therefore evolve to become inspirational places where *sukha*-driven leaders connect through LovInShip with their people, so that together they can realise the noble purpose of their organisation.

It is through self-knowledge and self-awareness that the leader senses and knows what others – colleagues, staff, stakeholders – really need. By shifting the focus from matter to humankind

– from the sensate material world of the lowest level to the divinity of the highest *sukha* level of self – leaders will be better able to understand and make contact with the people in their organisations and will feel less constrained to hide behind the logic of facts and figures. The worth of the leader must no longer be assessed in terms of pure material value, but in terms of the extent to which he or she can encourage people to give of their best, based on their own authenticity and genuine inspiration. In this way, we will create organisations where the organisational dynamic will be *sukha*-based instead of *dukha*- or matter-based. This requires a fundamental shift from KPIs to CPIs.

4. CPIs – Caring for People Indicators

'We do not have too much intellect and too little soul,
but too little intellect in matters of the soul.' (Robert Musil)

In today's material-based world of business, KPIs (Key Performance Indicators) are a tool widely known and used by organisations and their leaders. In fact, it is often the only tool that leaders know and feel comfortable with. KPIs make it possible for them to measure objectives. Of course, there is nothing wrong with that. We need KPIs so that results can be quantified, processes followed, and the value of actions checked in a logical and objective way against the expectations of the organisational strategy and the desired levels of performance. But if, as an organisation, we allow ourselves to be kidnapped by the artificial diktat of KPIs, people within the organisation become no more than pawns on a complex KPI chessboard of power and LeadershiT, repeatedly moved from one square to another by an invisible hand.

Organisations are still far too often evaluated by the extent to which they reach (or fail to reach) their KPI targets. This frequently results in a transactional style of leadership, in which the KPIs are the only yardstick. The KPIs are achieved? Fantastic! The KPIs are not achieved? Crisis!

Much less (or rather too little) attention is paid to the way in which people are required to reach their KPIs and how the leadership supports and inspires them in this task. Leaders must encourage their people to step out of their comfort zone and give the best of themselves to achieve the (often challenging) targets they have been set, a process which, in my opinion, must be dedicated to the service of a noble purpose.

At GINPI, we regularly see that people in organisations are in need of greater connectedness, trust, clarity, support and the feeling that they are contributing towards something worthwhile. We believe that you cannot accomplish this through a KPI-focus alone. If we are right in this assumption, KPIs actually become an obstacle to success, because following them up is tiring, uninspiring and unedifying. Or that, at least, is the case for the large majority of people in the organisation. And, of course, it is this majority that helps or hinders the creation of the organisation's added value.

For this reason, I advise companies to build up their systems and culture around CPIs: Caring for People Indicators. As the name implies, these indicators measure how much care you, as the leader, give to your people. How much do you care about your people as people and not simply as employees doing a job? How much attention do you pay to their welfare in the work environment; to their expectations to be treated as normal human beings in all circumstances; to their uncertainties, doubts and fears? How do you ensure that they strike the right balance between challenges, competencies, interest and the development of autonomy? By using Caring for People Indicators, you create a basis for their support, demonstrate your engagement, and focus your leadership on what is human, rather than on processes and results. CPI-driven leadership allows you to build the foundations of a culture that will help people to extend their personal boundaries by allowing them to explore and exploit their potential, which will encourage them to release their maximum work energy. This will lead to significantly improved performance.

But to benefit from this boost in positive work energy, energy which ensures that the right things are done in the right manner, organisations first need to adopt a new style of leadership. I mean, of course, LovInShip, in which the KPI-focus is subordinated to a CPI-focus. What's more, this change will also ensure that your KPIs become more sustainably achievable, because people will feel more engaged by and committed to their work. Why? Because engagement and commitment are generated through human interaction and appreciation, not by a 'command and control' approach in which power and hierarchical position are more important than the authenticity and honesty of the leader. Being willing as a leader to guide your people on the basis of CPIs rather than KPIs demands both courage and humanity. These are characteristics that only leaders who have at least reached the *dukha* level of consciousness will possess. Leaders who are still locked in the material level will therefore also remain locked in KPI-driven leadership. Or to look at it from a slightly different perspective: the leadership style adopted by the leader-as-human-being will make it possible to identify his or her level of consciousness: *dukha*, *sukha* or material.

KPIs = turnover, number of sales conversations and/or meetings, percentage of new customers, percentage of reduced logistical costs, created added value, percentage of staff who need to be brought from 'on target' to 'above target', market share, number of sold products per category, etc.

CPIs = number of motivation conversations and their measurable quality, the number and measurable quality of initiatives designed to increase and maintain individual engagement, the number and measurable quality of initiatives designed to improve the group atmosphere and allow people to collaborate autonomously and spontaneously, the listing of all behaviours and decisions that can negatively affect staff motivation and proposals, the replacement of these behaviours and decisions with more positively motivating alternatives, the extent to which people feel supported when they lose their way and experience moments of difficulty, etc.

Research has shown that people in organisations are only prepared to make available 15 percent of their total work energy under what I call 'command and control' leadership: in other words, BlooderShip, which effectively 'forces' people to work through the use of hierarchy, status and power and the creation of scarcity ('If you don't do this, you won't get that'). Under a leadership of this kind, people do not work because they want to or are inspired to do so, but because they are afraid or, at best, are transactionally motivated. What's more, the low percentage of effort made by their employees means that transactional organisations are missing out on huge opportunities. The potential added value of the unreleased employee energy is equally huge. In this respect, it is worth repeating the results of the previously mentioned poll carried out by the American Gallup[43] research bureau in 2017. They discovered that a staggering 85 percent of respondents in 142 countries said that they felt no real connection with their job, which means that only a small minority are enthused by their work and feel committed to it. In other words, there are a few billion people somewhere on earth who are not really happy, because their work fails to inspire them and/or they feel no empathy with their organisation. Viewed from both a social and a macro-economic perspective, this means that massive gains can be made if we can secure the engagement of this disenchanted workforce, by giving them the feeling that they are contributing something relevant towards achieving the noble purpose of the organisation for which they work.

	2009-2010	2011-2012	2017
Actively disengaged	27%	24%	18%
Disengaged	62%	63%	67%
Engaged	11%	13%	15%

Massive disengagement SOURCE: GALLUP

So what should leaders do? The best way to motivate your people is by moving away from a KPI-focus and replacing it with a CPI-focus; by providing encouragement to them based on who you are as a person and what you stand for as a leader; by letting people see your real, *sukha*-based divine-self, which will shine through in your communication and all the things that you do.

If organisations, no matter what their size or location in the world, wish to evolve towards sustainable systems with an engaged work-force, my strong advice is to rebuild your culture around a new noble purpose and to demonstrate to your people how much you value them through the care for their welfare that you show. When talking to leaders on this subject, I like to use the sentence: 'Tell me how much you care, and I'll tell you how much I know'. People in general, and certainly the millennial generation, want first and foremost to feel valued. It is only then that they will be prepared to commit themselves 100 percent to their work. Not before!

It takes courage for leaders to show themselves to others as they really are. It takes courage to stand up in full authenticity against the old paradigms, with their outdated expectations of what a leader should be. It takes courage as a leader to make clear to your people that you love them, in much the same way as you make it clear to your children and friends.

And because it takes so much courage, and because I nevertheless expect leaders to make the switch from KPIs to CPIs, we now need to look at the question of vulnerability. But vulnerability as a strength, not a weakness.

5. Vulnerability = strength

'It is only when we can experience vulnerability as a strength and not as a weakness that we will be able to move beyond shame.' (Brené Brown)

The use of vulnerability is an essential part of LovInShip: daring to show your uncertainty, daring to express your doubts, daring to ask for support and advice. Above all, daring to stand up for your opinions, daring to respect and have others respect your own values, daring to challenge behaviour that is incompatible with your organisational culture, daring live your Life according to your noble purpose. Viewed in these terms, vulnerability is something very different from weakness. On the contrary, this kind of 'daring' demands great strength. I have met many top leaders who are only willing (or able) to reveal a mere fraction of their true identity, their *sukha*, for fear of being excluded if their real views are seen as being too outspoken. They are worried that by having ideas and values that run against the mainstream of shareholder and stakeholder opinion in their organisation, they will be pushed to one side.

From my in-depth conversations with dozens of top executive and managers – often very pleasant and discreet discussions around my kitchen table, with a refreshing cup of tea or a glass of fruit juice – I have come to realise just how difficult it can be for leaders to find the courage to doubt. They are reluctant to tell people that perhaps they don't know all the answers. Instead of being open about their vulnerability, they go to the opposite extreme, adopting a 'my-way-or-the-highway' approach that allows them to be kidnapped by their own LeadershiT. By letting them talk about this difficult subject, which for many of them is healing, I can bring them to a higher level of awareness about the ways in which they actually benefit from truly being (or remaining) themselves, so that there is no reason for them to avoid their vulnerability. On the contrary, it is by showing their vulnerability that they grow in strength.

Brené Brown,[44] a research professor in social work at the University of Houston, has inspired me greatly with her ideas on vulnerability. In particular, her TED talk[45] is a mine of useful basic information.

The essence of vulnerability is that we, as human beings, have a need to be able to connect with others. Think, for example, about the piece I wrote on synchronicity, back on page 205, where I explained that we all need interaction with others in order to become more truly ourselves. It is vital that we do not allow ourselves to be kidnapped by our conviction or our fear that we are not 'worthy' of (or, conversely that we must not lower ourselves to seek) connection with others. This takes courage – a word derived from the Latin cor, meaning 'heart'. And what is the link between courage and vulnerability? Vulnerability requires you to tell your own story about who you really are with your whole heart. As I have already said, it takes guts to say openly what you stand for and what your values are, and to do so in the full knowledge of your own imperfection (because, after all, no-one is perfect!) and in full awareness that others will have different perspectives to your own and may judge you accordingly. Believe me, it is no easy thing to put your heart on the line and tell your own authentic story, while accepting the possibility that your people might not like that story or be willing or able to find a place in it. That being said, the reaction of others is not the most important thing. The crucial factor is how we deal with our vulnerability. It is thanks to our vulnerability and our belief that we are vulnerable that we become stronger, by embracing that vulnerability and not pushing it away because we are afraid of extreme reactions. I am certainly not saying that accepting and sharing your vulnerability with others is easy, but it is indispensable if you wish to develop relationships of quality. As such, it is one of the cornerstones of LovInShip and of any attempt you wish to make as a leader to create a CPI-focus.

In the construction of our House of Noble Purpose, we have now looked at the importance of having a noble purpose in organisations and the type of new leadership this requires. The noble purpose and the leadership are the sources of inspiration for a new organisational culture, which forms the foundations (the values) and the walls (the principles) of the house. And it is these foundations and walls that carry the weight – the noble purpose and LovInShip – of the roof.

The foundations and the walls are an essential part of the House of Noble Purpose. Together, they form the organisational culture – and that will be the subject of this chapter. I will not be talking about the different schools of thought that exist and the different theories they put forward about organisational culture. Instead, I will offer my own insights and observations based on my own experience as a leader, an entrepreneur and an adviser. I will also make use of research we have conducted at GINPI to see how culture relates to our ideas about the new noble purpose paradigm.

So, what exactly is it, an organisational culture? If I ask this question at conferences, the most common answers I get include: values, how we should behave, what we share, what procedures exist within the organisation, a reflection of the leadership, the rituals and stories we have in common, KPIs and strategy, purpose, symbols, etc.

As by now you might expect, I have a different theory on the matter. Let me explain with reference to a story about apes. As part of an experiment in the 1970s, scientists put five apes in a cage. In this cage, there was a bunch of bananas hanging from a tree. There was also a ladder propped up against the tree. As soon as an ape attempted to climb the ladder to take a banana, he and the four other apes were all sprayed with cold water. Of course, the surprised, confused and very wet ape climbed down, but his four companions were equally unhappy. Even so, after a time – once hunger or impatience had got the better of them – one of the other apes decided to try his luck on the ladder. Same story: a cold shower for everyone. The experiment continued until none of the apes were prepared to risk climbing the ladder or else were prevented from doing so by the others: our simian friends are not great lovers of ice-cold water. But this is where the experiment got interesting. One of the five apes was replaced by an ape that had not so far taken part in the experiment and therefore had no idea about the water. When this ape understandably made a move for the ladder, he was held back by the four others. This led to a degree of arguing and aggression, not to mention confusion in the new ape. Some time later, a second of the original apes was replaced by a newcomer. The new boy was again tempted by the bananas but was again held back by his cage mates. Gradually, the three originals that still remained were also replaced one by one, so that a position was reached in which none of the five apes in the cage had experienced the cold shower or knew of its risk. Even so, none of the five was prepared to climb the ladder and take a banana, even though by now they were very, very hungry.

You can see a parallel in this story with the way things work in organisations (not that I am comparing the people in organisations with apes! Heaven forbid!) In particular, the behaviour of the apes helped me to reach my definition of organisational culture as: 'how someone must think and act in order to be one of them, to be included in the group, to belong'. 'Them', of course, in this context means the wider organisation. What's more, I am talking very clearly here about behaviour. What behaviour is acceptable and what behaviour is not acceptable? What behaviour is stimulated and rewarded, and what behaviour must be avoided and condemned? In other words, company culture has a strong behavioural orientation. And if you want to guide the behaviour of people in complex systems (which, by definition, organisations always are), there is only one effective way to do it: through values and principles. They have the ability to align people in the manner you want.

Over the years, I have come to the conclusion that organisations with a positive and robust organisational culture are generally strong organisations, in the sense of being quick, correct, efficient, sustainable and passionate to book good results and/or discover and develop new things. Thanks to this strong culture, everyone in the organisation is gently shepherded in the right direction and held there. And it is on the basis of this same responsible culture that the organisation acts. In one respect, this is just common sense: having the 'right' culture is a strong competitive advantage that can set you apart from other similar organisations. It shows people who you are, what you do, why you do it, and why this makes you unique. It is enough to compare just two or three organisations of the same kind to understand why one acts quickly, is innovative, finds good solutions for customer problems, recruits people easily and keeps them, facilitates inter-team collaboration and inter-divisional support, etc., while the others do not. Why, for example, were Volkswagen, Toyota and Renault highly successful in launching new products and booking excellent financial results during the period 2005 to 2012, whereas PSA almost went bankrupt in 2013? All four were vehicle manufacturers, who built more or less the same cars – so why the difference? How can we explain that the Indian JET Airlines went bust in 2019, while the American Southwest Airlines continues to make a profit year after year, seemingly against the odds? Both of them fly people from A to B in planes, don't they? Why should the once so successful RSC Anderlecht, the most iconic Belgian football club, be struggling so badly, when clubs like Paris St-Germain, PSV Eindhoven, AC Milan and Manchester United continue to shine? At least for now! Surely, aren't they all similar football clubs? And how can it be that the governments in Scandinavia, Switzerland and Canada can function efficiently and proactively, while the authorities in, say, Italy, India, Congo or Myanmar cannot? Aren't they all countries with citizens who want more or less the same thing? Why is one team in a company a success and another team a disaster? After all, they both have the same employer. And so on.

The only explanation is the culture of the company, airline, football club, government and team involved. And the same explanation applies, by extension, to every existing system in which people work and collaborate. It is the culture of one organisation that sets it apart from another. The culture of one organisation promotes the right behaviour, while the culture of another promotes the wrong behaviour, or at least behaviour that is not appropriate for the realisation of its noble purpose, ambitions, objectives and strategy.

So, what is the 'right' organisational culture? It is a culture where the sum of the whole is significantly greater than the sum of the parts, and where this sum makes it possible to achieve the organisation's noble purpose through a clear strategy, efficient processes and fixed procedures (the latter forming the tactics or strategy implementation). If I were to compare an organisation visually to an iceberg, it is probably fair to say that the biggest mistake most leaders make is to focus too much on the financial results, which, in my comparison, represent the 15 percent of the iceberg you can see above the water. This is where most of the attention goes, often in the form of KPIs. But we know, of course, that the 15 percent of the iceberg above the water can only stay there because it is supported by the 85 percent under the water. If the 85 percent was not there, the 15 percent would sink. Applied to organisations, the 85 percent under the water is the organisational culture, which makes it possible for the 15 percent above the water to generate results.

If a company is failing to reach its objective, it needs to dive under the surface and look closely at the 85 percent. What is the basis of its culture? How do people act and behave, and why? Is this action and behaviour appropriate in relation to the expected results? And at a deeper level, further under the waves: what do people believe in; what do they stand for; how are the organisation's values experienced; are its main principles respected? If not, why not?

The diagram below shows the iceberg comparison and the way it translates into an organisational culture.

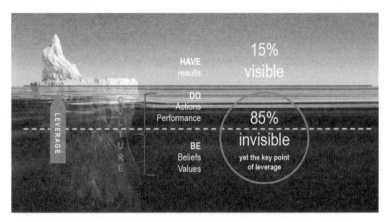

It is what an organisation says and does that determines its result

An organisation's culture is a combination of everything that the organisation stands for – all the convictions that exist among its people, its values and its fundamental principles – and the way the organisation behaves. (It is worth noting here that an organisation itself can achieve nothing. It is the organisation's people who do that! In a following book, about the spirit and soul of organisations and their organisational dynamics, I will say something in more nuanced terms about the 'own self' of organisations and the laws that govern them as living things.) When the people who form an organisation want to realise a particular noble purpose by implementing a strategy to bring about a desired result, they will first need to be aware of who they are as members of that organisation and must know in what they believe and how their values have been integrated. Who they are will determine what they do. And what they do will determine what they achieve as their result.

Most of the messages that people receive about their organisation's culture are non-verbal. They see what their leaders do and don't do, what they value and don't value. And in order to belong, and so that they can continue to belong, they slowly adjust their behaviour to what they feel is expected of them. In an ideal world, it is in this way that behaviour is guided by values. But more of that later.

First, I want to explain why this chapter is called 'The Nicky factor'. The most common theory about organisational culture, and the one I personally support and defend, is that it is made by the people at the top of the organisation. The lower echelons of the organisation look up to the management, and the management looks up to the executive committee and the board. The people lower down in the hierarchy therefore mirror the behaviour of those higher up that hierarchy. For this reason, it is vital that the behaviour of those right at the very top is exemplary and inspirational. Do you remember the earlier section on impact? It is the majority of the organisation's people, its base, who will experience the culture as positive, providing that culture is constructive, just as it is the majority who will be weighed down by the culture, if it is negative. Sadly, there are many organisations, both large and small, international and local, where a negative and depressing culture makes it unpleasant to work. It is not without reason that 85 percent of the world's working population feels no real engagement with their jobs!

Fortunately, in some organisations, visionary people are taking the lead to introduce a new kind of leadership. If these brave initiatives (brave, because they often go against the tide of organisational opinion) are successful, they will hopefully gain visibility and win support. These innovators are frequently regarded as trendsetters, allowing them to create a leverage effect. Entire organisations can sometimes be prodded into much-needed action by the vision and determination of a single person to try out a different approach or a new form of leadership. In other words, it is individuals who play the key roles in the major transformation of their organisation. My point? Even if cultural change ultimately occurs from the top down, there is nothing to stop people at any level from having the courage to take the initiative and try something new, in the hope that it will percolate upwards and be accepted. Following which, it can then work its way back down again. And this is where the story of Nicky comes in.

When I first got to know Nicky in 2013, she was a 'number 5' in her organisation. She reported to an irrelevant boss who was trapped in his LeadershiT, someone who had had his day but still refused to accept it. He, in turn, reported to a manager who was known for her BlooderShip and was later removed from her function. This manager reported in her turn to a member of the executive committee, the CHRO, who was open for the initiatives Nicky wished to take and was charmed by her vision and persistence. At the top of the chain, the executive reported to the group CEO.

Nicky believed strongly in the power of noble purpose and a correct organisational culture. As the person responsible for leadership trajectories within her multinational group, she had developed the idea to roll out a promising new programme that would support the necessary and revolutionary development of top talent within the organisation. This would help these talents to deal with the far-reaching transformation that had recently been initiated following the appointment of a new CEO. GINPI was consulted and we brainstormed with Nicky and her team about the possible content for the new programme. A strong basis was eventually agreed and sent up the hierarchy for approval. Her immediate boss thought that her proposal was too ambitious and tried to have it blocked. He simply lacked the courage to match the ambition that Nicky showed and the organisation needed. The manager above him saw more in Nicky's idea, but also lacked the courage to make a decision, preferring to leave this to the CHRO. Happily, we were at last able to convince him of the importance of what was on the table. On a side note: thanks to this actually, the then CHRO (and now top leader at the French La Poste) started being intrigued by the relevance and impact of noble purpose. All we then had to do was get the group CEO on board.

During a memorable meeting I had with him in April 2014, he became so passionate about the proposed programme (which was the direct result of Nicky's vision and ambition) that he agreed to make the necessary resources available to implement it and agreed to be present at its kick-off. In this way, he made himself the co-promoter of the project and what it stood for, referring to it on more than one occasion as an example of the organisation's need for responsible leadership within a result-oriented performance culture.

Nicky's vision and ambition, allied to the ambition and courage of CEO Carlos Taveres, helped to lay the foundation for a change of mentality and a paradigm shift at PSA. The group, which in 2012-2013 was on the point of bankruptcy, is today respected as amongst the best performing vehicle manufacturers in the world. The work of transformation is not yet complete, but it is staggering how much has already been achieved in a relatively short time. How can we position this within our iceberg comparison? In a conversation I had with Carlos Tavares, the kind of in-depth discussion I have with many CEOs and company owners, I explained that the problem with PSA was not its results (its visible 15 percent), but what the organisation had become; in other words, the things in which it believed, the values it maintained, and the fundamental principles that influenced its behaviour (its hidden 85 percent). These were no longer appropriate neither to meet the needs of a changing customer market and nor to deal with the technological revolution that the car industry was undergoing. The programme devised by Nicky – thanks to her persistence, even though she was relatively low down in the hierarchy – was an important step towards making the transition to a fit-for-purpose and resilient organisation.

Another friend of mine, the Frenchman Vincent Monziols, has accomplished something similar at St-Gobain. Vincent is a transformation leader, who succeeded, thanks to his own inspirational leadership style, in installing self-steering management and innovation at the heart of his organisation. He adjusted the vision and procedures, provided the necessary instruments for effective change, and converted an outdated culture into an innovative and forward-looking one, inspired by his own passion for start-ups. His method of working attracted the attention of the global management of the group, by the way in which he was able to achieve a paradigm shift in such a traditional company as St-Gobain. Today, Vincent is asked by other divisions in the group to assist them with their own transformation processes and it is clear that the group CEO and the global executive committee have all been inspired by his example. What once would have been unheard of at a company like St-Gobain is now the basis for new leadership and transformation.

1. Taking corporate values from the walls and into hearts

As mentioned earlier, the behaviour of people in organisations is directed by their shared values. In other words, it is the values of an organisation, together with its guiding principles, which form the foundations of our House of Noble Purpose. Values are organisation-specific: every organisation has its own set of values and both the choice of these values and the way they are implemented are characteristic of each individual organisation.

It is through this choice and implementation that organisations can differentiate themselves from other organisations. For example, what the Spanish family company Almirall hopes to achieve through its value of 'caring' is different from what that other Spanish reference company – the white goods manufacturer Teka – hopes to achieve with its value of 'care'. Similarly, BSH (the Munich-based Bosch Siemens Home Appliances, the number 1 in Europe and number 3 in the world) and the French vehicle constructor PSA both want their people to be resilient and have a strongly developed sense of initiative. With this in mind, BSH lists 'initiative and determination' as one of its values, whereas PSA's value statement refers to 'agility'. Both companies mean the same but have different ways of expressing it and putting it into practice.

I regard values, together with noble purpose, as the most sacred element of any organisation. Why sacred? Because values have an extremely deep meaning and are assumed (rightly) to be the basis for the actions of billions of people in companies worldwide. Put simply, this assumption asserts that, ideally, people are prompted to act by virtue of their experience of the values in their environment. As such, values are the behavioural compass of every organisation. Or at least they should be. But what do we at GINPI often see? We see that far too many people, often including people in very senior positions, know little or nothing about their organisation's values, never mind that they actually experience them. We have seen many times that the definition of values is the umpteenth element of the umpteenth strategic exercise, which results in the values being summarised in a neat, formal – but essentially lifeless – document. Once the exercise is finished, a copy of the document is framed and hung in the entrance hall of the headquarters building... but that's about all. Only very rarely is there meaningful follow-up. When I talk about cultural transformation at conferences and seminars and ask the participants to tell me something about their organisation's values (how many, what, etc.), you would be amazed how often (almost without exception, in fact) my question is met with blank stares from my audience. For many, it is a highly confrontational moment. The majority know nothing about them. Even the minority who can name them (or some of them) have no idea about their real meaning. In short, values are not widely experienced in the organisations that pretend to proclaim them. At best, they are observed, and then generally from a distance. Do the test yourself. Ask yourself if you know what your own organisation's values are. What do they mean and what do they want to achieve? Hopefully, you will score better than the many thousands of people who have attended my lectures and speeches. But, to be honest, I wouldn't bet on it.

In my work, I frequently make reference to the way in which the top of an organisation deals with values. If you want an example of precisely how not to deal with them, you need look no further than the notorious Enron scandal. It's long ago but it remains a great 'business case' example of how bad things can go. At the start of the 1990s, the corporation began to specialise in the delivery of gas, but also invested billions in supply contacts for other fields, such as water, the internet and insurance. Enron seemed to be doing well, but that way only superficial: the 15 percent of the iceberg above the waterline. In reality, the CEO Jeffrey Skilling and the CFO Andrew Fastow, with the connivance of other senior executives, had managed to hide huge losses through a series of 'clever' financial constructions – including tax evasion and bribery – and by offloading them onto subsidiaries. In so doing, they blatantly deceived (i.e. lied to) their own board of directors and audit committee. The company's external accountant, Arthur Andersen, also played a key role in the deception, thanks to some very 'creative' bookkeeping and the provision of false declarations. When Enron inevitably collapsed, it furthermore became apparent that the management had siphoned off millions of dollars into their own pockets. In view of all this, it may surprise you to learn that the value statement framed in Enron's head office included words like 'integrity' and 'respect'. But clearly the CEO and his executives had never read them.

Fortunately, there are also many good examples of how you should deal with values. We will now look at some of them, which I have chosen on the basis of their great authenticity and originality, which allowed the organisations in question to generate a major mentality switch and to create a real social movement, both inside their organisation and beyond.

The Danish family-owned Maersk, the world's largest container shipping company and owner of a huge conglomerate of other logistical subsidiaries, has a set of five value-driven principles that systematically direct all its operations in whatever field of activity. The five are: 'constant care' (not only for today, but also for tomorrow), 'humbleness' (listening, learning, sharing and giving space to others), 'uprightness' (a promise is a promise, we do what we say), 'our employees' (creating the right environment for the right people), and 'our name' (we embody our values, while continuing to strive for better; we radiate the sum of our values to the outside world). Although these values were only officially formalised in 2003, they have governed the company's operations throughout its 110-year existence. In an interview, Ane Mærsk Mc-Kinney Uggla, chairman of the A.P. Møller Foundation, expressed it as follows: 'The five values were integrated into our DNA by our founders, the Møller family, and they have now been our guide for more than a century.'

The American (online) shoe company Zappos has as its noble purpose: 'Creating memorable experiences for the greater good'. The company has a much-praised culture that is embodied by the conviction of Nick Swinmurn, the founder of Zappos.com. This conviction has been translated into ten core values. As Zappos themselves say: 'Our ten core values are more than just words; they are a way of life. We know that companies with a strong culture and a higher goal perform better in the long term. And while we grow, we continue to ensure that our values grow with us and remain a living part of the company.' The ten values are: 'Deliver WOW through service, embrace and drive change, create fun and a little weirdness, be adventurous, creative and open-minded, pursue growth and learning, build open and honest relationships with communication, build a positive team and family spirit, do more with less, be passionate and determined, and be humble.' This proves that values can be much more than a few boring words hung in a frame on a wall. At Zappos, their values are the Life energy of the organisation. People at Zappos live and experience these values, talk to each other about them and are proud to work for an organisation that believes in them. True, ten values is a lot, and it is no easy task to recognise and experience them all, but at Zappos, it works. The values are so relevant and generate so much energy that they have acquired an almost spiritual significance: they are the essence – the DNA – of the Zappos culture.

Although airlines in general tend to be regarded as organisations that provide bad service and are staffed largely by disgruntled employees, the American Southwest Airlines has proved that this does not have to be the case. Their clients have testified time after time that SWA's personnel are happy, friendly and always ready to help. Southwest, which is listed on the New York Stock Exchange under the symbolic registration code 'LUV', has a long history. It was founded some 50 years ago by Rollin King and Herb Kelleher. Since then, it has succeeded in conveying its vision and objectives to successive generations of employees, who have always formed a tight-knit team. This is due in no small measure to the fact that Southwest gives its people the autonomy to do whatever is necessary to keep its customers satisfied by projecting its organisational image. As a result, SWA is one of the companies that has made a real difference in recent aviation history, on a much greater scale than Brussels Airlines, which I mentioned earlier. They have achieved this by living out and living up to their noble purpose: 'To connect people to what's important in their lives through friendly, reliable and low-cost air travel'. Their values are encapsulated in two catchy slogans: 'Live the Southwest Way' (a warrior's spirit, a servant's heart and a fun-LUVing attitude) and 'Work the Southwest Way' (work safely, wow our customers, and keep costs low).

Last but not least, I think that the TED conferences also deserve mention. TED first saw the light of day in 1984, based on Richard Saul Wurman's observation that there needed to be a strong convergence between Technology, Entertainment and Design (TED). With his TED talks, he built up a community of people who went in search of a deeper understanding of the new developments that were beginning to shape the world. They believed – and still believe – that strong ideas have the power to change attitudes, lives and, ultimately, the planet. The community has as its noble purpose: 'How can we best spread great ideas?' They do this by initiating thought-provoking and sometimes controversial conversations. On TED.com, they bring together the wisdom and words of some of the world's most inspiring speakers, while the TED talks and conferences unite people from across the globe to think about the ideas and problems that affect us all. Like all value-driven organisations, TED does what it says it will do – and all without a profit incentive.

In contrast to Enron and Arthur Anderson, and many other organisations that deal with their organisational culture in a highly transactional manner, at Maersk, Zappos, Southwest Airlines and TED values truly are experienced and lived, by everyone associated with them.

And precisely because values have such remarkable power, I would urge you to take them down from the wall and start making them real, through the behaviour and efforts of your people. Values are a matter of the heart, not a matter of the mind. Values must make people – and, by extension, the organisation as a whole – vibrate with energy. Values are so much more than mere transactional words, which we learn by heart. Values are the glue that binds everyone in an organisation together, from the boardroom to the workplace and back again. Values create your organisation's cultural 'perfume', which allows you to be distinguished from everybody else.

How can you tell if an organisation attaches genuine importance to its values? There are a number of things you can check; look at the prominence given to values on its website and in its recruitment strategy; notice how often values are mentioned by its top people in their communication and public pronouncements; try to spot evidence of the values in the wider behaviour of the board of directors, etc. It is the sum of all these elements and many more that will make or break an organisational culture.

2. Balancing IT – WE – I

Finally, in this chapter about organisational culture, I would like to look at an important model that we use in almost all our GINPI interventions. This model, which is based on the Integral Theory[46] formulated by Ken Wilber,[47] helps to understand the dynamics of an organisation and the place of the individual within them. One of the main virtues of the theory is that it attempts to synthesise the wide diversity of thinking on this subject within a single framework. In this sense, it is an integration of matter, body, reason, soul and spirit.

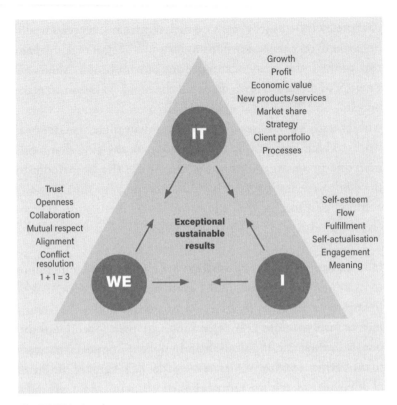

The IT-WE-I-triangle

If I ask leaders what, in their opinion, are the main reasons for their organisation's success, the answers I most often get are: good products and services, a good strategy, ambition, acquiring and keeping good market share, innovation, an attractive customer portfolio, having the right processes and procedures, etc. I hear much less about: inspirational leadership, a good company culture, a pleasant working atmosphere, a motivated workforce, shared values, etc. And I hear nothing at all about the noble purpose for which the organisation stands (or should stand) and the way in which people are able to realise themselves through their own specific way of creating added value in the service of that noble purpose.

From research, from my many contacts with top leaders and from our many GINPI interventions in many kinds of organisations worldwide since 2010 – from start-ups to hundred-year-old multinationals, from NGOs to cultural and social institutions, from political parties to parliaments and international organisations – I have learnt that most leaders concentrate on what I call the 'IT'. The 'IT' is the material dimension of business: turnover, results, market share, products and strategy. They hope to achieve their material and/or financial objectives by making their policy and their leadership subservient to (and even dependent on) these matters. In terms of our iceberg, they focus on the visible 15 percent associated with goals and results, often without taking account of the 85 percent below the surface.

The outcome of this approach almost has the inevitability of an immutable law: the organisational culture turns sour, the collaboration between colleagues becomes unpleasant, the gulf between management and workforce grows, people are less able to believe in what the organisation stands for, etc. The result is confusion, growing disinterest and, ultimately, total disconnection. In the diktat of the 'IT', the only things that count are all intangible and uninspirational transactional things. In reality, of course, transactional things like financial results should never be the objective of leaders and their teams, but should be the beneficial side-effect of their activities on behalf of the organisation's noble purpose.

If organisations wish to evolve towards improved performance, book sustainable results at a level never previously seen and make a sustainable contribution towards societal progress, they must focus first and foremost on securing the welfare and deep engagement of their people. They need to feel happy in themselves before they can be expected to give maximum effort and they need to be convinced that they are adding relevant value to something that goes beyond the purely material. People look for meaning in their work and in Life. They need to find enjoyment and fulfilment in their job, creating a balance between the three spheres we discussed earlier, and must be able to achieve their own self-realisation through what they do and how they do it. This means that leadership must focus as a matter of priority on the 'I' or the personal dimension of our triangle model: the dimension of the individual and of matters relating to the individual within the organisation. The leader must ensure that the right people are recruited and kept; that they can find purpose in their tasks; that the right balance is struck between giving responsibility and allowing it to be taken; that autonomy is encouraged and competencies developed. In nearly all organisations that have been able to transform themselves successfully into systems, this 'I' dimension is given the right amount of attention. Of course, this does not imply that people can do whatever they like and however they like. Giving the right attention to the 'I' dimension means that, as a result of receiving this stimulating attention which promotes their self-realisation, your people will be able to work better, more independently, more quickly, more focused, more innovatively and more creatively. And will feel happier and more fulfilled because of it.

In the second place, attention need to be given to the 'WE' or interpersonal dimension. This involves, among other things: encouraging efficient and spontaneous collaboration; setting positive challenges; providing mutual support and help; giving constructive feedback; effectively reconciling contradictory interests in the interest of the organisation as a whole; learning to talk about the best way to achieve the noble purpose and the strategy that will make this possible. However, it is important to note that a crucial underlying factor is also at play in this dimension: namely, that the 'WE' dimension can only develop its full power if the 'I' dimension is first in place. A strong 'WE' feeling is only possible if it is based on the sum of a whole group of strong and satisfied 'I' feelings. The reverse is also true. If someone does not feel happy in their work or comfortable in the organisation, if they need to fight every day for recognition, if they are not certain whether they will still have a job at the end of the month, if they do not know what the company stands for and do not know what is expected of them, then it will be impossible for them to deal with others in a direct, transparent, driven, authentic and convincing manner. And without this, there can be no 'we' feeling.

The message is clear: if leaders want to achieve good results, see turnover increase, see innovation blossom, see their strategy succeed – in other words, if they want to realise their 'it' – this will only be possible if they switch their organisational focus to the 'i' and the 'we'. I like to depict this 'it-we-i' model as a triangle: the 'i' and the 'we' form the base on which the 'it' dimension is supported. In effect, the triangle is like a three-legged stool. Imagine what would happen if one of the legs was missing. At worst, the stool would fall over. Even at best, a stool with just two legs would be uncomfortable to sit on. No, none of the three dimensions can really manage without the other two. Whoever is kidnapped by the 'it' will remain trapped in the old paradigm of BlooderShip and will regularly be confronted by his own LeadershiT. Conclusion? Every leader who wishes to develop a clearly defined and sustainable 'it' must concentrate on an equally sustainable 'i' and 'we'.

There is only one exception to this rule, and that is when an organisation finds itself in crisis. If your house is burning down, you need to put the fire out. There is no time for brainstorming and discussion. You need to act and act quickly, with almost military precision. This is the only kind of situation where 'command & control' is desirable. But only temporarily! By placing a sharp focus on the 'it' dimension, all your 'troops' will be lined up behind the same objective, so that all your organisational energy can be used to symbolically extinguish the flames that are threatening your existence. But once this has been achieved, the focus of your attention needs to be switched back to the 'I' and 'WE' dimensions. Check on how people are feeling, now that they have escaped from the fire. What do they need to get them back in tip-top condition? How can you help them to contribute towards the rebuilding of your fire-damaged house?

I have often seen in the past that many leaders fail to take this final step. Why? Because the sharp 'IT' focus temporarily gives an enormous boost to the organisation's energy, so that performance increases and fantastic results are booked. This persuades leaders – and certainly leaders who are not well versed in (or simply ignore) the principles of LovInShip – to carry on in the same transactional way, even after the crisis has passed, so that they become trapped in the temptations of 'IT'.

Maintaining too long a focus on the 'IT' dimension, so that the organisation's leadership and culture eventually become too 'materialist', can cause huge damage. People become exhausted and lose their engagement. Performance declines, enthusiasm disappears, objectives become blurred, frustration increases, sickness absence and burn-out reach new heights, results fall…

In these circumstances, the 'diehards' do the one thing above all others that they must not do: they make the focus on results even sharper. People are put under pressure to perform better. Teams are played one against the other. Internal competition between departments is escalated. This is not good. What the leaders should be doing is to provide their people with breathing space, allowing them the opportunity to develop new competencies and learn new ways of collaboration, so that they can find their proper place in your newly rebuilt house. In fact, what you really need to do is apply the principles of top sport: train hard in preparation for a top performance, then give that winning performance, and then wind down, relax and celebrate before moving on to the next challenge. Sadly, in many organisations, we see too little preparation in advance and too little relaxation afterwards: the focus is on top performance at all times. But this is very, very hard to achieve.

Noble purpose eats strategy for breakfast

Peter Drucker[48], one of the most highly praised management gurus of all time, once said: 'Culture eats strategy for breakfast. Over and over again!' By this, he meant that no matter how strong the strategy of an organisation might be, it will never be possible to implement it in the desired manner as long it does not match the organisational culture it serves.

This section is therefore about the final part of our House of Noble Purpose: the strategy and tactics to achieve it. Together, these form the organisation's 'what'. You can see them as the rooms of the house, symbolically enclosed by the roof of your noble purpose and the walls and foundations of your culture. Or to put it more simply: no meaningful strategy is possible without a culture and a noble purpose.

If we at GINPI have made a substantial contribution towards changing the mentality of leaders and transforming their way of inspiring others, then we have done so in the first place by persuading them to see the value of this philosophy. And in keeping with the philosophy, we teach them how to act in pursuit of a powerful and appropriate noble purpose. For me, noble purpose must be the leading force in any organisational system and the strategy must be aligned with this force, and not the other way around. In other words, we have turned the traditional business model on its head. It is no longer strategy that leads the way, with everything else following; strategy is now inspired by a noble purpose and achieved through a matching culture.

In other words, noble purpose is the reliable compass that guides the organisation in the right direction. The purpose of the strategy is to make sure that this direction can be followed. And when the weather becomes stormy and the seas get rough – perhaps through changing customer needs, organisational problems or unexpected market adjustments – you must be ready to trim the sails of your strategy accordingly, steering the best possible course that will allow you to get to the destination you have already set. It is important to remember that this course must not be random, but must be a course based on knowledge of the situation, a feel for shifting trends and a great deal of LovInShip. These are all variables, but from your ultimate destination – your noble purpose – you must never vary!

It goes without saying that strategy and tactics – the 'IT' dimension – nevertheless remain an essential part of any organisation. No company, department or individual can function effectively if the 'IT' has not been defined. Organisations that have a powerful noble purpose but fail to develop a strategy and the tactics that will allow them to realise it, will never progress beyond the realm of dreams and ideals. This is no use to anyone! For this reason, in our dealings with leaders we at GINPI focus on the urgent need to transform dreams and ideals into reality and to anchor them in a concrete manner by selecting the right series of positive actions. We do this by helping to define an appropriate organisational strategy, which serves the organisation's dreams and ideals, as expressed in their noble purpose.

Fortunately, there are many good examples of good examples to show you what I mean!

When Ernest Solvay,[49] the Belgian industrialist and chemist, in 1861 developed a procedure for the large-scale production of sodium carbonate (soda salt), he had much more in mind than the 'simple' realisation of a vision. His scientific ambition was transformed by the right strategy into what has now become the worldwide Solvay[50] concern.

In 1976, Anita Roddick[51] founded The Body Shop[52] in Brighton, a cosmetics company dedicated to the production and sale of ethically responsible beauty products. At the time, this linking of cosmetics with a moral standpoint was a revolutionary approach. But Roddick had a clear vision of what she wanted and started The Body Shop in a modest store with just 15 product lines. She later opened a first franchise in Brussels and her company eventually grew into a world-famous chain with numerous branches, its own production facilities and more than 300 different product lines. In 2006, the entire organisation was sold to the French L'Oréal group. In 1990, Roddick founded Children On The Edge, a charity for helping deprived children in Eastern Europe and Asia.

Elon Musk[53], the South African-born multi-entrepreneur, is sometimes depicted by his critics as being nothing more than a dreamer with a few screws loose. In fact, this kind of thing is often said about forward-looking thinkers and visionaries, because the ordinary mass of people is not (yet) able to understand their futuristic insights and their desire to help both society and the world. But Elon Musk is anything but crazy. Many of his dreams and revolutionary visions are currently changing our way of thinking about our planet, particularly in the fields of mobility, payments and energy. What he has achieved with PayPal, Tesla, SolarCity, SpaceX, the hyperloop and many other ideas is nothing short of outstanding.

However, Musk is by no means unique. There is no shortage of entrepreneurs or people who didn't see themselves as entrepreneurs, but did very entrepreneurial things, who have brought about great changes, thanks to a brilliant strategy linked to a noble purpose: Thomas Edison, Henry Ford, Coco Chanel, Walt Disney, Richard Branson, Steve Jobs, Bill Gates, Oprah Winfrey, Jeff Bezos, J.K. Rowling, Jack Ma, Paul Polman, to name but a few.

Nor is this combination of strategy and vision confined to the world of business. In the mid-20th century, Nelson Rolihlahla Mandela,[54] the South African freedom fighter and politician, led the call for the abolition of apartheid in his country. Strange as it may seem today, this humanist conviction – that people of different races and colours should be treated equally – was regarded as being revolutionary at the time. But for Mandela, this conviction was more than a just dream and he was prepared to put his Life on the line for his beliefs, although his actions were always peaceful. In 1963, he was arrested, tried and sentenced to life in prison. Even so, he never lost his faith in the rightness of his cause and continued to focus on what would one day happen in the future: the ending of apartheid. His strategy was based on remaining respectful to those who held him captive, while simultaneously seeking to bring about a non-violent change of mentality in world opinion. In 1990, he was finally released and his political party – the ANC – was legalised. In 1993, Mandela, together with the South African president, F.W. de Klerk, was awarded the Nobel Prize for Peace, for their joint efforts to bring about a peaceful end to the apartheid regime and for laying the foundations for a new and democratic South Africa. In 1994, he was elected as the first black president of the country he had always continued to regard as his homeland. It was the culmination of one of the most remarkable stories in the 20th century.

Once again, there is a long list of other political leaders, social visionaries and spiritual inspirers who have used powerful strategy to turn their vision into a reality: Martin Luther King, Gandhi, Angela Merkel, Pope Francis, Barack Obama, Bono, Geoffrey

Canada, the Dalai Lama, Christine Lagarde, Al Gore, Angelina Jolie, Mary Robinson, and many more.

And in order to realise your dreams and ideals, in whatever field, you need a strategy that can be given a boost by your own behaviour as leader and by the behaviour of others in your organisation.

In 2011, as part of an important intervention we carried out for the leading HR community of the international French bank, Société Générale, I had conversations with a number of the bank's management board directors and with the CEO, Frédéric Oudéa. The main focus of the discussions was the implementation of a new strategic plan that McKinsey had developed some time earlier for the group. From a visionary and a technical perspective, the strategy seemed excellent. It took account of all the relevant market trends, proposed the necessary new segmentation and identified growth potential in specific countries and regions. This entailed a significant degree of reorganisation at Société Générale. But after the implementation of the initial stages of the five-year plan and abundant communication on the subject, things had not yet been fully achieved as the CEO would have liked. So, what was wrong? I soon discovered that the culture of the organisation had not been sufficiently attuned to the new strategy they wanted to pursue. At that time, the SG culture was dominated by many egos, having a silo mentality and pushing for inter- departmental competition, and by people who very often worked for the bank because it was a guarantee for climbing the social ladder. In this kind of rationally-led organisation, it was a complex task to try and make everyone see that, to be a success, the new strategy had to be supported by the internal culture and a noble purpose. There was still huge potential in the organisation and many good people still worked there. But in our analysis, we concluded that Société Générale had lost years of market strength and efficiency through its failure to act quickly enough to adjust its organisational culture to match the direction in which the leadership wanted to travel.

This was regrettable, but what is currently happening to the American Sears chain of department stores is much worse and seemingly irreversible. Founded in Chicago in 1893, the company has lost many millions in recent years as a result of a series of disastrous strategic decisions. When Eddie Lampert, the former CEO, decided in 2005 to merge Sears with Kmart, the focus was placed primarily on clever financial engineering to create a financial added value. It is open to question whether or not this was a wise strategy, since the results do not make it clear. It is certain, however, that it would have been a better strategy to make the investment in both brands that they urgently needed. The company also missed the e-commerce train, so that important business was lost to their main rivals, including Home Depot and Lowe's. Sears is now on the point of bankruptcy. A 125-year icon is set to disappear, and all because of strategic errors and a short-sightedness that ignored the values of the company culture, which had proved their relevance long before Eddie Lampert ever arrived on the scene.

Organisations are often led on the basis of this kind of short-term perspective. Too few leaders think seriously about the impact of their actions on the longer future. For this reason, I believe the time has come to think about inviting the younger generations into the boardroom.

Inviting the next generation into the boardroom

'Too many people overvalue what they are not and undervalue what they are.' (Malcolm Forbes)

In this chapter on Houses of Noble Purpose, we have discussed the importance of noble purpose, the need for the right organisational culture and the role of strategy.

I would like to finish this section with a philosophical observation that in my opinion is by no means irrelevant.

Let me start with the questions I often ask leaders who have doubts about their willingness to transform their organisations on the basis of a noble purpose. These questions are as follows. What would it mean if your organisation would no longer exist in 10, 20 or 50 years time? How would the environment in which you operate, no matter how big or small, be different? To what extent would people miss the things for which your organisation stands?

Remarkably enough, no leader ever says that his company will not be relevant, that the world will not be different and that people will not miss them. But if I dig deeper, a more nuanced picture starts to emerge. If I question them closely about the relevance of what they do, about alternative products and rival organisations that are emerging, and about possible economic and societal paradigm shifts, I often see the first signs of confusion and fear start to appear. Confusion about the best way to move forward. Fear about the potential finiteness of their organisation if they carry on as they are currently doing. With all the changes that the world is facing in the years ahead, leaders need to ask themselves much more often: why do we do what we do?

This question is designed to offer an answer to what has been the essence of this chapter: how can we build organisations that are successfully sustainable by virtue of the manner in which people in those organisations are able to realise themselves through the added value they create in the service of a better, more harmonious and finer society. In other words, in the service of an inspiring and authentic noble purpose.

Put simply, this is a question about the future. About the future of our children and their children. About the world in which they will play, grow up, work, live and die. About the society in which we hope that the positive effects of what we are doing with our organisations now will be seen and felt in concrete terms. About how we today can make a worthwhile contribution to the hopes and dream of tomorrow.

Everything that we, organisational leaders with impact, now do must be done with respect for the current and future generations. The time for thinking only about ourselves is over! The focus on short-term success and material gain no longer works! The call for change and positive action from the young people of the world is getting louder and louder. And they are right!

For this reason, I would like to give the world's leaders a piece of valuable advice: leave an empty chair at your boardroom table. A very important and special chair. Because this chair represents the future generations. I would also advise them to fix a name card to this chair, so that no-one forgets who is sitting there. The future generations must be given a symbolic voice in every boardroom. By daring to ask these generations what they think about the decisions that are on the table, leaders will be able to take a very different approach not only to how they make those decisions, but also to strategy, to the things for which they stand, and how they wish to be remembered.

Asking the question about what future generations will think of the men and women who direct the organisations of today is both purifying and humbling. It compels directors to take socially relevant and correct decisions without delay.

In short, if we wish to make the House of Noble Purpose methodology truly relevant and to allow it to have maximum impact, we need to ask ourselves and keep on asking ourselves how our Houses of Noble Purpose can best be organised and used to serve the interests of future generations.

6

A World of noble purpose

'Nothing is more dangerous than an evil thought in the mind of a fool.' (Karl M. Verstraeten)

Because people realise themselves through meaningful work in organisations that are driven by a noble purpose; because organisations will become ecosystems which, also driven by a noble purpose, will attract people who will in this manner achieve self-realisation; because people need organisations and organisations need people; because of all these things, we need to build a society that facilitates, encourages and supports this interdependency.

When individuals, organisations and society are all aligned around a noble purpose, ably led by holistic and long-term thinking leaders from the national and international world of politics, from the public sphere and from the media, who aspire to raise humankind to the next level of its evolution, only then will it be possible, in my opinion, to drastically change our world and push it in a more positive and hopeful direction.

When I speak about political leaders, I mean mayors, governors, members of parliament, government ministers, premiers, presidents and heads of state. When I speak about leaders in the public sphere, I mean the heads of multinational organisations like the UN, the EU and NATO, but also the leaders of international federations or NGOs, like FIFA, UEFA, the International Olympic Committee, the Red Cross, Doctors Without Frontiers, Greenpeace, etc., but not forgetting the top people in every other kind of organisation, whether great or small.

In this chapter, I will describe how noble purpose can and must be made to serve the interests of humankind and society and will suggest ways in which this can be achieved.

The beast is dying

Let us first take a look at how things stand today. To do this, I would like to refer to an article I wrote back in 2016, when I was the vice-chairman of LEAD-IN, which at that time was the Belgian think-tank for leadership. What did I conclude then and what do I believe now?

Worldwide, we are seeing enormous shifts in society and in the way political and societal leaders are viewed. Our current systems (organisations, governments, political parties, religious institutions, NGOs, etc.) are losing the plot and are increasingly confronted with a feeling of chaos and their own impotence. This leads to ever-growing discontentment and to visible societal frustration and pain. These developments are reported in great detail and even further encouraged by the media, which set a focus on everything that is going wrong.

I regard this as evidence that the world order is undergoing a seminal transformation, in which the old is slowly but surely being replaced by the new. And as with every transformation, in which the deep identity of the transforming system is substituted by a new identity, with no possibility of returning to the old ways, so this societal transformation will also be experienced as painful. What's more, this pain will be accompanied by unrest, tumult, opposition, exasperation and violence. The caterpillar is turning into a butterfly, gradually but irreversibly.

I compare the tension, discomfort and uncertainty resulting from this intense societal transformation with the demise of a kind of prehistoric monster. This monster was able to grow unchallenged for many years, allowing it to become powerful but also resulting in huge societal distortion. It is the symbol for an era when roaring to demonstrate your power was normal, when everyone with a different opinion was shouted down (or worse) and when the only focus – either from a selfish survival instinct or from a more predatory hunter instinct – was on your own path through the jungle.

But humankind, people, are becoming more self-aware and more vocal, are less afraid to stand up for the things and the principles that mean something to them, and are better informed than ever before by the virtual connections we now all have with each other. As a result, they have had enough of the kind of leaders who keep the 'monster' alive by feeding it with human sacrifices. Men and women are now starting to question this old world order. The scales have fallen from their eyes and they can now see the old system – the monstrous beast! – for what it is, with all its many uncertainties, imbalances and injustices. They realise that there is an urgent need for a new system, in which transparency, sustainability, respect, citizenship and general well-being must be the central pillars. Growing awareness of the discrepancy between the old and the new, and the fear that this engenders, cuts people to the quick. It is this that has prompted them first to resist and then to actively fight in whatever way they can against the old system, in the hope that a new and better system will emerge.

The monster is now being fought more fiercely and more openly by those many people who wish to join together to rid the world of the evils of the past. All this human effort is causing the monster to totter, as it struggles – with increasing hopelessness – against the ever growing power of new social order. Its frantically beating heart, a symptom of its last desperate attempt to gather together its remaining energy for the final battle of survival, will soon give out, conquered by the incessant and unquenchable spirit of humankind, which wants to see something new in its place.

It is against this background that we are seeing increasing criticism of the inefficiency and ineffectiveness of institutions like the European Union, the United Nations and NATO. The same groundswell of opinion also explains the backlash of the majority against narcissistic potentates like Trump, Erdogan, Putin, Assad and Orban. The advent and rapid growth of political parties on the far right and other extremist groups, which offer people spurious 'assurances' and attempt to convince them of the danger of 'the other', raises even bigger questions, which we fail to address at our peril. This is why climate change deniers are being challenged by a growing number of ordinary people; why criticism is also growing of selfish entrepreneurs and billionaires, who only think of themselves and the interests of their own organisations, while shamelessly raping responsible economic principles, society and the planet; why the *gilets jaunes*, the *podemos* and the anti-globalist have all grown from small groups of pioneers into full-scale popular movements.

All these tendencies are proof of a society in rapid evolution; a society that is looking for a new and more humane world order, with more respect, less chaos and better leaders. All the outrages of the old system, with the inefficiencies of its leaders and the extremist rantings of its politicians, are simply the last symbolic thrashings of a dying monster that is bleeding to death.

It is high time for a new group of political and public leaders to come to the fore, acting in the genuine interests of society as a whole and using this noble purpose to develop, at the very least, a medium-term vision for the future as builders of a new world order.

A new paradigm

'If you believe it will work out, you'll see opportunities. If you believe it won't, you will see obstacles.' (Wayne Dyer)

Even if we might have the feeling that we are living in difficult times, many important parameters are nevertheless still positive. General prosperity and global well-being have made huge progress during the past century. The gap between rich and poor has been significantly reduced and the general health of the majority of humankind is now better than it has ever been. In other words, people are not only living for longer but are also enjoying a better quality of Life. At the same time, illiteracy has fallen, access to information is almost universal and the chances of a newborn child dying from hunger or disease have been limited (but, sadly, not yet eradicated).

In the meantime, the industrial revolution has been replaced by the technological and knowledge revolutions. The quantum leap forward created by artificial intelligence, robotics, innovation, new economic concepts, social awareness and the information goldmine of the internet has set in motion an evolutionary process the like of which (and the speed of which) the world has never seen. And as part of this stratospheric evolution, there is one other element whose crucial importance we must not overlook: the value of noble purpose. The questions about why we live and what quality we want to give to that Life are fundamental. For me, the manner in which we will be able to evolve towards a noble purpose-driven humankind, society and world are just as vitally relevant as the evolution from an agrarian to an industrial society that took place some 250 years ago. Some people may find it utopian to argue that the world must become a giant House of Noble Purpose. But why shouldn't it? What is stopping it? Who doesn't want to live in a society and on a planet where everything is viewed from the perspective of whether it has meaning and whether it can contribute to the general good? Just as people in organisations where the work is meaningful are happier and more engaged than people working in organisations where the work is transactional, ephemeral and material-driven, so citizens in towns, regions and countries where long-term collective interests take precedence over short-term political egotism will also feel happier and more hopeful than citizens elsewhere.

The criticism that this ideal is 'utopian' is often expressed by those who draw their energy from negativism and the power of impossibility. These are people who do not have the vision, strength or personal inner harmony to contribute to a noble purpose-inspired city, administration, society or international institution. Besides, 'utopian' does not necessarily means impossible: this is what they said to Martin Luther King, Mahatma Gandhi, Nelson Mandela, Vigdis Finnbogadottir, Simone Veil, Michael Gorbatchov, Benazir Bhutto, Muhammad Yunus and so many others, who succeeded in turning an existing paradigm on its head or throwing it completely overboard. These were all enlightened souls who were not put off by the supposedly utopian or (in some eyes) 'undesirable' nature of what they were planning, but instead achieved great things, even in some cases at the cost of their own Life.

It is my hope that the concept of societal noble purpose, which at the present time might seem utopian to some, will one day, like the ideas of the great thinkers of the past, also become a reality.

I want noble purpose to become the cement of parliaments, societies, economies and all the other fundamental systems that shape the direction of the world in which we live, work, play, grow old and die. The place of noble purpose in the world is of the very greatest importance, forming as it must the basis for future progress, prosperity, peace and joy.

Without having the pretension or the desire to be a King, Gandhi or Mandela, but firm in my belief that noble purpose is ultra-essential for the further positive evolution of humankind, I am convinced that the years ahead will be fascinating and groundbreaking ones, in which the momentum we need to make a paradigm shift will be finally reached. This will be a revolutionary shift, which ensures that the things people need to be happy, connected and self-fulfilled, in symbiosis with others, the environment and nature, can be given to them, providing we make noble purpose central in everything we do.

A world of noble purpose

Let us first assume that a world of noble purpose is a question of transformation and evolution; the transformation of old mentalities and paradigms into a wholly new way of thinking and doing. Let us also assume that the evolution is progressive, not a big bang that will miraculously transform our existing purposeless society into a noble purpose society overnight. It will take time; people's hearts and minds need to be prepared, certainly for the scale of the irreversible changes that are necessary to build the kind of world I envisage.

In this noble purpose world, all major initiatives and all strategic decisions will be taken at all levels – local, regional, national, supranational, global – in relation to their ability to contribute to the measurable and sustainable evolution of all humankind, the society in which people live, and the planet on which we depend. And therefore no longer in the purely limited interests of a city, a region, a country, a public authority or an international organisation. In the mature noble purpose world the decisions of all governmental authorities, from the local to the international level, will be attuned to each other in function of the universal higher purpose. It will be a world where widespread hunger, disease and poverty will no longer be tolerated. The wasting of our natural and human resources will likewise no longer be accepted. The raping of nature and the planet (it is not without good reason that we call her Mother Earth) will be brought to an end, as will the exploitation of certain population groups. Discrimination on the basis of skin colour, gender, sexual preference, nationality, age, social origins or ethnicity will be eradicated. The abuse of children as sex slaves, sometimes with the knowledge and connivance of the authorities, will be eliminated. The encouragement of children to smoke, take drugs or drink unhealthy drinks will be outlawed. The overproduction of food – half of which is never even consumed and the other half of which goes to only a limited part of the world's population – will be abolished. The destruction of nature in the interest of a handful of companies will be prohibited. And so on.

Everything that governments, public authorities and supranational entities decide will be measured against the positive contribution they make to the noble purpose that each city, region, country or group of countries has defined. I am strongly in favour of the development of an organic system of collaboration for all authorities, from the most local to the most global, which must enable taking conscious decisions at all levels that contribute proactively to the paradigm shift towards a noble purpose-based society. Whatever is decided at one level must be attuned not only to its own noble purpose, but also to the universal noble purpose. This can only happen as a result of a paradigm shift, which will herald in a new age when, amongst many other things, slavery will no longer be tolerated, when CO_2 emissions will be radically reduced, when the use of harmful substances in foodstuffs has been forbidden and when the possession of nuclear weapons is strictly controlled or abolished.

And as the years and decades pass, so more and more adjustments to the universal noble purpose will take place. This must be broad enough and very clearly defined. It will not be enough to have a general slogan like 'a desire to serve the world's population'. This is, of course, a fine ambition, but it is too vague to be meaningful. Precisely how the world population can be served must be described in such a way that a contribution can be made at even the smallest operational level, which may only be a village or a community.

There must, of course, also be a mechanism for validating the noble purpose, just as there must be a mechanism for measuring its implementation. This implementation must be made of people's own free will, but with the knowledge that failure to implement will have a significant human, ecological and economic price, a price that must be substantially more than the cost of implementing the noble purpose in the first place. The payment of this price must be enforceable. There is no point in creating a kind of United Nations of noble purpose, where no-one is responsible for ensuring implementation and where there is no real recourse against those who block sensible and worthwhile proposals for their own selfish reasons.

Global joy index

In order to motivate political and public authorities to implement the noble purpose philosophy, one possibility is to use a Global Joy Index (GJI). This would measure at regular intervals and in accordance with a universally accepted methodology, the extent to which joy is present in each city, region, country or group of countries. Instead of using the gross national product or some other economic parameter as a yardstick of 'success', from now on we should use the GJI. This accurately determines the amount of holistic joy – in other words, joy across a broad range of factors – which is experienced by each inhabitant in each geographical unit. This takes due account of the quality of Life, the quality of work, how safe people feel, how much hope they have, and the presence of poverty, poor schooling and inadequate upbringing for young people. The different levels of joy must be made concrete and clearly defined in advance, so that there is no possibility of any ambiguity or inconsistency. These definitions must be linked to the realisation of the noble purpose of the geographical unit concerned, which in turn must then be linked to the universal noble purpose. In the future, progress will no longer be determined by the dominance of economic parameters, which are only of interest to part of the population, but by matters that are deeply felt by everyone who wants to live in decent and humane conditions: in other words, the amount of joy in Life. Of course, I am not saying that economic parameters are no longer important. What I am saying is that for far too long economic parameters have been the be-all and end-all of everything, so that for years, in my opinion, we have been measuring the wrong things. Above all, we have been staring blindly at economic growth, but without seeing the negative side of this 'success': sickness, burn-out, psychological dysfunction and the huge discrepancy between who people are and what they do.

If we have an active working population worldwide, 85 percent of whom do not feel connected to what they do each day or to the organisation that employs them, then we must conclude that this is not simply an economic problem, but first and foremost a massive social problem, the costs of which are incalculable. Economic growth has boomed dramatically during the past 100 years, but work happiness and the welfare of people in the workplace have not been able to keep pace. It is certainly true that there is less outright slavery, exploitation and abuse than a century ago, but there is still far too much 'modern' slavery, too much economic exploitation, and too little pride, satisfaction and happiness in the way the majority of people are expected to work. This is a huge challenge for the political and public actors of the future.

Harmony

As a result of this purely economic logic, which has had an ever-present and dominating influence so far throughout the history of humankind and society, certain interested parties developed a very short-term form of reasoning, which they turned into an equally short-term approach to strategy, serving only their own purposes. This led to the growth of different needs between the different layers and classes of society, so that it became normal for one class to exploit another. Large and often contradictory interests began to emerge between minorities and majorities in individual countries or regions, and also between national and international players on the world stage. At the same time, some groups had full access to information, knowledge, knowledge acquisition, decision-making powers and power in general, while other groups had no access at all. Some groups even developed strategies to deliberately keep other groups starved of information or to feed them information that was wrong. The division of society into the 'haves' and the 'have nots', and the self-proclaimed 'right' of the haves to decide what should happen to the have nots, resulted in major forms of dehumanisation, creating in their wake growing inequality, tension, fear and the disappearance of hope.

I said earlier that it is no longer acceptable that one part of the world should live in relative luxury, while the other part of the world lives in abject poverty. It is no longer tolerable that children in some countries have no access to clean water, while children in other countries play in swimming pools filled with it. It is no longer morally permissible that some parts of the world show great concern for human rights, for the rights of women and the rights of the LGBT community, while in other parts of the world people are being imprisoned or even killed because of their ideas, race, gender or sexual orientation. We can no longer stand idly by and watch how some countries and regions treat the environment with great respect, while others contaminate and exploit it, as though there were no such things as global warming and a hole in the ozone layer. I could go on like this for some time. The key point is that over the years the harmony that is inherently present in the completeness of our being human, in our human relations and in nature, has been ignored, eliminated and despoiled. What's more, this disharmony has become institutionalised in systems, official bodies, public authorities and parliaments. As a result, disharmony is now the rule rather than the exception, and forms the basis for the power and legitimacy of many political and public leaders.

If we wish to install noble purpose in society and the world, we must first restore harmony in that society and the world. This means first restoring harmony in the hearts and minds of our political and public leaders. This will require a huge paradigm switch, whereby people consciously evolve from fear and division to acceptance, inclusion and holistic thinking. The power of harmony is the power we will need to make progress towards our noble purpose ideology. Put simply, there can be no noble purpose without harmony – and the harmony I envisage is one that involves all stakeholders, by which I mean local, regional, national, supranational and global leaders, together with all other authorities that fall under their jurisdiction.

Collective before individual

This means that individual political and public interests must be subordinated to the common interest. This immediately introduces an important new parameter into society, which will then be transformed from one based on division and polarity to a new version that is based on (and will further evolve from) the power of the collective.

I am not saying that we should pretend in future that there are no such things as differences. That would be naive and dishonest. There will always be differences between races, between the sexual preferences of heteros and homos, between people who want to work for others and those who wish to be self-employed, between cultures from the North and the South, etc. These differences are both wonderful and necessary: they are what make us so much more tolerant, human and interesting, more special as people and more fascinating in our interactions. Differences are simply differences, no more and no less. It is thanks to our existing differences that we humans have been able to develop (and will continue to develop) various visions of Life, which has made it possible for us to evolve more quickly and more effectively as a species. These differences do not automatically imply 'better than' or 'worse than'. Just because someone is different from us, this does not mean that they are wrong. Just as we are not wrong, if we are the ones who are different. We share our differences with each other, and that is what makes the world such an exciting and cosmopolitan place, a universal patchwork of diversity.

The political and public leaders of this world must build constellations in which differences are welcome, providing these differences contribute to our positive progress and evolution. Women must have just as many rights as men. White-skinned people must not be seen as being more or better than those with yellow, black or brown skin. Homosexuals must have just as much right to be proud of their sexual orientation as heterosexuals and bisexuals. Of course, it goes almost without saying that differences between people and groups must never be allowed to result in the limitation of one group by another. For example, using the Koran to spread violence and hatred, with the intention of dividing cultures and religions, rather than bringing them together, is wholly unacceptable. Likewise, the proclamation of laws that restrict the voting rights, the free choice of career and the autonomy and integrity of women within the family system are equally abhorrent, even though such legislation is still firmly embedded in the cultures of some countries. This also applies to the use of young children as cheap labour in some regions of Asia, Africa and Latin America, where again it is part of local tradition and custom. Just as despicable is the tendency in many lands to deny the LGBT community the free choice and free expression of their love. And I could go on like this for hours. In short, our new noble purpose world will need to be aware that any population group, ethnic group, culture or society that argues in favour of limiting the rights of others, simply because they do not conform to their tradition, is potentially dangerous and harmful, if this tradition preaches discrimination, exclusion or the denial of the right for people to evolve. How can this problem be solved? There is only one answer. We need to develop a new and universal way of thinking that embraces the concept of evolution, while at the same time valuing the concept of diversity.

Serving humankind, society & the world

What is the reason for our existence? Is it trivial and random, or does it have some deeper meaning? I believe in a deeper meaning. I believe that people must try to develop the best possible meaningful existence for themselves in the service of the collective. I believe that each of the 8 billion of us on earth has an important role to play in helping to create a better and more balanced society, in which evolution, harmony, sustainability and joy will be the results. To make this possible, we must use all the resources that are available to us as human beings, not least our intelligence, our willpower, our skill and our resilience. We must do this with respect and from a sense of sustainable inter-connectedness, in symbiosis with nature and the animals. The interests of our individual units of existence, starting with us human beings, must be made subordinate to the general good, by which I mean the general good of the whole, the earth, the universe and nature. If we persist in developing systems of production in a manner and at a pace that risks damaging our own precious resources, we are committing a crime against the universal laws of harmony. In this sense, the climate crisis is not just about the climate, but is a symptom of a deeper crisis in humankind, a humankind that can no longer see or no longer cares that our humane and ecological ecosystem is the source of and basis for our continued existence on this planet.

This brings me to the noble purpose that each of us must have, whether we are worker, director or head of state; whether we are black, white, red or yellow; whether we are Jew, Christian, Muslim or Hindu; whether we are man or woman; whether we live in the city or in the countryside; whether we are rich or poor, aristocratic or commoner; whether we were born in Niger or in Belgium, in Canada, or Iceland, on the Maldives or in Spain. There is a reason why every one of us was brought into this Life. And depending on our social, societal and geopolitical context and on our own sense of purpose and willpower, we will each of us be able to realise, to a greater or lesser extent, the things that are inherent in that reason, things that go beyond our own mere self-interest and make possible our connectedness with a noble purpose.

If we wish to transcend our own self-interest in this way, it is first necessary to have our basic material needs satisfied in terms of health, food, education, shelter and security. At the same time, everyone on earth must also be given the opportunity to develop and satisfy their higher (than basic) needs. In my opinion, all political and public leaders therefore have an obligation to use their role and responsibilities to make a contribution towards the personal development of every person, via the principles of universal harmony and noble purpose. This further implies that they must translate this obligation into concrete measures and applications for each city, region, country or group of countries of which they have charge.

Put simply, this chapter is about the way that public and political leaders must be inspired to use their noble purpose to make a better society and a better world, by first bringing harmony into their own Life and then into the systems for which they are responsible and in the contexts and places where they are able to influence people.

From political LeadershiT to political humanity

This evolution will only be possible if political and public leaders start to act with a high degree of self-awareness and self-respect, and display within themselves a deep affinity with the warm universal principles of appreciation and humanity. Whoever feels in this manner a sense of responsibility towards the general good and has respect for the universal laws of harmony, will be sure act on the basis of exalted thinking and collective engagement. Once this paradigm shift has taken place in the heart and minds of our leaders – so that their own interests and needs or the interests and needs of small groups give way to the wider interests of humankind (no matter how local or global) – it is to be expected that this will lead to a general paradigm shift among the world's population. But to achieve this, the leaders will first need to leave their own fears behind and learn how to take action based on hope.

In the chapter on BlooderShip in the section on Houses of Noble Purpose, I spoke about LeadershiT. I explained how business leaders often carry across the 'shit' they experienced during their youth into their organisations, and how this then finds expression in their leadership. This same principle applies to political and public leaders. Each political leader has his or her own past, a rucksack of experiences that will help or hinder him or her to become an effective statesman or woman, working for the benefit of the general good and the realisation of a noble purpose. Whoever enters politics or public Life as a leader is obliged to inspire others and encourage them to reach a higher level of achievement. Consequently, we do not expect our public leaders to sow division, promote fear or take away hope. Whoever takes on a political or public role is also obliged to serve the interests of humankind, and not his or her own interests or the interests of a small elite. Consequently, we expect our leaders to be humane, wise and motivating. Why do we expect these things? Because what they do and the policies they pursue will have a huge impact on us all. This impact can be either positive or negative. To show what I mean, here are some pairs of opposites: Barack Obama versus Donald Trump; Nelson Mandela versus Jacob Zuma; Mikhail Gorbatsjov versus Vladimir Putin; Aung San Suu Kyi versus Thein Sein; Angela Merkel versus Adolf Hitler. In other words, it is highly desirable – essential, in fact – that our leaders are good people, who have a clear noble purpose for society. It is the level of awareness and humanity in our political and public leaders that determines the level of awareness and humanity they will be able to inject into society. Or to put it in slightly different terms: whoever takes on an impactful role in the political or public arena usually does so on the basis of the things that strongly inspire, influence or concern him or her. A leader who yearns for recognition, will pursue a policy of recognition. A leader who is plagued by fear and doubt, will pursue a divisive policy devoid of hope and expressed in radical language. In contrast, a leader who believes in the power of collectivism and our ability to find creative and collaborative solutions for problems will pursue a policy of respect, humanism and tolerance.

The political and public leaders, who are first and foremost human beings, must therefore learn how to deal with others and with each other in a purer, deeper, fairer and more meaningful way. They owe this to themselves as impactful leaders; they owe it to our present-day society, which is desperately searching for meaning; and they owe it to future generations, whose fate is always in the hands of the political and public leaders of their past.

In my view of the world, each human being has four bodies: physical, mental, emotional and spiritual. I assume that in principle – by which I mean when our basic human needs have been satisfied – each and every one of us is capable of connecting with our spiritual body, the body where our noble purpose is housed. For this reason, I expect the political and public leaders of the future, because of the importance of their role and the level of their societal impact, to make contact with this spiritual body. This is the only way in which they can increase the level of their consciousness and their humanity, so that they can act in the general interest and to the benefit of their noble purpose. This will lead to the development of strategies and the taking of decisions that will build a new society in which every once can live in a decent manner.

Reinventing politics

Political leadership must become a calling, a temporary calling to bring about substantial change in the service of the general good. It must cease to be an institutionalised, life-long, paid occupation. Political leaders must be chosen through democratic systems and must be held accountable on the basis their step-by-step realisation of the policy for which they have been given a mandate. I no longer expect political leaders to say one thing before their election and then to say or do something else afterwards (often immediately afterwards). Nor do I expect them to change course somewhere along the way, claiming that the context has changed or that they have been forced by others or by circumstances. If they wish to alter their policy away from the mandate they have received, they must first check their new proposals against the general good and then seek the permission of their citizens and any others who may be involved.

I further expect political leaders to stop telling lies. If they persist, based on an objective lie-detection system, they should be demoted or turned out of office. It is no longer acceptable to say things that then fail to match what is effectively done. Or that things are done which are not explained or indeed cannot be explained afterwards. This is a straightforward question of taking responsibility. In my opinion, a politician who sends a tweet with a false accusation or an inappropriate comment, even if he later says that this was never his intention, has no place in the new kind of politics we need in our new society. If the British politician Nigel Farage, someone who is no stranger to a lie or two (not least in the Brexit referendum of 2016), attacks a highly respectable man like Herman Van Rompuy, who at that time was the first President of Europe, by saying that he has all the charisma of a damp rag, then I believe that Farage should have his political mandate withdrawn. If Donald Trump, a man from the same mould as Farage but in a super-charged form, continues to talk and act in the same offensive, divisive and unpresidential way, then I hope that he will be systematically declared an irrelevant *persona non grata* by his own people and by the rest of the world. If the Saudi crown prince, Mohammed bin Salman, (almost certainly) had the journalist Jamal Kashoggi murdered and dismembered in his country's embassy in Istanbul, then he must be made to face the hard consequences of his actions, so that this kind of disgusting practice can be publically condemned and shamed. The time has come in the world when we must be prepared to challenge, correct and sanction the things that are unjust, unfair or downright wrong.

From now on, I expect the words and deeds of all political and public leaders to be beyond reproach. Whoever takes on the most responsible role in society – the guidance and fulfilment of our fellow man – cannot do so half-heartedly or without the necessary feeling for nuance and respect. Their way of doing things must be characterised by a high degree of awareness and humanity. Together with entrepreneurs, philosophers, artists, scientists and researchers, they are amongst the most powerful and inspirational forces in our society, and their noble purpose must encourage people to greater respect for themselves, respect for others and respect for nature.

Continuing my list of expectations, I also expect that political leaders will stop contradicting and blaming each other. If you analyse recent political campaigns and debate, they essentially boil down to promising the earth to voters, while castigating other parties for failing to understand, doing it wrong or not listening to the electorate. To my mind, this is evidence of a redundant political system that has had its day and is totally lacking a powerful noble purpose. Whoever acts on behalf of a noble purpose, which for a political leader by definition must be to the benefit of humankind and society as a whole, does not need to lower himself or herself to the level of cheap accusations and insults. Instead, I expect political leaders to focus constantly on their noble purpose, how it can serve the general good, and how they propose to bring this about. They must stop focusing (as is currently the case) on trying to get the better of their opponents. Rather than attempting to prove the 'unsuitability' of these opponents, the politics of the future must concentrate on the authentic pursuit of an own noble purpose, which is clearly visible in the coherent Life of the politician concerned. The time has come for politicians to define their policies exclusively in terms of their noble purpose and how it can contribute to the general good. We must put behind us empty promises and opposition for opposition's sake. Our society needs to move forward, and this requires a positive rather than a negative political approach. Or as they say in English: 'Instead of opposing, start proposing!'

This brings me to another important point. We need to get away from 'zero-sum' politics, whereby one side wins and the other side loses. This philosophy of 'everything for me and nothing for the rest' is no longer appropriate in this day and age. I therefore expect politicians to find ways to work together with each other, if necessary in shifting alliances and majorities. They must take account of all the relevant parameters, and not just their own party political parameters. They must involve all stakeholders and ensure that they are able to work towards the realisation of a common goal, each on the basis of their own abilities. Politicians must stop wasting all their time and resources on working against each other, instead of doing all they can together to increase the size of the societal cake of opportunities. They must serve the interests of us all, rather than simply trying to satisfy their own supporters or boost their own image.

For this reason, we need to find the largest possible common political denominator, but must be careful that it does not become so vague and all-embracing that everyone can find something positive in it, but only at the cost of it failing to make a contribution towards the solving of real problems that benefit the common good. If, for instance, serious climate objectives are set, I assume that there will be no deviation from these objectives, even if this means that certain vested interests need to give ground. Once decisions have been agreed and taken, they must be honoured. This is part of the same principle that makes the parts subservient to the whole. In the same way, the health of the population must take priority over everything, including the interests of certain industries and certain types of economic logic. This approach would put an end to many of the ridiculous things we see in politics today. How is it possible, for example, that politicians encourage people to stop smoking without tackling the tobacco and other related industries, and putting an end to their repugnant economic activities. Of course, the role played by the politicians in all this is equally repugnant. They fail to take action to stop the terrible consequences of smoking, resulting in countless deaths each year, simply because they cannot see an alternative to plug he whole in their budget that tobacco so conveniently fills.

Equally illogical, if less dramatic in its effect, is the policy of offering employees healthier alternative ways to travel to and from their work, but without putting a stop to the practice that sees organisations provide company cars, for which they also receive fiscal benefits. In the new era of politics, I expect that political leaders will have the courage and the determination to put an end to this kind of nonsense. For example, I expect that they will sit around the table with the food industry to determine health norms in respect of the calorific composition of foodstuffs, which all concerned will then apply coherently and consistently to the benefit of world public health. I also expect the same high standards from the leaders of other national and international organisations such as FIFA and the IOC, organisations that represent an exalted ideal and have the ability to influence billions of people positively, by again coherently and consistently applying the highest ethical and humane principles, in a manner that makes clear that they condemn all possible conflicts of interest, including self-interest. The assuming of a political or public leadership role is of such huge importance that the thoughts, words and deeds of such leaders must be beyond reproach and must display a noble purpose of the very highest order.

For me, the noble purpose-driven politics of the future must therefore search together with every possible stakeholder, no matter how great or small, for sustainable and positive solutions that serve the needs of humankind, society and the world. The starting point for this new politics must be collectivism and the desire to further enhance and improve this collectivism through a non-stop collaborative process, but without naivety and without falling back into bad habits. By believing in the possibility of this new kind of politics, new political and public leaders will emerge who will once again do things that we are no longer used to, even though they were often done by the more inspiring leaders of the past.

Making the impossible possible

Just as Martin Luther King, Gandhi, Mandela and numerous others leaders have achieved the most remarkable things, so I expect the political and public leaders of the future to seek, determine and pursue a noble purpose, even if most people regard them as impracticable or even impossible. A calling of this kind is only reserved for men and women who are made of the sternest stuff and live their Lives according to noble principles. Their authenticity and integrity must be beyond question. Being average or even good is not enough; they must be outstanding.

I expect that leaders in the new paradigm will appeal to the universal principles of respect, humanity and humanism. They must have the courage to stand up for these principles and for other clear moral points of view that will not always be easy to explain or implement, knowing that this is the best way to serve the general good in both the medium and long term. The short term does not interest them; they are thinking of the future. For this reason, their arguments will be based on honesty and transparency, not on manipulation and corruption.

This is not an unachievable utopia. It is what humankind in the 21st century badly needs, and therefore we must all work to make it a reality. We must raise our banners high in optimism, not lower them in pessimism. New hope needs to be injected into society and into people's hearts. All forms of intolerance must be banished. We must no longer be willing to tolerate the intolerable. The dominance of the economic paradigm that makes possible a multitude of abuses – some hidden, some open – must be broken. It demands courage and determination to go against current trends of long-standing, but it is now the only right thing to do. This means that our new leaders will be required to take huge steps, perhaps even giant leaps forward and they will need to hold fast to the principles of humane and universal integrity, if they wish to succeed. Because these are the principles that will ultimately bring harmony back into society and the world.

It will not be easy to initiate the kind of paradigm shift that this involves, but if we stay where we are we can be certain that in the long run we will crash and burn against the wall of our own finiteness. It is much better that principled and inspired men and women should now stand up and come to the fore, clear in their approach and determined to develop political strategies based on noble purpose as the best hope for all our futures.

Is there really hope? Of course there is! There are already clear correlations between politics based on long-term collective interests and feelings of satisfaction and joy in people's Lives. It is not without good reason that countries like Sweden, Norway, Denmark, Canada, Switzerland and Iceland, who all have a political decision-making process with a high collective focus, also have high GJI scores and broadly happy populations. In contrast, countries where the political leaders are notorious for their corruption and self-interest are nearly all at the bottom of the class when it comes to the level of joy and security among their often impoverished peoples.

Bringing noble purpose into town halls and parliaments

I expect our new political leaders to bring noble purpose into local town halls and national parliaments, where they must develop clear and explicit policies in pursuit of those purposes. It must become a new trend to unite citizens and stakeholders around the noble purpose of a city, region, country or group of countries.

Who does not want to live in a city or country where the political leaders talk inspirationally about the noble purpose that they have in mind for that city or country? Who would not want to take part in and help realise that noble purpose, even if in the short term a price has to be paid in order to reap the rewards in the long term?

The power of the media, 'new style'

I am well aware that much of what goes wrong today is the fault of the superficiality and manipulation of the media. And by that I do not mean just social media. I also mean newspapers, magazines and television. I expect that in the new noble purpose-driven paradigm the fourth estate, as the media are often called, will also make their contribution to noble purpose. They have a major obligation in this respect, by virtue of all the negative news and unnuanced reporting on which they have concentrated in the past, often at the expense of more positive messages.

The media need to think carefully about their future role in the informing and educating of people, and in particular their ability to boost levels of hope, while maintaining an accurate sense of reality. As one of society's most crucial stakeholders, the media must help positively to further build a new and noble purpose-based society, by developing in their readers, viewers and listeners a higher level of consciousness

It is too easy an excuse to say that bad news sells better than good news. And it is too ridiculous for words to argue that news items should be chosen on the basis of their likely popularity ratings. The media need to decide – and soon – whether or not they are serious about the role they want to play in the new society as an educating force for good, rather than the destructive force they currently are. This would require them to drop their focus on 'doom and gloom', switching instead to a priority on positive and praiseworthy initiatives and human dramas from which people can learn.

Politicians and the media also need to learn, so that they can work together to build a society that is founded on more exalted principles than the short-sightedness of self-interest and temporary economic success.

The key question is: which political, public and media leaders will be willing to take the difficult steps that can lead to this change of mentality – and therefore to a better society and world?

7

What now?

'Beauty is what remains when all else passes.'
(Vincent van Gogh)

We have seen that it is up to each of us to ask the key question about what we want to achieve in our Life and through our different roles and responsibilities in that Life.

Do we wish to contribute in some way or other to the positive evolution of humankind? Or do we only want to focus on our own self-interest? What are the personal motivations that will persuade us to make these essential choices?

We have also seen that living in accordance with a noble purpose offers us far more perspectives and can make us happier, more balanced and more fulfilled. We know from research that people achieve self-realisation through the work they carry out for organisations with a noble purpose to which they can make a real contribution. For this reason, all organisations must become Houses of Noble Purpose, where loving leadership rules and where appropriate strategy is embedded in a clear organisational culture.

To this end, organisations must be triggered by political leaders who wish to build a new society based on collective interests and the general good. In this noble purpose-driven society, different stakeholders will work together to achieve common objectives. There will no longer be an 'us against them' mentality. It will be replaced by an 'all for one and one for all' mentality to the benefit of the noble purpose.

My hope is that during the next two decades we will evolve into a world in which the majority of the power centres – cities, regions, countries and groups of countries – will base all their activities on a universal noble purpose. Where will we find this universal purpose? It is contained in the universal declaration of the rights of man, the universal principles of humanity and humanism, and the universal principles of sustainability and respect.

For me, noble purpose is both an objective and a philosophy of Life. It is thanks to noble purpose that humankind, society and the world will make progress in a respectful and sustainable manner. Why? Because a noble purpose is never against something or someone; it is always for something or someone, based on the conviction that every person and every organisation has something unique to offer, which must be realised to the benefit of all.

This makes necessary a local, regional, national and supranational mentality that focuses on the collective and the general good. This is something else that the installation of a noble purpose can achieve.

The time has come for us to regard a noble purpose as a basic right of every human being.

The time has come for us to regard noble purpose as the inspiring new economic principle of every organisation.

The time has come for us to regard noble purpose as the foundation on which every city, region, country or group of countries is built.

The time has come for us to regard noble purpose as the universal right of each of us and the universal obligation of every political and public leader.

A word of thanks

I never imagined that writing a book, certainly a first book, would involve such a confrontation with myself. It immediately taught me how to put things in perspective and made me more aware than ever of just how essential and precious Life really is.

For that reason, in this work I would like first and foremost to bring an ode to Life, to my Life. The opportunity each new day brings to add something to the journey of Life is a wonderful gift. As is the freedom to do what I want to do, when I want to do it, where I want to do it and with whom I want to do it. For these things I am truly grateful, every day.

This Life would never have been what it is, were it not for my parents. Out of love and with great devotion, they gave to my brothers and me so much of their passion, energy and time, so that we grew up to be decent, complete, ambitious and respectful men. It is thanks to my parents that I received my foundations for the later beauty, joy and harmony in my Life. It is thanks to them that I have become the person I am.

My grandparents also played an important role in my development. In particular, Nana and Parrain were a strong presence in my Life for a long time and made a huge contribution to who I am today. In her own unique way, Nana was a friend with whom I could have intimate and highly motivating conversations. She always encouraged me to rise above mediocrity. Right from the very beginning, she believed in me and quickly saw that I was different from all the other boys, with gifts that were rooted in a deep humanism.

My thanks also go to my numerous friends and other loved ones, who have occupied and still occupy a special place in my Life. Some of our meetings and conversations played a hugely formative role in who I have become, what I have done, and what I have still to do.

Likewise, I am most grateful to all my many business relations and GINPI clients. Over time, I have developed personal bonds, even bonds of friendship with many of them. Bonds which I cherish immensely, and to which I attach enormous importance. The opportunity to experiment with new ideas and methods for them and with them and to give them guidance and direction, often at crucial moments in their Lives, was and is a great honour, which gave and still gives me great energy.

Thank you also to the many hundreds of other remarkable people who I have met at a more personal level in my Life and who were able to touch me and move me, in one way or another. The conversations I have had with these people in the four corners of the world were truly inspirational. Mountaintop walks at night, mediations by day, virtual exchanges of ideas with people on the other side of the globe, creative sessions in artistic settings, intimate dinners in castles and palaces, even the simplest but often most essential interactions with people on the street: they have all influenced the way I look at the world.

My thanks also go to the many thousands of people who came to listen to me and ask questions. This gave me the chance to step outside my comfort zone and give the best of myself, while I attempted to bring them deeper insights and encouraged them to take a more noble purpose-driven approach to their Lives.

What I gained most from all these meetings was the inspiration to 'colour outside the lines', to go beyond the norms and dare to say and advise what needed to be said and advised, while always remaining myself but also learning more about who I am.

My deepest appreciation and gratitude also go to my partners in CoBrAS. It is a partnership that has allowed us to make a substantial contribution to a better society and economy, thanks to our systematic work in domains that are very close to my heart. Our conversations and meetings have always been an exceptional source of inspiration for me.

Naturally, I would like to thank my publisher, LannooCampus, for their unfailing belief in me and for their willingness to share my vision that noble purpose can change humankind – and therefore society, the economy and the world – for the better. Their support and advice throughout the entire process of writing this book was invaluable, as was their 'push' to get me to set down my ideas on paper. Their ambition to make *The Book of Noble Purpose* a reference is something that, for me, is beyond value.

Last, but certainly not least, my heartfelt thanks go to my partner Luciano, the man of my Life. I am so grateful for his acceptance and tolerance when I am away on business (again), when I am working late at the office, when I am attending another conference or business dinner, whenever I am called in somewhere to give some urgent last-minute advice. When love and ambition find each other, they create a wonderful and very important cocktail of progress. The beauty of purity is the purity of beauty!

Endnotes

1. https://www.youtube.com/watch?v=UF8uR6Z6KLc
2. https://nl.wikipedia.org/wiki/Mark_Twain#Verandering_van_inzichten
3. https://nl.wikipedia.org/wiki/René_Descartes
4. https://nl.wikipedia.org/wiki/Dag_Hammarskjöld
5. https://nl.wikipedia.org/wiki/Alexander_de_Grote
6. https://nl.wikipedia.org/wiki/Marie_Curie
7. https://nl.wikipedia.org/wiki/Carl_Gustav_Jung
8. https://nl.wikipedia.org/wiki/Synchroniciteit
9. https://nl.wikipedia.org/wiki/Karma
10. If I talk about 'things', I usually mean in the broadest sense of the word. This can cover matters as diverse as ideas, services, products, goods, concepts, etc. In fact, everything that can be regarded as the results of the actions of an individual.
11. https://nl.wikipedia.org/wiki/Milton_Friedman
12. https://stevenpinker.com
13. https://www.gallup.com/workplace/238079/state-global-workplace-2017.aspx?g_source=link_NEWSV9&g_medium=TOPIC&g_campaign=item_&g_content=State procent2520of procent2520the procent2520Global procent2520Workplace
14. For reasons of confidentiality, I have substituted Irene for her real name and have not revealed the name of the organisation where she works as the chairwoman.
15. https://nl.wikipedia.org/wiki/Viktor_Frankl
16. Belgacom, the current Proximus, where I worked for 5 years under the inspiring CEO & president John Goossens and had various leadership responsibilities.
17. The Belgian state today still holds 50.1 percent of the shares and can still count on a substantial dividend each year.
18. When I worked as a young manager in the Customer Service Department at Belgacom Directory Services in 1994-1995, a subsidiary of Belgacom, GE Directories, Singapore Telecom, Danish Telecom and an investors consortium, which produced telephone directories and was in direct competition with Promedia/Yellow Pages, the words 'War Room' were pinned to the management board room door!

19 Corporate values are the behaviour of all the people in an organisation that will lead that organisation in the right direction, so that the way in which people work and collaborate takes place in a manner that matches the organisational culture.

20 VUCA is an acronym for Volatility, Uncertainty, Complexity and Ambiguity, and was first used by the American army in the 1990s to describe the increasing complexity of the world following the end of the Cold War.

21 http://rajsisodia.com

22 www.consciouscapitalism.org

23 Firms of Endearment assumes that companies that are more than just a set of financial KPIs with a focus on short-term profit will ultimately do better than the companies that are exclusively focused on financial results to start with.

24 https://bcorporation.eu/about-b-corps

25 In the meantime, Brussels Airlines has been taken out of the Lufthansa low-cost subsidiary German Wings, with which it was intended to be integrated. There is a new CEO and largely a new management committee, so that the Brussels Airlines culture is now changing.

26 From 1923 until November 2011, Sabena NV (Société Anonyme Belge d'Exploitation de la Navigation Aérienne) was the Belgian national airline, the oldest national airline in the world at the time of its foundation.

27 Groupe PSA (previously PSA Peugeot Citroën), PSA for short, is a French vehicle manufacturing group responsible for brands that include Peugeot, Citroën, Opel, Vauxhall and DS Automobiles. In 2018, PSA produced some 3.9 million vehicles, had a turnover of 74 billion euros and a workforce of no fewer than 212,000 employees.

28 https://www.heritage-b.com/en/

29 Founded in 1924, the TEKA Group is a leading kitchen and bathroom decorator, with more than 100 million customers worldwide. The group produces high-quality built-in appliances, kitchen sinks and faucets in 13 factories in Europe, Asia and America, as well as a wide range of bath fittings and decorations. TEKA has subsidiaries in 33 countries and sells its established brands TEKA, Küppersbusch, Intra and STROHM in more than 110 lands. https://teka.com/global/about-us/

30 'Almirall puts Science at your service. We believe in constant innovation and strong investment in R&D. That's what we do now, and that's what we'll continue to do in future. Because at Almirall, we care.' (Jorge Gallardo, President) https://www.almirall.com/en/about-almirall/about-us/history

31 https://www.unilever.com/about/who-we-are/our-vision/
32 https://www.patagonia.com/company-history.html
33 https://www.natureetdecouvertes.com/fr/qui-sommes-nous#histoire
34 For more details over the different forms of love: https://westcoach-ingblog.wordpress.com/2019/01/27/de-acht-lessen-van-de-griekse-liefde-de-oude-grieken/
35 https://nl.wikipedia.org/wiki/Abraham_Maslow
36 http://www.guibertdelmarmol.com
37 https://nl.wikipedia.org/wiki/Desoxyribonucleïnezuur
38 http://www.sambodh.org/B/sb.html
39 Ashram is an Indian name for a community and meeting place for the adherents of a religion in India. It is often a kind of hermitage, monastery or other place of religious significance. Usually, an ashram is a place where a sadhak (holy man) lives, and the name often refers to this man or to the location of his abode. In olden times, ashrams were situated far away from the inhabited world, in remote woods or mountainous regions, since this was more conducive to meditation. Ashrams are now used for wider spiritual purposes, such as reflection and yoga, often under the guidance of a guru or mystic teacher of some kind. https://nl.wikipedia.org/wiki/Ashram
40 https://nl.wikipedia.org/wiki/Carl_Gustav_Jung
41 https://nl.wikipedia.org/wiki/Synchroniciteit
42 https://nl.wikipedia.org/wiki/Karma
43 https://www.gallup.com/workplace/238079/state-global-work-place-2017.aspx?g_source=link_NEWSV9&g_medium=TOPIC&g_campaign=item_&g_content=State procent2520of procent2520the procent2520Global procent2520Workplace
44 https://brenebrown.com
45 https://www.ted.com/talks/brene_brown_on_vulnerability?language=nl
46 http://www.kenwilber.com/Writings/PDF/Introductiontothe IntegralApproach_GENERAL_2005_NN.pdf
47 http://www.kenwilber.com/home/landing/index.html
48 https://www.drucker.institute/perspective/about-peter-drucker/
49 https://nl.wikipedia.org/wiki/Ernest_Solvay
50 https://www.solvay.com/en/our-company
51 https://nl.wikipedia.org/wiki/Anita_Roddick
52 https://www.thebodyshop.com/nl-be/a-propos-de-nous/heritage
53 https://nl.wikipedia.org/wiki/Elon_Musk
54 https://nl.wikipedia.org/wiki/Nelson_Mandela

This book was originally published as *Het Noble Purpose boek*,
LannooCampus, 2019.

D/2019/45/440 – ISBN 978 94 014 6372 0 – NUR 801, 807

COVER DESIGN Compagnie Paul Verrept
INTERIOR DESIGN LetterLust | Stefaan Verboven

LannooCampus Publishers is a subsidiary of Lannoo Publishers,
the book and multimedia division of Lannoo Publishers nv.

LannooCampus Publishers
Vaartkom 41 bus 01.02
3000 Leuven
Belgium
www.lannoocampus.com

P.O. Box 23202
1100 DS Amsterdam
Netherlands